Growing up with Down's Syndrome

BILLIE SHEPPERDSON

CASSELL EDUCATIONAL

Cassell Educational Limited
Artillery House
Artillery Row
London SW1P 1RT

British Library Cataloguing in Publication Data

Shepperdson, Billie
  Growing up with Down's syndrome.
  1. Mentally handicapped children—
  Care and treatment 2. Down's syndrome
  I. Title
  362.3   HU891

  ISBN: 0 304 31407 2

Phototypesetting by Chapterhouse, The Cloisters, Formby, L37 3PX
Printed and bound in Great Britain at The Bath Press, Avon

Last digit is print no. 9 8 7 6 5 4 3 2 1

Contents

To William Renwick Heather

Acknowledgements

I wish to express my appreciation to all those who have helped with these studies. The 1972 work was funded by the Social Science Research Council. The 1981 study was funded by the Joseph Rowntree Memorial Trust. The Joseph Rowntree Memorial Trust is to be thanked particularly for its on-going interest and generous support of the 1981 project.

In Swansea University College I must thank Maurice Chazan, Roy Mapes and Bill Williams for their advice and encouragement. There are special thanks to Jean Cleary and Bill Bytheway for their unstinting help throughout the project.

Outside University College I should like to thank David Lane. In addition, I am grateful to Bramwell Stratford and Gareth and Maureen Hughes for reading the manuscript. I am particularly indebted to Cliff Cunningham for his detailed and useful comments on some of the chapters.

The manuscript was typed, through several drafts, by Pat Al-Salahi, June Burtonshaw, Carol Cook and Caryl Johnston.

Needless to say, my greatest debt is to those who took part in the study. I am grateful for the kindness shown to me by teachers in the schools I visited, and for the patience and tolerance of the parents and children themselves.

Introduction

This is a research account of a two-part study of Down's syndrome children and their families which was carried out in South Wales in 1972 and 1981. The research had three main aims:

1. To describe the variations in how families cope, emotionally and practically, with the fact of having a Down's syndrome child. The focus of the work is on the different ways in which families cope at two points in the child's life: the beginning and the end of the school years.

2. To ascertain how far families with a Down's syndrome child receive similar services and, where they do not, to assess the extent to which allocation of service help has varied according to the needs of the child and the family, rather than according to other, less relevant variables (e.g. location of residence, or how persistent families themselves are in mobilising help).

3. To examine the experience of community care for one cohort of Down's syndrome youngsters. The first two aims of this study, when linked, describe the reality of community care for these families. The account, to some extent, presents the ideal of a community care, in that the teenagers were brought up in their own families, and it is this ordinary family lifestyle that service providers nowadays wish to encourage where it is possible, or emulate where it is not. The care is less than the ideal in that, at the time the cohort was born, there were few services and, moreover, the study took place in a deprived region of Britain. The account illustrates how far ordinary family life does in fact foster the aims of independence and integration into the community for teenagers with Down's syndrome.

Whilst the text contains obvious lessons, it does not seek to be an instruction manual for parents or professionals; rather, it aims to describe the lives of families who have a Down's syndrome child and to give an account of how they perceive their situation.

DOWN'S SYNDROME CHILDREN

Down's syndrome children were selected for this study because they are likely to form the largest identifiable category within the mentally handicapped population. (Craft (1979) suggests they form one-third of those with an IQ of under 50.) Parents of such children are also likely to have many experiences in common.

Since Langdon Down produced the first formal list of physical characteristics of the syndrome in 1866, Down's syndrome people have been a popular choice of subject in many studies, but the emphasis over the years has changed considerably. At first the studies, which were often confined to the medical literature, tended to be simple descriptions of stigmata and symptoms, but nowadays there is greater concentration on ways of ameliorating the condition. These methods include medical and surgical intervention, both for obvious life-saving purposes and also – more controversially – for the removal of some of the facial signs of Down's syndrome through plastic surgery (e.g. Lemperle and Radu, 1980). Other methods are concerned with the education and training of the child and his or her family (e.g. McConkey and Jeffree, 1975). The provision of suitable services has also received increasing attention. Interest in all aspects of Down's syndrome shows no sign of abating, and in 1984 a new journal – *Trisomy 21* – devoted to 'reporting main areas of research, care and training of Down's syndrome people', began publication from the Division of Human Genetics, University of Manitoba.

CHANGES IN APPROACH TO MENTAL HANDICAP

Services for mentally handicapped people have undergone radical changes in the last three or four decades. Early services were concerned to contain, protect and care for mentally handicapped people and this was achieved at the expense of encouraging them to develop their full potential. Partly as a result of these aims, services were provided which effectively isolated mentally handicapped people from others. Those cared for away from their families were incarcerated and isolated in subnormality hospitals and even those at home were denied access to normal ways of life. For instance, it was not until 1970 that severely mentally handicapped children were given the right to education.

In the post-war period the inappropriate nature of the care being offered in institutions, especially for children, was recognised. It was shown that normal children who were brought up in institutions were disadvantaged by their abnormal lifestyle (e.g. Spitz and Wolf, 1946). This was seen to apply equally to mentally handicapped children, who became additionally disadvantaged after a period of institutionalisation (e.g. Baumeister, 1968). Down's syndrome children were often used as subjects in studies that demonstrated this effect.

Furthermore, it was questioned whether a hospital was an appropriate setting for people who simply required a home. King *et al.* (1971), comparing various types of institution, concluded that nursing training was inimical to providing a home-like atmosphere for children. Oswin (1971) starkly described the arid life of handicapped children in some hospitals, pointing out that the safeguards and checks governing the care of children did not apply to those cared for in hospitals. Miller and Gwynne (1972) compared the 'warehousing' and 'horticultural' regimes of care in homes for physically disabled adults. The models described by them have relevance for other types of institution. Scandals about treatment of patients in long-stay hospitals brought some institutions into unwelcome prominence.

Meanwhile, the plight of families who had struggled alone and unaided to care for their mentally handicapped members at home began to receive consideration. Several studies highlighted the difficulties, both social and financial, for families in this position (e.g. Schonell and Watts, 1956; Holt, 1957; Tizard and Grad, 1961; Moncreiff, 1966; Younghusband *et al.*, 1970).

The emphasis on home care and the growing publicity about the problems of families who were providing it led to an explosion of help in the 1970s. The 1970 Education Act brought all children in England and Wales, whatever their mental status, under the care of local education authorities. A practical result was that all of them thereafter had a school place at 5 years as a right and no child was classed as 'ineducable'. In addition, financial help became available for many families. The attendance allowance was introduced in 1971, the Family Fund in 1973 and the mobility allowance in 1975.

Family care is still seen as the most appropriate care for handicapped children, but nowadays the trend for mentally handicapped adults is to look beyond the family towards integration into the wider community. 'Community Care' is the current choice for dependent populations – the mentally handicapped, mentally ill, elderly and severely physically disabled. This trend is linked with the wish for all people, regardless of disability, to enjoy normal patterns of life. The impetus for this movement came from Denmark, where the first legislation for normalisation and integration in services for mentally handicapped people was introduced in 1959. 'Normalisation' for mentally handicapped people was popularised by Wolfensberger (1980) and was extended to include 'the use of culturally valued means to lead culturally valued lives'. For all disabled people, including mentally handicapped people, the current intention is that they should take their place in the community and possess the same rights to education, housing, leisure activities and employment and enjoy the same legal and personal freedom as everyone else.

BACKGROUND TO THE SOUTH WALES STUDY

The emphasis on family care led to an interest in how families did cope with a disabled member and several studies have described the way of life of families caring for children with a variety of disabilities. Hewett (1970) compared families with a cerebral palsied child with those who had not, and Gregory (1976) carried out a similar study with deaf children. Carr (1975) and Gath (1978) both made intensive studies of families with a young Down's syndrome child and compared them with families that had normal children only. Pringle and Fiddes (1970) examined families with thalidomide children. Hannam (1973), Kew (1975) and Wilkin (1979) gave more general accounts of the impact of a disability on families.

The study carried out in South Wales and reported here has two major differences from most of these other studies. Firstly, it concentrates on the differences between those families who have a Down's syndrome child, instead of emphasising the differences and similarities between them and families who have either normal children only or a child with another type of disability. There are, of course, problems associated with this. Not least of these is that caution must be used in interpreting the results: any particular aspect of behaviour cannot be automatically assumed to be the result of having a Down's syndrome child. A study by Boles (1959) illustrates this point. He found that mothers of cerebral palsied children scored highly on measures of guilt and anxiety. It is obvious how such findings could be interpreted and used. However, he found that his matched control group of mothers of normal children also had high guilt and anxiety scores. While this is a useful caveat against drawing causal connections, simple differences between both families and children themselves are of legitimate interest, and such an approach does avoid making stereotyped generalisations about 'families with Down's syndrome children'. It must also be said that, by the teenage years, some differences between Down's syndrome teenagers and their normal peers are so marked that comparative figures merely state the obvious. For example, not one Down's syndrome teenager in this study in South Wales had ever travelled on a bus without supervision, almost half needed help with dressing and only one or two were *suspected* of having had any sexual encounters (of the mildest nature). We do not need an elaborate study to show us that this is unlike the life of most non-disabled youngsters. It is when services and trends for Down's syndrome adults are such that normalisation becomes a reality, at least for some people, that comparative studies will usefully show the gains that have been made.

Secondly, although this study deals with two periods in the lives of Down's syndrome children – the beginning and end of the school years – its primary emphasis is on the teenage years. This is because parents of younger Down's syndrome children have already received a lot of attention (Carr, 1975; Gath, 1978; Cunningham, 1982; and in the professional journals), whereas the literature on teenagers is relatively scanty.

It should be emphasised that the teenagers in this study do form a population, i.e. everyone who fulfilled the criteria of being a Down's syndrome child born in 1964, 1965 or 1966 and living at home in a defined area in South Wales qualified. They have not been identified as users of a particular service, which can bias results (e.g. applicants to the Family Fund, pupils attending special schools or members of the Down's Children's Association). The children were, however, all known formally or informally to professionals working in the education services.

The book is divided into three parts. The first part describes the research methods and gives background information on the families and the children. The second part describes variations in the emotional and practical responses of parents and the third part assesses variations in the help given by services to families.

Part 1
A description of the methods, families and children

1 Research Methods and Characteristics of the Families and Children

This chapter outlines the methods that were used in the Down's syndrome study and describes the families and children who took part. Masculine pronouns will be used throughout because boys outnumbered girls in this study.

RESEARCH METHODS

The families studied

The 1972 sample

The aims of the research have been set out in the Introduction.

Down's syndrome children who were at the beginning of their education were selected for the study but, in order to obtain a sufficiently large sample, selection had to range across three years of birth: 1964, 1965 and 1966. All such children identified and living with their parents in the defined area in South Wales were included.

Permission was sought from local education authorities (LEAs) in the area to approach schools where there were Down's syndrome pupils and to contact their parents. Schools were visited and parents were sent a letter, or approached by the head teacher, asking if they would take part in the study. Since the study was firmly linked to schools, children not attending school, or in schools that were not approached, could have been missed. In 1981 it was found that this was the case. Before parents were even approached, however, there were some losses from the sample:

1. One LEA was unwilling to cooperate in the study.
2. A more serious loss was four children attending one assessment unit. The head mistress was willing to have the children tested and all school records studied but would not allow the parents to be approached. Since the children could not be treated in the same way as the rest of the sample they were, reluctantly, excluded.

Two parents refused to cooperate. In both cases they had been approached by the head teacher rather than by letter. In all there were 37 children in the 1972 study.

The 1981 population

The intention in 1981 was to follow up the children who had been studied in 1972 in order to see children and their families at the beginning and end of their school careers.

It was possible to add a further 19 children to the 1981 study. It was discovered that five children had simply not been identified in 1972. Four families had moved into the area through migration or boundary changes. The previously uncooperative LEA gave

3

permission to carry out the study in 1981 (an example, perhaps, of changing attitudes) and so a further 7 children could then be included. Similarly it was possible to visit three of the four families whose children had attended the assessment unit that had restricted access in 1972.

There were also losses. Two parents refused to cooperate. In addition, two mothers who had been visited in 1972 did not want to continue with the 1981 study. This was unfortunate since both had been particularly articulate and sensitive respondents. One child in the 1972 study had died by 1981. There were also three families who had moved out of the area since 1972, but it was possible to trace and visit them. A total of 53 teenagers were visited in 1981, 34 from the 'original sample' and 19 in the 'new sample'; together they form 'the population'.

Table 1.1 gives details of the children in the population and the year in which they were born.

Table 1.1 *Year of birth and number in sample (% in brackets)*

Year of birth	Original sample (1972)	(1981)	New sample (1981)	Total population (1981)
1964	15 (41)	15 (44)	4 (21)	19 (36)
1965	10 (27)	9 (27)	4 (21)	13 (25)
1966	12 (32)	10 (29)	11 (58)	21 (40)
Total	37 (100)	34 (100)	19 (100)	53 (101)

The discrepancy in size between the 1972 and 1981 samples is an important difficulty. Apart from the five children who were originally missed, this was unavoidable but it does mean that the longitudinal aspect of the study is weakened. It is particularly unfortunate that, by chance, the additions, particularly those from the LEA that earlier had refused to cooperate, contained a disproportionate number of bright children. Consequently, the 1972 results are biased towards the less able children, and this should be borne in mind when considering the results.

Methods of enquiry

In both 1972 and 1981 there were two main methods of enquiry:

1. An interview with carers – usually the mother. The word 'mother' is normally used when referring to general responses since it reflects the reality of the situation for most families. Other carers are identified where necessary.
2. Ability tests on the children.

The carers' interview

The basic teenage interview schedule was modified for use with the new sample so that, where appropriate, information that had been gathered from the original sample in 1972 could be obtained for the new sample also. The interview generally followed the pattern of the schedule although mothers were not stopped from discussing matters that should have come later; the questions were simply repeated as they came up so that mothers could add to or qualify statements already made. Some questions were intended simply to introduce a topic for discussion. All interviews were tape-recorded and this had the distinct advantage of allowing a flexible, conversational approach. Most interviews, in both 1972 and 1981, lasted between two and two and a half hours.

The interviews with mothers were meant to be wide-ranging in order to give as complete a picture as possible of the homes of these children. This did mean, inevitably, that for some issues the picture is not exact. For example, information on the help given by the father would have been better if questions had been based on 'what happened last week', etc. It was recognised at the time that the questions asked were not of this nature, but it was felt that to concentrate tediously on these minor issues would have tired mothers and taken up time from more important questions. However, for definitive answers on these sorts of issues exact questions are needed and this limitation should be borne in mind.

Some of the problems associated with the analysis of the interview information are given in the chapters dealing with the relevant sections. One general point can be made here. All information is based on what mothers said happened. Although it is obviously desirable that this should have some relationship with what did happen, it cannot be taken for granted. Where it was known that a mother's statements were grossly contradicted by the facts, this is stated, and sometimes a mother's interpretation of the facts was not accepted. Carr (1975) discusses similar difficulties with her own work on Down's syndrome children.

The problem is related to a more fundamental one of using verbal response (rather than observation) in order to find out what people think or how they behave. When differences between people are being studied, it is open to question whether some disparity is due simply to differences in the use of language or to differences in what a person is prepared to say. Some examples illustrate this point:

1. An inarticulate mother would perhaps be unable to express her thoughts and feelings and so would not be credited with having any that were worth mentioning.
2. One mother might feel irritation towards her child but think this was only 'normal' and so not worth mentioning. Another might feel the same amount of irritation but assume it was the result of her own feelings and so report it as important. In other words, before the interviewer receives any information it has been selected, by a non-standard person (viz. the mother in each case), each with her own idea – conscious and unconscious – of what needs to be told and withheld.

Some of the problems of interpretation of answers are discussed by Oakley (1974; pp.66–70). She relates dissimilarities in answers coming from different social classes with the work of Bernstein. There are two main points:

(a) The working-class speech code makes 'the presentation' of individual feelings difficult (relevant for example 1 above, perhaps);
(b) Both working and middle classes relate their answers, not to what is the fact, but to their expected norm (possibly relevant for example 2), so a mother could feel, say, rejection towards her child but be unwilling to admit it. These are sensitive areas but possibly the same happens on less emotionally charged issues. For instance, the question 'Are you strict?' could be answered quickly with what a mother saw as the 'usual' response rather than with an answer based on her own opinion.

What a mother sees as the interviewer's expectations also makes a difference. The Newsons (1963) in their study of 1-year-olds found that mothers gave different answers to the same questions from health visitors and university interviewers.

These points obviously have implications for the research, especially since social-class differences were often apparent. It may, for instance, account for the large numbers of mothers in social classes IV and V (semi- and unskilled workers) who, in 1972, denied any change in the relationship with their husband. (See *OPCS* 1977 for an explanation of social-class classifications.) However, a response to one question was rarely taken on its own but was classified according to the other answers and the whole tone of the interview. Most answers had additional evidence to support their inclusion in a particular classification. Some of the problems encountered are discussed in more detail in the relevant sections.

All classifications of mothers' responses were made after the interview, in the light of the interview information as a whole. In most cases the chi-squared test was used to test frequencies for significance. Goodman and Kruskal's γ was used where appropriate (Goodman and Kruskal, 1954). It is important to point out that a relationship that is non-significant does not necessarily imply that there is no relationship between the variables. What it indicates is that the sample is not sufficiently large and/or the relationship is not sufficiently strong for the relationship to be proved statistically significant. The object of the research is to provide a description of the strength of relationships, as well as to apply tests of their significance. The insistence of some schools of thought on a ritualistic hypothesis testing can become tedious and, indeed, misleading if this becomes the arbiter of what is relevant and what is not (Bytheway, 1975). Percentages are rounded to the nearest whole number. Consequently, percentages do not always add up to 100 in tables.

In 1981 the Malaise Inventory was administered to all but one carer, as a further and more objective test of mental well-being. This is a simple test of 24 questions, mostly concerned with health. (Rutter *et al.*, 1970). It has been used with other mothers of handicapped children (e.g. Bradshaw, 1980; Pahl and Quine, 1985).

In 1972, 36 mothers were interviewed in their own homes and 1 was interviewed at school. They were usually alone, although in seven instances fathers were present for some or all of the interview.

In 1981 all 53 interviews were conducted at the home of the Down's syndrome child. Forty-eight were with the teenagers' natural mothers. Two interviews were with fathers (as sole carers) and in both cases another sibling was present. One interview was with a sister and her husband, who looked after the Down's syndrome teenager now her parents were dead. One interviewee was a maternal grandmother who cared for the Down's syndrome teenager because her daughter was dead. Another interview was with a stepmother, although the natural father answered questions to which she could not have known the answers. In one instance the interview with the mother, who was not British, took place using a brother of the Down's syndrome teenager as interpreter. One interview, which it was not possible to reschedule, was not satisfactory because it was conducted patchily, with a brother at one point and the parents at a later short meeting. Six fathers and one stepfather were present for the whole of the interview; ten fathers were present with the mother for part of the interview; ten fathers were either dead or no longer living with the mother of the Down's syndrome teenager.

The tests

In both the 1972 and 1981 studies a further aim was to find out whether home background influenced the achievements of the children in any measurable way. These results are given in Appendix 1.

The children were tested with the Reynell Developmental Language Scales and the Gunzburg Progress Assessment Chart, Form 1 (Gunzburg, 1963).Only the Gunzburg results will be used in the discussion of the teenagers' lives. The Gunzburg PAC is a measure of social competence and designed specifically for ESN(S) children. The test includes detailed questions under the following headings: table habits; mobility; toilet and washing; dressing; language; differences; number work; paper and pencil work; play activities; home activities; dexterity and agility. Scores were compared within the population rather than with Gunzburg's own norms because the focus of the work was on differences between the families and children in the study, rather than between them and others.

Teachers or, where appropriate, Adult Training Centre (ATC) staff completed the forms and therefore all items on home behaviour, which they might not have known about, were excluded. Consequently, the maximum possible score on the Gunzburg PAC was 107, rather than 120. The fact that teachers may not score accurately of course presents a major problem. It is clear that a variety of people with different standards and rating different children, may produce a variety of results. All that can be said is that the teachers were often familiar with the forms and usually knew the children well, and the correlation between the Gunzburg scores and test results carried out by the researcher were high. (Spearman's ϱ for the Gunzburg and Reynell tests was .79.) The test results are simply used in this report to give some idea of the abilities of the children under discussion. Table 1.2 shows the mean and range of scores of the children in 1972 and 1981. In 1981, in addition to the Gunzburg PAC, teachers were asked to supply details of the numeric and reading ability of the teenagers in their class.

Table 1.2 *Gunzburg PAC mean and range scores, 1972 and 1981*

	n	Mean	Standard deviation	Range
1972	36	29.02	15.24	2–57
1981	53	61.6	27.42	0–107

The comparative study in 1981

In 1981 a study was also made of young Down's syndrome children, living at home in South Wales and born in the years 1973, 1974 and 1975. The methods used in 1972 were repeated. The purpose of this study was to enable a direct comparison to be made between those Down's syndrome children and their families who were at the beginning of their school careers in 1972 and those in the same situation in 1981. One mother refused to cooperate, leaving 26 children in the study. The results of this subsidiary study are presented briefly in Appendix 2.

CHARACTERISTICS OF THE FAMILIES AND THE CHILDREN

This section describes the families and the Down's syndrome children who took part in the study. Since one of the main objects of the research is to illustrate the range of ways in which families cope with similar situations, it is important to outline the differences and similarities between the families and the children.

Characteristics of the families

In 1972 the day-to-day care of the children was the responsibility of the mother in all cases. In 1981 this was still largely true and details given here refer to the mother where she was the person primarily responsible for care, the father where she was not, and to the sister of the girl whose parents had both died.

Marital status of the parent responsible for care

The marital status of the parents in 1972 and 1981 is shown in Table 1.3. The following changes had taken place since 1972 for parents in the original sample. Of those who had changed from a married state two mothers were divorced, one father was widowed and one wife had left. The widower and one divorcee were about to remarry. One widow had remarried since 1972, and the woman who was separated in 1972 had become a

Table 1.3 *Marital status of responsible parent (% in brackets)*

	Original sample		New sample	Total population
	(1972)	(1981)	(1981)	(1981)
Married and living with husband	28 (76)	20 (59)	14 (74)	34 (64)
Divorced/widowed and remarried to father of Down's teenager	2 (5)	2 (6)	1 (5)	3 (6)
Widowed	2 (5)	3^a (9)	2^b (11)	$5^{a,b}$ (9)
Widowed and remarried, not to father of Down's teenager	0	1 (3)	0	1 (2)
Separated	1 (3)	1^a (3)	2^c (11)	$3^{a,c}$ (6)
Divorced from father of Down's teenager	3 (8)	6 (18)	0	6 (11)
Divorced from father of Down's teenager and remarried	1 (3)	0	0	0
Both parents dead	0	1 (3)	0	1 (2)
Total	37 (100)	34 (101)	19 (101)	53 (100)

a Includes one father.
b Includes one father; child in the daily care of her maternal grandmother.
c Includes one father with common-law wife.

widow. The mother who had been divorced and remarried in 1972 later divorced her second husband, went on to marry a third but again the marriage ended in divorce. Another woman who was divorced in 1972 remarried but was divorced again by 1981.

Age of parents

The likelihood that a woman will give birth to a Down's syndrome child increases with age. Consequently, Down's syndrome births are related to patterns of fertility within a population. In the 1960s, when the population was born, women in the vulnerable age range had often completed their families. So, while the rates of Down's syndrome births to these women were higher than to younger women, in absolute numbers there were normally as many Down's syndrome children born to younger as to older women. The trend is now changing: there are fewer births altogether nowadays and even fewer to older women. Amniocentesis has also played a part in reducing Down's syndrome births to older women. Murdoch (1984) found that, whereas before 1970 70% of mothers in Scotland were over 35 years at the birth of their Down's syndrome children, after 1970 the position was reversed and 70% of Down's syndrome babies were born to mothers under 35 years old. Carr's (1975) study of Down's syndrome children born in 1963-64 found the average age of mothers at the birth of their Down's syndrome children was 36.6 years. Gath (1978), looking at 1970–71 births, found the average age of mothers at the birth to be 31.6 years.

In this population of teenagers, the age of the mother was known for 50 women. The average age of mothers at the birth of their Down's syndrome child was 33.1 years. This compares with a mean age of women at childbirth in England and Wales for 1966 of 26.8 years. The percentage of women over 35 years was only 49%, much lower than the 70% reported by Murdoch for pre-1970 births. This may be because births in the Scottish study were not confined to those that took place in the 1960s.

Since the age of fathers in the United Kingdom normally correlates highly with that of their wives, paternal ages can also be expected to be raised for Down's syndrome children. Fathers in Gath's study (1978) had a mean age of 33.9 years at the birth of the children compared with the fathers of her normal controls, who had a mean age of 30.5 years. Fathers of the South Wales population in the study had a mean age of 35.7 years at the birth of their Down's syndrome children.

Language

Table 1.4 shows the main language used by the parents of the Down's syndrome teen-agers. More parents claimed to know Welsh *tipyn bach* (a little bit) and would use odd words and phrases, but this is discounted.

Table 1.4 *Language spoken by parents (% in brackets)*

	Original sample (1972)	(1981)	New sample (1981)	Total population (1981)
English-speaking	24 (65)	22 (65)	18 (95)	40 (76)
One parent Welsh-speaking	6 (16)	5 (15)	–	5 (9)
Both parents Welsh-speaking	6 (16)	6 (18)	–	6 (11)
Other	1 (3)	1 (3)	1 (5)	2 (4)
Total	34 (100)	34 (101)	19 (100)	53 (100)

Total Welsh speakers 1971: 20.8% (Welsh Office, 1978).

Social class

Table 1.5 illustrates the social-class composition of fathers of the population and compares them with the general population in Wales, and with studies by Carr (1975) and Gath (1978) in England.

Table 1.5 *Social-class composition of fathers of Down's syndrome children (% in brackets)*

Social class	Wales (1966)	South Wales (1964–66)	Carr London & Surrey (1963–64)	Gath Oxford (1970–71)
I and II	(20)	12 (23)	16 (37)	14 (47)
III	(46)	28 (53)	17 (40)	11 (37)
IV and V	(35)	13 (25)	10 (23)	5 (17)
Total	(101)	53 (101)	43 (100)	30 (101)

The table shows that the social-class composition of families in the Down's syndrome population did not differ substantially from that of the general population (see Shepperdson (1985a) for a further discussion of social class and Down's syndrome births).

Religion

Carr (1975) found that over a quarter of mothers in her sample were Roman Catholic compared with only 1% in her control group.

Table 1.6 shows the religious affiliation of carers in the study population. In this study, too, Roman Catholics appear to be over-represented. Estimates of Roman Catholic affiliation in the United Kingdom are of the order of 5.4% of adults in 1980 (CSO, 1983).

Table 1.6 *Religious affiliation of mothers (% in brackets)*

	Original sample (1972)	(1981)	New sample (1981)	Total population (1981)
Roman Catholic	8 (22)	8 (24)	1 (5)	9 (17)
Church of England/Wales	14 (38)	12 (35)	12 (63)	24 (45)
Nonconformist	15 (41)	14 (41)	5 (26)	19 (36)
Salvation Army	–	–	1 (5)	1 (2)
Total	37 (101)	34 (100)	19 (99)	53 (100)

Employment

Table 1.7 compares the employment status of fathers in 1972 with that in 1981.

In 1972, 81% of fathers who were living at home were in full-time employment. For the teenage population in 1981, only 63% of fathers at home worked full-time (54% for the original sample).

Table 1.7 *Employment status of fathers (% in brackets)*

	Original sample		New sample	Total population
	(1972)	(1981)	(1981)	(1981)
Full-time worker	21 (58)	11 (32)	11 (58)	22 (42)
Self employed	4 (11)	3 (9)	2 (11)	5 (9)
Part-time/retired	–	1 (3)	–	1 (2)
Retired early	–	1 (3)	1 (5)	2 (4)
Unemployed	2 (5)	5 (15)	2 (11)	7 (13)
Invalided	4 (11)	4 (12)	–	4 (8)
Retired	–	1 (3)	1 (5)	2 (4)
Father absent	6 (16)	8 (24)	2 (11)	10 (19)
Total	37 (101)	34 (101)	19 (101)	53 (101)

[a] Including husband of remarried woman and brother-in-law of orphan teenager in care of her sister.
Percentage of men in full-time employment in United Kingdom 1971: 76.7 (CSO, 1983)
Percentage of men in full-time employment in United Kingdom 1981: 81.4 (CSO, 1985)

Table 1.8 shows that some families had incomes supplemented by a mother's earnings.

Table 1.8 *Employment status of mothers (% in brackets)*

	Original sample		New sample	Total population
	(1972)	(1981)	(1981)	(1981)
Full-time worker	5 (14)	4 (11)	3 (16)	7 (13)
Part-time worker	5 (14)	10 (29)	7 (37)	17 (32)
Has no outside work	27 (73)	18[a] (53)	8 (42)	26 (49)
Mothers absent	–	2 (6)	1 (5)	3 (6)
Total	37 (101)	34 (99)	19 (100)	53 (100)

[a] Including sister of orphan teenager
Percentage of women in employment in England and Wales 1971: 43.9 (CSO 1985)
Percentage of women in employment in England and Wales 1981: 47.5 (CSO 1985)

It is clear from the figures that more mothers had returned to work as their children became older. However, most of those working were only able to take part-time employment, which, for the most part, carries with it all the disadvantages of little security, few pension and sickness benefit rights and, sometimes, lower pay and status.

It is not true to say that women come into the employment field when their menfolk are unemployed or absent since, as Table 1.9 shows, it was women with husbands in full-time employment who were significantly more likely to be working themselves. The average age of non-working mothers was a little higher than that of women who did work outside the home (51.4 years compared with 46.5 years) but there were about as many women over 55 years working as were not.

Table 1.9 *Employment status of fathers and mothers 1981 (% in brackets)*

Fathers	Mothers				
	Full-time	Part-time	Not working	Absent	Total
Full-time	4 (15)	13 (48)	8 (30)	2 (7)	27 (100)
Not working	1 (6)	3 (19)	11 (69)[a]	1 (6)	16 (100)
Absent	2 (20)	1 (10)	7 (70)	–	10 (100)
Total	7 (13)	17 (32)	26 (49)	3 (6)	53 (100)

[a] Including sister and brother in law of orphan teenager.
Full- and part-time workers compared with those not working: $\chi^2 = 5.57$; df = 1; p < 0.02.

Family size

Table 1.10 shows the total number of children born to mothers of the population by 1981.

Table 1.10 *Total number of children born to mothers of Down's syndrome population (% in brackets)*

Number of children	Number of mothers[a]
1	4 (8)
2	10 (19)
3	19 (37)
4	8 (15)
5	5 (10)
6	3 (6)
7	2 (4)
8	1 (2)
Total	52 (101)

[a] Age of one mother not available.

In the original sample only one mother had given birth to one more child since 1972. The average family size for the whole population including the Down's syndrome child was 3.4 children. This is rather higher than that of the United Kingdom as a whole and is probably accounted for by the fact that some older women had a Down's syndrome child after they fancied they had completed their families. Only 17 (46%) women in the 1972 original sample had planned the birth that produced the Down's syndrome child. The average age of these women was 29.2 years, but it was 38.1 years for the 54% who had not intended to have more children.

The average number of children did not vary substantially with social class. The mean family size for social classes I and II was 3.1, and 3.5 for social class III, and classes IV and V. This compared with 2.0, 2.1 and 2.3 children respectively after 10 years of marriage for the population of the United Kingdom (Dunnell, 1979).

In 1972, 32 (94%) of the 34 Down's syndrome children with brothers and sisters had at least one sibling still at home, but, in 1981, only 37 (76%) families in the population had a sibling remaining in the household. In 15 of these 37 families all the siblings were over 18 years old and consequently could be expected to leave the parental home in the next few years. This has implications both for the stimulation to which the Down's syndrome teenager is exposed in the house and also for the parents who are manifestly required to go on with their caring role beyond the normal expectation.

Characteristics of the children

Age of the children in 1972 and 1981

The teenagers were born in 1964, 1965 or 1966. In June 1972 the age range of the children was 5 years 7 months to 8 years 4 months; in June 1981 the range for the whole population was 14 years 7 months to 17 years 4 months.

Sex

The sex distribution of the 1972 sample and 1981 population is shown in Table 1.11. This gives a sex ratio of 1.12 males per female. This is rather lower than that of 1.24 given for one-year-olds by Carter (1958). A slightly higher mortality rate of Down's syndrome

Table 1.11 *Sex of the teenagers (% in brackets)*

| | Original sample | | New sample | Total population |
	(1972)	(1981)	(1981)	(1981)
Male	24 (65)	23 (68)	5 (26)	28 (53)
Female	13 (35)	11 (32)	14 (74)	25 (47)
Total	37 (100)	34 (100)	19 (100)	53 (100)

females has been noted (Record and Smith, 1955), but the difference between the sexes in this population was very slight.

Place in the family

The tendency in the 1960s for the Down's syndrome child to be the youngest in a family is undoubtedly partly a result of older mothers having Down's syndrome children. Carr (1975) reported that the siblings of the Down's children in her study tended to be older than those of her control children.

The position of the Down's child in the families from South Wales is shown in Table 1.12. It can be seen that, if singletons are ignored, then the average age of mothers at the birth of their Down's syndrome children rose with the position of the child in the family.

Table 1.12 *Birth order and average age of mothers at birth of Down's syndrome child (% in brackets)*

	Number of children	Average age of mother at birth of Down's child
Only child	4 (8)	38.3
Eldest child	8 (15)	23.4[a]
Middle child	10 (19)	28.6[a]
Youngest child	31 (59)	36.1[a]
Total	53 (101)	33.1

[a] Age of one mother not available.

Health of the children

Fundamental to the quality of any person's life is health. It has implications for enjoyment, stimulation and development and, where a child is involved, implications for the amount of work and worry that will be involved in bringing the child up. The fact that Down's syndrome children are likely to be disadvantaged in this respect is well known. In general, the younger the child the greater is his vulnerability. (Aumonier and Cunningham (1984) give a detailed account of the health and medical problems of Down's syndrome children up to two years old.) The health of the children, as reported here, relies totally on what mothers said, or thought, or remembered about their children's health.

The young children In 1972, 20 mothers out of 37 (54%) reported difficulties of some kind with their babies in the first three months of life. Medical problems ranged from slight jaundice to severe heart problems.

Some of these babies, though they were not ill, presented considerable management problems. Feeding difficulties were commonly mentioned although Aumonier and Cunningham (1984), who have investigated this area far more thoroughly, found that only 27% of Down's syndrome babies took longer than a week to learn to suck well. However, the babies in their study were receiving good health-visitor support. They found that those who presented difficulties for longer had been tube fed and this supports the comments of one mother in the South Wales study who vividly recalled the problems she encountered with tube feeding. The following quotation illustrates the very real management problem which a baby, who is not defined as ill, can still present. The lack of support that was available for this mother in the 1960s is apparent in what she says.

> Every half hour of the day we had to tube feed him . . . it was continuously all through the day and all through the night . . . pumping it in – we could only get one ounce into his system every half hour. I couldn't seem to do anything but feed, feed, feed – you know. . . . No, they wouldn't take him in [to hospital]– he wasn't ill, they told me. Then he seemed to turn. Every hour then, for three months. Then I tried three times a day and he came all of a sudden on these feeds. I felt better then because I was having my sleep. My husband was awake half the night – you know – taking it in turn . . . . I would sleep on the settee and then my husband would take over. I didn't undress for six weeks, I was too tired to undress. I used to sit there and feed, feed, feed – no help at all, we were on our own.   (1972)

By 1972 fewer children were presenting serious problems but mothers were sometimes surprisingly vague about the exact medical status of their children, even when the conditions were potentially serious. For instance, not all were sure whether a heart defect had been found, or a diagnosis given, and the implications of a 'weak heart' or 'heart murmur' were not clear to some parents. It highlights the poor communication that could exist between mothers and doctors in those days and it is one of the areas that had improved for parents in the comparative study (see Appendix 2). Apart from coughs and colds, which were often dealt with promptly by prescriptions (sometimes, it should be said, without the doctor seeing the child), many of these problems had cleared up or improved. Six children had undergone operations; these were for heart conditions, cataract removal, pyloric stenosis, circumcision and teeth extraction.

In 1972 seven children had continuing problems: four had serious heart complaints, two were having convulsions and one had a problem with vision. Another was thought to be deaf, although this had been discounted by the time that the family was visited in 1981.

The teenagers By 1981 the improvements were even greater than those made in early childhood. Twenty-eight (53%) mothers felt their children's health had improved since early childhood and only a few (8%) thought it had deteriorated. No change was reported by 21 (40%) but, of these, 15 said their teenager's health was good and six said moderately good and no one reported bad health, implying that most of these children had always enjoyed good health anyway. Asked to rate their teenager's health as Good, Average or Poor, 38 (72%) said it was good, 13 (25%) average and only 2 (4%) said poor – and in fact these two did not display any obviously worse symptoms than some of the others.

All nine teenagers who scored well on the Gunzburg test of social competence (i.e. over one standard deviation above the mean) were rated by their parents as enjoying good health. This compares with 71% of the teenagers with an average score and only 50% of the 10 who scored badly (i.e. over one standard deviation below the mean).

Heart problems Smith and Berg (1976), reviewing available studies, found that the incidence of heart defects in the Down's syndrome population as a whole is likely to be between 40 and 60 per cent. Of the children sampled by Aumonier and Cunningham (1984) 47% had cardiac lesions. In the South Wales teenage population 70% of parents reported no problems, but this includes two teenagers who had had problems so slight their parents either discounted or were unaware of them. For some, heart complaints were a constant worry and one mother withdrew her son from school for three years when she realised the severity of his condition. Another remarked that she had become falsely optimistic until the doctor said, 'Don't think it couldn't happen again' (i.e. cardiac arrest). Her reaction reflected the depression she felt on hearing this: 'It puts you back to square one. You shove it to the back of your mind and then someone brings it up again.'

Chest complaints By their teens 55% were free of any major chest problems and only five teenagers presented severe problems. A third of them still tended to get more frequent or more severe respiratory problems, given a normal person of that age, but most parents coped with this, especially since there was, for many, a marked improvement from the early days.

Convulsions Smith and Berg (1976), reviewing the evidence, found that epilepsy occurs in 1–10% of the Down's syndrome population and suggest that even 10% is a smaller percentage than is usually found in similarly retarded populations. The incidence in the normal population is much smaller. Thompson (1971) suggests that 5% of the population will have a fit of some sort during their lives but only 0.6% will have chronic epilepsy. Veall (1974), taking the definition of epilepsy as those who had experienced a fit in the last two years or was on regular medication for earlier fits, found a prevalence of 5.8% in the Down's syndrome population. The prevalence under the age of 20 was 1.9%. He found no evidence that epilepsy in his study was related to Alzheimer's disease.

In this sample 7 (13%) children had had some sort of 'fit' at some time (diagnosed as such). Five of these seven children had had fits when they were babies and at least two of them were treated with drugs at this time; one had fits when she was vaccinated. One boy continued to have convulsions until he was 10 years old and his mother felt their cessation was linked with him beginning to lead a more active life.

In 1981 three boys were having fits: one of those with episodes in babyhood began to have them again at 16 and two others with episodes in babyhood began to have them at the age of 12 years. At the time of the interviews two of the boys were on drugs and this had controlled the problem (one had been having fits four times a day and the other two to three times a week). The other boy had small attacks only, every 3 months or so. Epilepsy had not been officially diagnosed but his mother was a trained nurse and had a lot of experience with mentally retarded children, and was unlikely to be wrong. As she said: 'They'll see themselves one day and then they'll believe me. They'll be telling me – I wouldn't be a bit surprised.'

Other parents described less typical symptoms. One boy would have some sort of attack during which he would lie down on the floor: his mother felt this was due to respiratory problems. Another mother described an episode when her daughter was 6 that she thought was a fit due to heat, but which had never been officially diagnosed as such. In addition to these cases mothers of two very severely retarded teenagers described 'attacks' resulting from temper or frustration, which probably did not have any physical basis.

Visual defects Aumonier and Cunningham (1984) found visual problems in 62% of their sample. In the South Wales study only 22 (42%) mothers were completely satisfied with their children's eyes and sight. Three mothers suspected that their teenagers had visual problems and the fact that none had been diagnosed did not reassure them because they thought testing could not be reliable in the circumstances. Nineteen (36%) of the teenagers had been prescribed glasses; a few when they were under 6 years old and the rest were at ages between 10 and 14 years (with the average age 10.3 years). Over one-third of the children refused to wear them or avoided doing so.

Two children had problems with cataracts. For one the condition was not sufficiently severe to need treatment but one girl had considerable problems. She had been operated on as a baby and, at the time of the interview in 1981, was undergoing further treatment for 'a bubble on the eye' and an ulcer and was to have a corneal graft in the future. Another girl sometimes had a 'lump' under the eye that had not been satisfactorily explained or treated.

Hearing defects Down's syndrome children commonly have problems with hearing because of constant ear infections (Hunton, 1979) but Evans (1973) also reported less easily detected hearing defects. It is disturbing, but consistent with Evans's findings, that Cunningham and McArthur (1981) found all Down's syndrome children in their sample had some aural problems and that half of these were not spotted in routine screening tests.

Ten (19%) teenagers in this study had some hearing problems. Three of them had had operations, which were probably putting grommets in their ears. Three teenagers had been prescribed aids but one had been advised to discontinue using his and the others were not regular users. Other teenagers were known to have, or suspected of having, slighter problems and it may be that more universal and thorough testing would have led to the identification of more problems. Parents again were not convinced that testing could be accurate.

Weight and mobility Smith and Berg (1976) in their review of available studies, conclude that Down's syndrome individuals are shorter than the normal population, the boys showing a greater discrepancy from the average than the girls, and Roche (1965) found a greater variability between Down's syndrome children of the same age and sex than exists between normal children compared in this way. Chumlea and Cronk (1981), using the information from three studies of Down's syndrome children, suggest that Down's syndrome children are commonly overweight and that this tendency begins to develop at around 2 to 3 years of age.

Of this population, almost half (46%) were considered by their parents to be overweight. They were aware of the problem when interviewed and talked of their teenagers being on diets, but it was clear that few felt a total ban on sweets and soft drinks feasible. For instance, one boy, supposedly on a diet, was given £6 a week as pocket money and he spent this principally on unsuitable additional food. Two mothers with teenagers at boarding school commented that they were always overweight when they returned home from school for the holidays. The fact that so few of the mothers were able to give an exact account of their child's weight would seem to indicate that many, as yet, were not taking the problem too seriously. A greater number of mothers of girls were able to give estimates of heights and weights than were mothers of boys: 12 mothers of girls compared with five mothers of boys.

Mothers with Down's syndrome children commonly report problems with mobility. In this population 23 (43%) mothers reported some problem. Five teenagers had extremely severe difficulties. Two had wheelchairs and, when in the house, one of these insisted on going on all fours and the other shuffled round on his bottom much of the time. A third girl was so overweight and so stubborn that taking her to town could be 'a nightmare'. The two other teenagers with severe mobility difficulties had heart problems.

Others had less severe difficulties. It was impossible to decide, for some, how far the teenager actually could not rather than would not walk, but the end result, for the

Table 1.13 *Reasons for limited mobility*

Reason	Number of times given
Tires easily	8
Refusal to walk	8
Overweight	7
Heart problems	5
Feet problems	5
Legs ache	3
Very slow	3
Odd walk	2
Medication	1
Total	42

mother, was the same. A few teenagers who refused to walk simply sat down when they wished to stop – a particularly trying problem for parents, since moving them was impossible.

Table 1.13 lists the problems which mothers considered limited the mobility of the teenagers.

Clearly overweight exacerbated problems, creating a vicious circle in which less exercise meant increased weight and so on. Table 1.14 shows the relationship between mobility and weight problems. Although the relationship does not reach statistical significance, weight was considered by some parents to be implicated as a major problem for their teenagers. The table is included because it suggests that, in spite of the failure to reach significance, there may be some association between the two problems (Bytheway, 1975).

Table 1.14 *Weight and mobility of teenagers (% in brackets)*

Mobility	Weight problems		Total
	None	Some	
No problems	18 (64)	10 (36)	28 (100)
Some problems	8 (40)	12 (60)	20 (100)
Total	26 (54)	22 (46)	48 (100)

$\chi^2 = 1.89$; df = 1; not significant.

Other health problems There were other less worrying problems. Skin complaints were not uncommon and eight (15%) teenagers had had boils or 'pimples' of varying severity, two had psoriasis and one eczema. Two boys had alopecia that had not responded to treatment. Two children had asthma.

Hospital admissions In 1972 the 37 children had experienced 37 hospital admissions between them. Forty-one per cent had not been admitted for any reason. By 1981 only 13 (25%) teenagers had never been in hospital but 22 (42%) of them had been in hospital only once. Table 1.15 lists the various reasons for all admissions to hospital after birth. Those who stayed in hospital straight after birth are not included.

Table 1.15 *Reasons for admission to hospital*

Reason	Total number of admissions
Pneumonia/bronchitis/chest	15
Heart	6
Gastroenteritis	6
Tonsils	6
Observation	5
Jaundice	4
Stomach conditions	3
Eye problems	3
Accident	3
Problems with passing urine	3
Appendicitis	3
Ear problems	3
Knee problems	2
Convulsions	2
Social reasons	2
Dental treatment	2
Others	9
Total	77

Seven mothers stayed in hospital with their children when they were admitted but another four mothers were not allowed to remain with their young children (aged 7, 4, 1½ and 1 year old). One mother in the new sample found that this separation produced more than a transient problem:

> That was a bad thing . . . she screamed when I had to put her down and leave her. Terrible. I asked [to stay] but wasn't allowed. They do stay with them now. After that she wouldn't sleep in a cot . . . in her little mind she thought she was back in hospital and that I'd just dumped her and left her . . . we had to have her in the bed after that.   (1981)

Only two mothers reported severe difficulties in hospital. One eventually had to have private treatment for her son's ears. This was the only example of private treatment in the population.

> The doctor was very stupid with him – he wore a mask and gown and Malcolm bolted. There was no chance of getting him back . . . . In the [private hospital] they made the same mistake, the anaesthetist came in in a gown. He said, 'Walk him down to the theatre.' Malcolm went berserk – he went into a corner and was fighting them off and he said eventually 'Do you want it done?' He knelt on his chest and Malcolm gradually inhaled. It upset me terribly.   (1981)

Hunt (1980) suggests that conditions that routinely would be investigated and treated in the normal population may be ignored in Down's syndrome children or attributed to their mental condition. There was an obvious example of it in this study. One mother spent three and a half years, until her son was 14 years old, convincing the hospital that treatment was needed for his constant 'dribbling' of urine.

> It must have been three and a half years we had it. They said you've just got to put up with it – well he was going to the toilet and I thought 'Well he wouldn't cry for nothing.' Every time he went to the toilet to pass water he cried and they said I worried too much. In the end I went down and said 'Well I'm not going from here until I have a second opinion', so they took him up to the ward and gave him a thorough examination and [after an operation] . . . he's been dry ever since.   (1981)

SUMMARY

There was some variation in the family experiences of the Down's syndrome teenagers. Within the population, children experienced a full range of family possibilities: some had very young parents and others parents were rather elderly, some were in small families and some large, some had one parent at home, others had two and one teenager had become an orphan. While this, in one sense, dismisses the notion of a stereotyped Down's syndrome family, on average Down's syndrome teenagers in this cohort did have families that differed from those of their normal peers. On average their parents were older than others with similarly aged children, parents had more children and the Down's child was more often the youngest child in a family. In common with other teenagers, however, most were being brought up in a traditional nuclear family.

These family characteristics can affect the lifestyles of Down's teenagers in a variety of ways – some advantageous and some not – but a negative factor in the lives of many of the families in the study was the Down's child's poor health. However, in spite of many having a poor start in life, most were in reasonably good health by their teens. Continuing poor health placed a few of the teenagers at a relative disadvantage.

2 Down's Syndrome Children Growing Up

This chapter outlines the levels of independence achieved by the children in various aspects of self-care in 1972 and 1981. The description concentrates on the teenage years because to date less information has been available about mentally handicapped teenagers and adults. Arguably deficiencies in teenagers are more important than in children. It is well recognised that a proportion of school-age Down's syndrome children will not have achieved mastery of all the necessary skills, but if as teenagers they are not yet independent in these matters then their ability to lead a normal life will be restricted. It is also likely that any discrepancies between a Down's syndrome teenager's performance in these matters will be treated with less tolerance in public.

The 1972 and 1981 studies are treated separately in this chapter because a different level of competence was accepted for the subjects as children than as teenagers. For instance, in 1972 a child was accepted as toilet trained if he could simply keep clean and dry by day regardless of some involvement of his mother in reminding him or taking him to the lavatory, but in the teens he was expected to deal with this aspect of his life himself and consequently mothers were questioned in some detail in 1981. Details of children being left in the house alone and bathing are included for the teenage but not for the childhood years, since parental involvement was expected to be inevitable for the younger group – although one boy apparently did bath himself from a very early age. The account attempts to show what children and teenagers did rather than describing capabilities.

THE CHILDREN IN 1972

Table 2.1 shows the level of independence reached by the children in 1972 in eating, dressing, toilet training, and going out alone.

Eating

Carr (1975) found that 69% of the 4-year-olds in her sample could feed themselves. Cunningham (1982), using material from his own and other studies, gives the average age for a Down's syndrome child to be able to feed himself as $2\frac{1}{2}$ years. Cunningham's averages may be optimistic since the parents in his study all had good early support and he excluded a few children who had additional problems from his averages.

In this study a generous interpretation of 'independence' was made in that no account was taken of the children who needed all, or part, of the meal to be cut up on the plate beforehand, nor of the children who preferred a spoon to a knife and fork. If he could, and would, eat without undue disturbance to others at the table this was

Table 2.1 *Independence of Down's syndrome children, 1972 (% in brackets)*

Function	Help needed			Total
	Always	Sometimes	Never	
Eating	2 (5)	8 (22)	27 (73)	37
Dressing	7 (19)	22 (60)	8 (22)	37
Toilet training (day)	6 (16)	6 (16)	25 (68)	37
Going out alone	13 (35)	12 (32)[a]	12 (32)[b]	37

[a] Allowed into the garden only
[b] Allowed out alone beyond the curtilage

counted as independence. Those who would only eat certain foods by themselves, ('only chips and bread and butter'), or only eat at school by themselves, were classified as having 'some independence' only. Needless to say, this may tell us more about the parents than the ability of the child but, from the point of view of work for families, it is the willingness to eat, rather than the ability, that counts.

Mothers who were determined to encourage independence had adopted very different training practices from one who patiently spent many months loading the spoon, lifting it to her daughter's mouth and waiting for her to take it, to another who 'used to plonk it down in front of him. I never cared how much mess he made'. A few made no efforts and were consequently surprised when children came home from school demanding to eat by themselves.

Dressing

None of the sample of 4-year-olds in Carr (1975) could dress independently. Cunningham (1982) suggests that the average age for dressing, excluding buttons and laces, is between 4 and 5 years old.

In this study very few of the children were totally reliable dressers and one of the eight who was able to do it only did so if her 'mood' was right. Of the 22 with 'some independence', a certain number could manage to an extent but would put garments on inside out, or back to front, or put shoes on the wrong feet. Others were simply beginning 'to try'. The mother who admitted to carrying out most of the dressing herself because of lack of time in the mornings was almost certainly stating the truth for many families.

Continence

In Carr's (1975) study 38% of the 4-year-olds were clean and dry in the day, and 18% were at night. Cunningham (1982) put the average age for Down's syndrome children 'using a toilet or potty without help' as between 4 and 5 years old.

In this study a child was classified as toilet trained simply if he could – reasonably easily – be kept clean and dry in the day. So, by these standards 25 (68%) children were reasonably reliable by day although four or five had a very occasional accident, or needed reminding to go some of the time. Where a mother had to be far more vigilant than this, and keeping the child clean and dry involved very regular efforts (e.g. 'I have to make him, he would do it in his pants'), he was classified as half-trained. Six (16%) had made no progress, although some of these mothers had optimistically put their children in knickers rather than nappies.

Eighteen (49%) children were not fully reliable at night. This includes three children who could be kept dry if they were 'lifted' in the late evening. There is one caution about this information. Two boys, apparently dry at night in 1972, were not so in 1981.

Since the mothers did not talk of any relapse, the most likely explanation may be that mothers themselves used a different standard in 1972; so that what was an acceptable lapse for a 6- or 7-year-old was not considered to be so for a teenager.

Going out alone

In 1972 it was already becoming a problem to decide how much freedom outside the home to allow the Down's syndrome child and differences between the children emerged very clearly. Needless to say, parents were influenced not only by what they considered to be desirable in this respect but also by the competence of the child and the dangers in their own area.

Despite the fact that Table 2.1 shows that 12 children had some freedom outside, only rarely was a child given all, and perhaps more, of the freedom given to a normal child. There were differences between the children that were not dependent on the situation of the house. In 1972, in the pilot study, two girls of similar age lived quite close to each other but whereas one was not allowed out at all the other wandered about quite freely: in fact she had been brought home twice by the police. This did not concern the parents, who quoted this to show the child's prowess. Both sets of parents were slightly shocked at the attitude of the others. Generally, for those who were allowed out, some caution was exercised and often there was a brother or sister who would keep an eye on them. They would go into the street to play or to nearby playing fields, for instance.

It is to be noted that some parents, even when their children had just started school, were making determined efforts to encourage independence in the child. From the earliest days some parents had a very clear idea of what they hoped to achieve in later years. In some instances this could cause friction between husband and wife.

> I still get very frightened. My husband insists that I should keep him in but I won't allow that. He's got to learn. [My husband] doesn't worry any more than I do – my heart's in my throat all the time I let him out, but I've got to do it. He's got to be allowed to develop as far as he can.   (1972)

Other mothers would pretend to want something at the local shops in order to let the child practise going out shopping.

For at least one mother in 1972, allowing the child out was the greatest problem she had. By 1981, though, this boy enjoyed considerable freedom and his mother had to be reminded what a problem this had been for her earlier. When she was first interviewed she had been extremely anxious and the topic came up again and again.

> I say, 'Terry got out again' and my husband says 'Give him a clip,' he says, 'and tell him he can't go out the gate.' Well, I mean he don't see him. He sees the girls playing out the front there and he wants to go out. Well, I mean [my husband] doesn't see what I see of him – you know – *crying* because he wants to go out and it really hurts because I don't *want* to keep him tied in – I mean, it's only for his own good that I've *got* to keep him tied in. Well, anyway, I lets him out. He's playing for half an hour and all of a sudden he's gone, . . . it isn't as if he just runs around here, it's as if he's got to go a long, long way. (1972)

This mother said her child could have been killed on one expedition by causing cattle to stampede. Like other parents, she had been unable to get any satisfactory advice on the problem. One mother remarked that she had been advised in the early days to keep her child at home but the adviser had now changed her mind and recommended the opposite policy.

THE TEENAGERS IN 1981

Although the range of independence achieved by the Down's syndrome teenagers was

Table 2.2 *Help Down's syndrome teenagers need with self-care (% in brackets)*

Function	Always	Sometimes	Supervision only needed	Never	Total
Eating	3 (6)	6 (11)	–	44 (83)	53
Dressing	22 (42)	11 (21)	8 (15)	12 (23)	53
Bathing	28 (53)	1 (2)	9 (17)	15 (28)	53
Shaving	8 (57)	–	–	6 (43)	14
Menstruation	13 (52)	4 (16)	3 (12)	5 (20)	25
Toilet training	10 (19)	11 (21)	3 (6)	29 (55)	53
Minding	33 (62)	20 (38)	–	–	53
Going out	29 (55)	6 (11)[a]	14 (26)[b]	4 (8)[c]	53

[a] Very limited freedom
[b] Limited freedom
[c] Unrestricted local freedom

extremely wide, the following account shows that almost all parents were still giving considerable help to their teenagers with everyday self-care. Table 2.2 summarises the help the Down's syndrome teenagers needed in this area.

Eating

It can been seen that, by their mid teens, the vast majority of these Down's syndrome children were able to feed themselves. Less than one in five needed any form of help and only 6% were dependent at every meal. The help needed was very slight too, cutting up meat for instance.

One child had been able to feed himself but, as he grew older, he became more disturbed and could not be left with food in case he threw it on the floor or simply 'slung it' in any direction. Two mothers, whose teenager children needed respectively no help and help with some foods only, remarked that their daughters were messy eaters and dribbled and dropped food 'like a baby – she gets it all over her mouth'.

With more encouragement many of the teenagers could have become more independent with feeding. For instance, one girl acquired the skill of feeding herself as soon as she went into residential care. As the mother said 'You get over-protective – you feel you must do it.' Again, one teenager would feed herself at school, but significantly, not at home.

Dressing

In comparison to their eating skills, which meant that most teenagers could feed themselves, only a quarter were able to dress themselves totally independently. As was the case with most items of self-care, parents might find themselves assisting with tasks the teenager could, if encouraged, manage himself. Another problem here was that dressing had to be done at the beginning of the day. Down's syndrome children are commonly slow in their actions and, faced with the choice of missing the school bus or encouraging independence, parents found themselves taking over more of the dressing than they would like. Parents could reduce the burden on themselves by a wise choice of clothing e.g. shoes without laces (a troublesome item for even relatively competent youngsters), and T-shirts without buttons. Zips, which might be expected to ease matters, could present problems. Most of the help consisted of helping with fastenings and making sure clothes were not inside out and back to front. Only four teenagers were completely helpless and even they would hold out arms and so on to assist with dressing.

Dressing could become part of a general discipline problem and one father described his own and his wife's efforts thus:

> As it is now she'll tell him what to do and he won't listen . . . she'll start shouting and ranting and raving as she does, and he'll sit on the floor and she'll try to move him – she'll try to drag him. She gets all sweaty and excited and he'll still sit there and he won't move. And she'll put his pyjamas on – he won't put 'em on. He won't put 'em on for me. I have to drag him out of the chair to put his pyjamas on. He don't want to put 'em on, so he won't put 'em on. So I clout him one and he may then decide he'll put 'em on. But he'll take his time about it and eventually I have to go: 'You have 2 minutes, get 'em on or [you'll get] a clout.' Two minutes will go to 5 minutes, or 10 minutes if you like – they're still not on. But my daughter will come in then, make a little fun and a joke and all of a sudden he's got them on.
>
> (1981)

It should be pointed out that we are talking here simply of the physical act of dressing and no other self-sufficiency in this area should be taken as implicit to the discussion. Only one or two teenagers could be relied upon to change their clothes at the appropriate time, some being content to wear the same clothes day after day. Only 24 (45%) were sufficiently interested or aware, or could be trusted, to choose their own clothes in the morning.

Bathing

Only 28% of the teenagers were able to bath themselves, but even here, while the question was not specifically asked of all, it became apparent that parents could still be involved with bathing in that they ran the bath and checked the water, fearing that their children would either scald themselves or have the water too cold. Although parents were not asked about cleaning the bath out it was almost certain that hardly any teenagers would be required to do this. These attentions could be extended even to the most competent of teenagers.

Shaving

At the time of the interview 14 (50%) boys were shaving and six of these coped with the activity themselves. Electric razors were popular with parents for obvious reasons.

Menstruation

All 25 girls had begun menstruating by the time of the interviews. Two girls began their periods as early as 9 and 10 years, 6 did not begin until 14 years but the majority (9) began at the age of 13. The average age of onset for the 23 girls for whom data are available was 12.4 years. The mothers did not give the exact month in which their daughters began their periods and so this average is only a guide. As with all girls the age of the onset of menstruation did seem to be linked with weight. The average age of onset for those whose mothers identified a weight problem for their daughters was 11.4 years (10.9 years for those with a marked problem) compared with 13.2 years for those without.

Only 5 of the 25 girls were left to manage their periods themselves. Three more could deal with the actual changing themselves but had to be reminded to do it. As with incontinent children, the work is not confined to those times when daughters need changing, but can also involve washing of sheets and clothes – and destroying of soiled clothes in some instances. Although the wholly incontinent girls in some ways presented fewer problems in that they were padded anyway the work could be unpleasant.

One mother described how she could, on occasions, be dealing with a bed soiled by urine, faeces and blood. Two of the girls were inclined to throw away their pads if given the opportunity. One mother whose child had been in a slow learning class visited the school at intervals during the day in order to change her and a grandmother kept the child away from school at these times.

Continence

Just over half the teenagers (55%) were able to cope with going to the lavatory them-selves. Two of these teenagers still did have accidents in the day because they delayed going – especially if they were out playing. One of these and two other teenagers could also have bowel accidents. For two of them the problem was commonly associated with swimming. One girl with both these problems could in all other respects be described as 'high grade'. Eleven teenagers needed help on some occasions and, for 10 of the 11, the help needed was with cleaning themselves after a bowel movement.

Of the 10 who always needed help, five were doubly incontinent and wore pads all the time, although three carers still attempted to 'catch' their children and encourage the use of the lavatory. Two of the incontinent children displayed abnormal behaviour – smearing or eating faeces and one would try to put his head in the lavatory if left unattended.

Twelve (23%) teenagers were not totally reliable at night. Three of them would be wet (and sometimes dirty) almost every night. Three others were wet at least half the time. The rest could be classified as having only infrequent accidents. One mother avoided the problem by 'lifting' the child once or twice at night and one boy was not dry until he was $13\frac{1}{2}$ years old, although this was at the same age as his normal brothers. One girl only had accidents if she was ill and another boy had had problems at an earlier period when he had convulsions.

None of the parents mentioned any attempts (e.g. with drugs or conditioning devices) to cure this problem of bed wetting and most seemed to accept it fatalistically. One mother spoke of 'only the odd accident that children get' about the bedwetting of her son of 17. The resignation parents showed was in spite of the fact that problems con-nected with elimination were felt to be particularly trying. There is no doubt that this was partly due to the fact that the most incontinent children were also the most severely handicapped, but this was not invariably the case. One extremely independent and competent boy was wetting the bed on average three times a week. This, together with the fact that he needed cleaning after bowel movements, was viewed by his mother as her major problem with the boy. No help had been given to her with this problem.

One boy had received help from nurses at the local hospital for mentally handi-capped people. Until he was 13 years old he would only use a potty but, over a period of 4 or 5 months, the helper 'got him off the potty, and into standing and doing it all tidy'. There were still problems with him wetting his underpants when he went to the lavatory (although he would change them himself) and inadequate cleaning after a bowel movement.

Minding

One of the most time-consuming aspects of caring for the Down's syndrome teenager was the fact that, with perhaps one exception, no teenager was left alone in the house for any length of time. That 38% of teenagers were left alone at all in the home gives a misleading picture of the freedom this gives the parents since the average time they were left was only 36 minutes. Nine of the 20 were left for periods of only 15 minutes or less and most of these parents would only 'slip to the [local] shop' or go next door.

Two of the most independent teenagers were girls. One would let herself in from school. Her mother was not happy about it, however, and intended to leave work – her comment on it was: 'It's a chance you don't like to take too often'. Clearly, leaving a child to come in to an empty house is a different proposition from leaving a happily occupied child in the house alone for 20 minutes. The other girl was exceptional. She attended weekly boarding school but, on Saturdays, her mother was able to leave her daughter in bed when she went to work. The 15-year-old was able to get up, dress, have breakfast, carry out jobs left on a written list by her mother and then join her mother at work if she wished to do so. This was wholly atypical of the rest of the population and it worked extremely well in this instance. The girl scored well on the tests but not exceptionally so. She had always mixed well with other children and had been treated very normally at home. During most of her childhood she had been brought up in a household of four adults who lavished much care and attention on her. Her condition had not been made known to her parents until she was over 2 years old. It is possible to speculate that, with a most cautious estimate, at least three or four of the other teenagers could have reached this level of independence if circumstances had made it necessary.

Most parents felt that their teenagers could not be relied upon in this way. Some teenagers had been left alone in the past but the results had been so disastrous – e.g. furniture had been ripped and one youngster had started a fire when everyone was in bed in the morning – that no further attempts had been made. Mothers of three girls expressed worries about people coming to the door. Another was afraid her daughter would start cooking and have an accident.

Nine teenagers were allowed out of the house alone but would not be left in it alone. Undoubtedly the reason for this stemmed in part from the fact that there was usually someone else in the house and in part because going out in the street could be regarded by parents more as an extension of the curtilage in which supervision was maintained, rather than an excursion beyond it.

Going out alone

Twenty-nine (55%) teenagers were not allowed out at all alone. The six (11%) teenagers who were given 'very limited' freedom only went as far as neighbours' houses or were 'watched' while they went to local shops and were never allowed out of sight for more than a few minutes. The 14 (26%) who enjoyed 'limited freedom' were allowed out for reasonably long periods, although mothers always knew where the teenagers were and when they were due back. The following account was fairly typical of these teenagers:

> We know where he is, you see. He used to go with [neighbour], but, if they used to be going somewhere, they'd let us know, so we'd know he'd be safe. Then, when he goes up to Martha [neighbour, half a mile away], we know she won't keep him too late – she'll send him back. Say if we tell him he's got to be back by half past five, he'll be back by half past five.... No, he doesn't actually know the time but he's got the sense of – he says sometimes, if he's going for half an hour to up to Martha's, or an hour – and we tell him, 'Come back half past five.' Perhaps he'll tell Martha, 'I've got to go back half past five.' (1981)

One of the most capable girls in this 'limited' group ventured further afield with friends but again her mother was very aware of what she was doing and where she was. Another boy went to a nearby disco alone but he was known to the man on the door.

The four teenagers (8%) who could come and go in a more relaxed fashion had all given rise to varying degrees of anxiety in their parents about their ability to cope during the time they were gaining this amount of freedom, as the quotation that is to follow shows. By the time of the interviews in 1981 parents were fairly confident. The quotation is from the mother of the 15-year-old girl mentioned in the last section.

> Well, I think the first time she said to me, 'Can I go shopping for you, Mam, down to A?' well, I nearly had a fit, I thought she'd be knocked down or run over, but I let her. I thought she could just as easily get knocked down crossing the road to Anne, they'd always gone together and I didn't know whether I'd let her go on her own. So I said, 'Well, cross on the crossing and just go as far as Spar and get me this and that and come straight home.' I was out of the door looking up the street and when she came back it was a relief, but she was all right.   (1981)

Even the four independent teenagers could not use public transport. Only one mother felt her daughter could have done so if she had lived in an area where it was necessary. Two of the boys went out on bikes. One could only use his bike in a limited way but the other boy, who had been encouraged from his earliest days to show maximum independence, was able to ride much more freely. Asked in 1981 how she had continued the considerable training efforts she was making in 1972 his mother replied:

> It's been very successful, very . . . well I wouldn't know how far he goes because I've no idea, but he's got a little bike – I hear all sorts of reports about him – he's been up to X and down to town. He goes a lot of places.

On dangerous roads the boy would go on the pavement, ringing the bell to warn pedestrians.

> Another time I asked him where he was going and he said he was going to watch cars and it turned out he was going to the town centre. Well, there's a dangerous crossing there, so I said to him, 'How do you cross the road? Do you go across where the flowers are?' 'No, Mam,' he said, 'red, green, orange.' Well there's a crossing by the school and so he was walking down to there and using the Pelican crossing. I thought that was extremely bright. He was doing what other kids won't bother to do . . . . Now, to be honest, every time he goes out my heart is in my mouth. I'm worried every minute he's out, but I'm not going to stop him. I think he's shown me he's got sufficient intelligence to care for himself as much as possible. And, after all, he's like other children, isn't he, you take a chance with any kids.   (1981)

The extreme dependence of most of the teenagers meant that, for any but the most limited outside activities, an adult had to be in attendance. This involves both time, trouble and extra expense for parents. A further aspect, which will only be touched upon here, is that this limited mobility has implications for the development and stimulation of the child. It followed that it was only those teenagers whose parents were prepared and able to provide life outside the home for them who could lead a life that approached normality.

Overall self-care

Table 2.3 shows how the teenagers fared overall in the seven items of self-care.

Table 2.3 *Range of independence of teenagers*

Total number of items achieved independently	Number of teenagers	(%)
0	6	(11)
1	12	(23)
2	8	(15)
3	6	(11)
4	8	(15)
5	4	(8)
6	2	(4)
7	7	(13)
Total	53	(100)

Any teenager who could go out alone at all or who could be left alone in the house for any period of time is counted as having independence in those areas, although it has been shown that for most teenagers who could do these things the actual independence was of a limited nature. In spite of the generous interpretation of independence in these very basic functions half the teenagers were independent in only two spheres or less.

Help from the teenagers

Independence involves more than being self-sufficient in personal care; it extends to keeping house. Mothers were asked how far teenagers helped with everyday tasks. As yet most of the teenagers were not making any substantial contribution to household work, as Table 2.4 shows. Twelve of the teenagers who did help would only do so if asked, or nagged: 'It's murder to get her to do things. She *can* make her bed, she *can* wash dishes. There's lots of things she's able to do but she doesn't.'

Table 2.4 *Help given in house by the teenagers (% in brackets)*

Frequency	Boys	Girls	Total
Often	3 (30)	7 (70)	10 (19)
Sometimes	17 (63)	10 (73)	27 (51)
Very rarely	1 (17)	5 (83)	6 (11)
Never	7 (70)	3 (30)	10 (19)
Total	28 (100)	25 (100)	53 (100)

The task most commonly undertaken by the teenagers was making beds, which was done by 17 teenagers (32%); three more helped with this task. Washing up or drying dishes was done by 16 children (30%), although often it was only tea things and there was at least one mother who redid them afterwards.

Teenagers were also involved in vacuuming (10) and dusting (9), and 6 were beginning to cook. Others were involved in simple jobs such as stirring gravy, but this was more of a treat for them than any genuine contribution. Surprisingly, only 6 children were involved in setting and clearing the table although it is possible that mothers simply forgot to mention this. A light meal – tea or supper – was made completely by only 4 teenagers. Other less common tasks included cutting lawns (2 boys), preparing vegetables (2 girls), helping with and doing ironing (2 girls), washing (1 girl) and fetching coal (2 boys). For some the extent of helping was only 'pouring me a second cup of tea', but others were described as 'genuinely useful'. In fact, of the 43 who did help, 21 (49%) were rated as performing some tasks 'well' and only 7 (16%) 'badly.' A few teenagers coped with what was required but lacked the concentration to finish the job. All the teenagers who 'often' helped did the work well and indeed one very helpful and capable girl hoped to get a job cleaning with her mother when she left school.

Many of the schools were encouraging the teenagers and training them to do household tasks and, in the same way that they had been surprised at the advances made with self-care through school training, some parents were beginning to have a new perspective about their children's capabilities. Only one mother did not appreciate this new training since she was 'scared to death' and certainly, in 1972, one mother felt that she was well able to give this sort of training herself and the school should concentrate on more traditional teaching.

The work from the parents' point of view

The preceding account has attempted to give an objective description of how much work is involved in the care of a Down's syndrome teenager but, for the parents, their subjective feelings may be crucial.

It was clear that for the few parents whose teenagers were incontinent this, not surprisingly, was difficult to bear, particularly as the child approached adulthood. The other task that was found particularly irksome was the constant attention required, particularly for the minority of teenagers who still needed active participation or entertainment from their mothers most of the time. Two mothers expressed it in this way:

> You have to be doing with him all the time.   (1981)

> It's a 24-hour-day job. Even if you sit and knit she won't let you. Five minutes, then she'll sit by me and pull the needles. She wants you to love her.   (1981)

Another expressed it more bitterly:

> I have to be doctor, a chiropodist and a haircutter looking after her – you name it – and I'm supposed to be a teacher as well now, according to the school – I'm supposed to play with her, keep her amused, talk to her – at 63 years of age.   (1981)

Table 2.2 showed how few of the teenagers were totally independent in many everyday items, but at least one mother made light of it:

> You tend to forget how much work is involved.   (1981)

But, in spite of all that mothers did, some were anxious to do more. One mother said,

> I'd like to do more for her. If I could teach her to do more for herself, I'd like to. I'm doing as far as I can to the best of my ability but I don't know if it's the best for Joan – if I'm getting all out of her I should. I'm feeding her, I read to her but is that enough? That's what I often think. If I'd had help when she was young, I'd know more about it now.   (1981)

A rather low level of independence has been outlined, but, this said, it did seem that many of the teenagers were in a transitional phase, and might be on the brink of a new independence. It was apparent that, as their sons and daughters became older, some parents emphasised the teenagers' new adult status in contrast to others who persisted in the use of such phrases as 'these little children', or repeatedly referred to the Adult Training Centre as 'school'. Clearly for those teenagers whose only adult characteristics were increased size and physical maturity, this was understandable, but such attitudes run the risk of influencing expectations and the degree to which parents feel independence in Down's teenagers can appropriately be pressed. Parents are usually sensitive themselves about how far independence is realistic for their children but a recurrent theme was that strides in self-care had come when a new situation presented itself e.g. a change in the full-time carer (a sister taking over from a mother, or a mother re-marrying), the child attending boarding school or the mother taking a job. Such changes could lead to a reassessment of what might be possible and result in greater independence for the teenager. Parents must also be aware of what the possibilities are if progress is to be made. The lack of progress of some of these teenagers on basic self-care must be considered in relation to the dearth of advice services available for these families, especially in the early years.

Accidents

It is not, of course, a perverse wish to sacrifice themselves or to hold back their children that leads parents to continue protecting and helping their children. Underlying the parental caution is the very real fear that if their children are not sufficiently mature to tackle a task correctly, then some accident will result. This is at the root of much of the extreme protection afforded the teenagers within and outside the home and plotting a reasonable course between encouraging independence and keeping a mentally handicapped child safe is not always easy. Newson (1976) points out that, although nine times out of ten experiments succeed, there is less margin of error with mentally retarded children so that, when something does go wrong, it can go disastrously wrong. Indeed, parents described many instances of potential danger from which the children had escaped unscathed. It was obvious that while a normal child gains discretion and awareness of danger as he becomes physically capable of carrying out more dangerous tasks, the mentally handicapped child, who is physically able, often continues to be unable to see the consequences of his actions or understand his own limitations. In addition, he retains the vulnerability of a child but lacks his advantages. A small child may wander but will be noticed before he encounters danger, but a mentally handicapped teenager may pass without comment until catastrophe draws attention to him. In view of the importance of reconciling the very real need to protect the child with the equally great need to encourage independence, it was a serious omission that this study did not include more discussion of occasions when the balance struck was wrong and accidents happened. The account relies, however, only on what arose spontaneously during the interviews.

Maintaining a close watch on Down's syndrome children was a greater problem in the early years when the youngsters were more active and venturesome. Children were apt to 'escape' whenever vigilance was dropped, as the following quotation from a mother in the new sample shows. This problem was not uncommon and could persist over several years.

> It was very difficult when we lived in a city. Once when she was about 5, we were in a supermarket and we were at the checkout and she was in the pushchair at the end and I was lifting the things in and then suddenly, she wasn't in the pushchair . . . she'd just gone out of the shop straight into the three-lane road and a man picked her up. He was hurling abuse: 'People like you don't deserve to have children . . . ' because he'd had a shock, you see, it was understandable. But it was a regular thing at that time in any shop, no matter how vigilant you were. (1981)

After the age of 10 years things improved for this mother because after one 'escape', which had included a bus ride, the involvement of the police in this incident had given the child a fright. Another mother in 1981 still had a major problem with her 17-year-old son. She had bought an armband for him that had on his name and address, since he had been known to go out even when everyone thought he was safely in bed.

> But I could be here and I could go up to the toilet upstairs and when I came back Alistair would be gone. If you went outside the door you wouldn't see sight nor hair of him – he'd be gone and you could be going that way and he'd be going this way, and he could be hours before he came home. (1981)

Obviously trips outside the home alone involved dealing with traffic and many parents, even of the most competent teenagers, judged their children to be insufficiently aware to be allowed complete freedom in traffic. In fact, only three parents reported road accidents and two of these were when the boys were only $3\frac{1}{2}$ years old. The other involved a teenager riding his bike and he had since been forbidden to use it on roads. This small number of accidents is, however, possibly only a reflection of the extreme caution of parents. This gives the children little opportunity to come to harm but also little opportunity to learn to cope. Another boy seemed to have avoided accidents only by extreme good fortune:

> He used to wander around when we first moved down here but not now, I think my husband's talked to him a lot not to wander off . . . he used to wander. He got into [a local factory] one night. The security from there came round with him . . . and they were asking him how he *did* get in. Well he couldn't tell them, but they've got television all around and they wanted to know *how* he got in . . . we called him the six million dollar man . . . . And he can drive a car . . . when I was living on the caravan site all the men there used to get him to go into the wagon, the jeeps and that and they taught him how to drive. He got into the lady's car across the road . . . he drove right to the end and she had to run after him to stop him.

And then he went into Spar's van – she was delivering the groceries. He got in, it was open, the keys were there and he was round the corner and left it there and came home. He knows the gears. Now they lock the doors.   (1981)

Other incidents were as follows. Two boys had started fires in the house when they were 10 and 12 years old respectively. One girl had accidentally turned all the electric cooker rings full on and another boy was inclined to play with electric switches. Further events included actual flooding of the house, unsupervised shaving with a razor and, one boy, misled by the animal picture on the can, sprayed the parrot with turtle wax. According to one mother her daughter used not to feel glass cutting if she held it broken in her hands.

It should not be assumed that it is the least able teenagers who are most at risk, and, arguably, in fact, the reverse is true. The majority of these incidents refer to boys, but it is impossible to say if they are indeed more venturesome, or more prone to accidents, or if mothers simply reported their exploits more. They did not have significantly more freedom than the girls. Similar percentages of the sexes were allowed outside alone and/or never left alone in the house. One mother exercised extreme caution with her daughter because she recognised that failure to avoid accidents would increase the already heavy burden on herself and she feared she would be unable to cope.

Personalities of the teenagers

There is more to sharing a house with someone than simply considering the amount of work they generate, and there have been various attempts both to verify and to refute the idea that identifiable personality traits are common among Downs's syndrome individuals. Some support for this has certainly been found. Silverstein (1964) found that Down's syndrome hospital patients were more 'mannerly, responsible, coopera-tive, scrupulous, cheerful and gregarious' than others. Different studies by Domino *et al.* (1965), Moore *et al.* (1968) and Johnson and Abelson (1969) have lent further sup-port to this, although Wunsch (1957) found more variability in behaviour and 14% of his sample showed 'aggressive hostile' behaviour. However, these studies have mainly been concerned with people in institutions and, in addition, do not use observation but tend to rely on the opinions and ratings of those in charge of the subjects, who could themselves have been influenced by the stereotype.

Holt (1957) studied mentally handicapped children living at home in Sheffield. He lists the 'most prominent characteristics' of the children and from this it is consequently possible to compare those characteristics attributed to Down's syndrome children with those of others. Down's syndrome children were described by a smaller range of behaviour than others. Forty-nine per cent were described as 'affectionate', 26% as 'sociable' and 28% 'wandered'. This compared with 5%, 13% and 8% respectively for 'imbeciles' in the study.

A more recent study by Gibbs and Thorpe (1983), with Down's children brought up at home, lends further tentative support to the notion of a Down's stereotype. In this study, the most common attributes were given as 'clownish', 'sociable' and 'affectionate'.

It seems likely that, although without doubt a large proportion of Down's syndrome children may indeed be affectionate and sociable, there is a wide range of behaviour. In this study, from the interviewer's subjective assessment, 20 (38%) teenagers displayed some characteristic that would militate against a normal, relaxed family life. These children were, by their parents' accounts, wilful or difficult to control or discipline, excessively demanding or disruptive or, from the tests, so retarded that anything approaching normal interaction was out of the question. However, it was apparent that most of these families had adjusted to any problems and did not feel oppressed by the situation themselves. When mothers were asked if their offspring were 'difficult' (which is not quite the same thing), only seven (13%) gave an unequivocal assent and only eight more (15%) felt that to some extent this could be said of them. Consequently, although the following account concentrates on the more difficult aspects, it did seem that parents themselves were in fact coping with, or had come to terms with, many of the problems. Indeed, it should be stressed that some mothers in speaking of their Down's syndrome teenagers compared them very favourably with their other, normal, children and one or two pointed out characteristics that could usefully be cultivated by others. Their Down's children's gentleness, lack of aggression and open, friendly manners, which extended to all, regardless of colour or class, were particularly picked out for praise. Mothers made the following comments:

> I think if I've ever met someone who's a truly Christian person, it's Malcolm. I've never known him do a cruel or nasty thing in his life and no matter how he is hurt he will always turn the other cheek. There's something odd about these children – or are we odd that we find it strange to recognise goodness – it's quite alien to us, isn't it?   (1981)

The mother of one of the most competent girls attending an ESN(M) school made the following remark:

> I wish she would be a bit more aggressive but she never rises to anything, Sophie, you know, she's a bit too gentle. I wish she would at school – fight back . . . . She's not handicapped, compared with other Down's, no, but compared with a normal person [she is] in that she's not going to be independent . . . she's so trusting and she doesn't see any malice in things. Perhaps as she matures, she might. It's a bit of a rough old world really.   (1981)

Generalisations should not be made on the basis of these comments any more than on the reporting of less desirable qualities. The range of reported behaviour was very wide, as were the teenagers' abilities.

At home some of the teenagers could be very little trouble – arguably too little trouble in that they were 'getting lazy' and were content 'to sit there all day and not move' or 'wouldn't move off the spot'. In others a similar disposition was shown in their unwillingness to leave home, or anxiety to be back when they did. Three of the teenagers were spontaneously described in exactly the same words by their mothers as 'home birds' and others spoke of the teenager's lack of enthusiasm about going out. 'I have to force him to come out these days.' It is perhaps this characteristic that leads to the stereotype of Down's syndrome people as being placid, and certainly over a third of the teenagers showed little activity at home and had little interest in outside activities. There were some mothers who welcomed and took advantage of this characteristic, others, though, felt that the contrast between their idea of a normal teenager's lifestyle and that of their own children was too great. Some of the teenagers also showed an ability to spend long periods in their own rooms occupying themselves. Some mothers encouraged this self sufficiency, and indeed provided televisions and record players to promote it, but others felt it was too unsociable a lifestyle to be wholly desirable.

> She likes living in the bedroom and she does like being on her own quite a bit, I find this. She shuts herself up in her bedroom for hours really. This is why I think I want to get her out now a lot this year because I don't want her to shut herself up. She's getting older and I just feel – well, it was all right when she was little because she couldn't go very far anyway but now we must try to take her out more.   (1981)

In contrast with the less active teenagers, however, and to illustrate further the dangers of making generalisations on this topic, some mothers found that their expectations of a placid and underactive child had been confounded. At least eight more teenagers were obviously leading very active lives and one boy, whose mother delighted in and encouraged his physical and emotional toughness, was extremely active in a wide range of sports.

Down's syndrome children are frequently represented as being stubborn, and certainly almost half of the mothers spontaneously said that their teenagers showed this characteristic. 'She'll do what she wants, you won't push her' and 'If Pat says "no", she means "no" ' were typical comments. Not all found this an unpleasing characteristic and at least one mother regarded it as showing her daughter had a mind of her own and so welcomed it.

In contrast, violent or aggressive behaviour was rarely mentioned. Eight mothers said their children could have temper tantrums when thwarted. Five teenagers broke ornaments and were at times destructive. One boy was growing out of these aggressive tendencies:

> Well I'm told by the doctor that violence is a very uncommon thing in a mongol . . . but, as I said, Roger isn't an ordinary mongol . . . when I compare him with the other mongols I've seen. I think he's more normal. . . . I think the cause of it is usually frustration . . . he was breaking things up, you know, windows and goodness knows what. In his temper he'd throw things . . . [but] he'll hurt himself rather than hurt someone else first, he's banging his head . . . he's a loving kid and will not hit out, he takes it out on things. (1981)

Another boy would smack his mother, if he was provoked. Five mothers felt their teenagers destroyed their own clothes or siblings' belongings because of 'frustration', although the cause of the frustration was explained variously as sexual frustration, inability to communicate and boredom.

Four children had shown a severe deterioration in behaviour and/or abilities. One severely retarded boy, who, in 1972, had been suspected of being deaf, reacted very badly when he moved schools at the age of 11 or 12 years, although it was not entirely clear that this itself was the cause.

> He's started hitting himself for some unknown reason . . . and a year last Christmas he started again and he hasn't stopped. He did go off and on before. He stopped for a while, you know, it was heaven . . . for 6 months at a time, but he hasn't stopped now this time. (1984)

Since he could mark himself if unrestrained, the problem could only be contained by binding his arms with tapes. He seemed quite happy with them on but would begin again the instant he was released. He had also started banging his head on occasions. His mother was sensitive and caring and the home was good. Professional help had been given but, in 1981, no solution had been found.

One girl, who had been seen in 1972 and was bright and responsive and had scored well on tests then had deteriorated into a teenager who did little and with whom it was difficult to communicate. Throughout testing in 1981 she ground her teeth or made repetitive hand movements. It was not clear why this change had taken place but her mother associated it with an injury to her teeth when she was on holiday. Conditions at home had also worsened and her parents were elderly and in poor health, but cause and effect cannot easily be disentangled. The family had not had professional help.

Two of the severely retarded teenagers showed abnormal crying patterns, one crying silently and for no apparent reason and the other never crying at all, although her mother would have been 'glad many a time if she'd cried'. The mother of this girl reported that her abilities had deteriorated in infancy and she was certainly very retarded in 1981. Since she was in the new sample she had not been seen in 1972. There seemed to be nothing in the home circumstances to account for any deterioration.

A boy, also not seen in 1972, likewise showed some abnormal behaviour at home, perhaps largely because he was shown no other way of conducting himself. He was allowed to crawl round the home, naked from the waist down because of incontinence, without any apparent effort to introduce more normal behaviour or provide him with occupation. He had hardly attended school at all.

It has been said that very few mothers considered that their teenagers could be left unattended in the house for long, but this did not mean they needed constantly to be amused. Most, though not all (as we have seen), were able to occupy themselves, albeit not always in a wholly relaxing manner (for the parents, that is!).

> He likes living at home, he doesn't like going to school – he'll play, he'll turn the place upside down . . . he's got a habit at the moment – he cuts everything up with scissors, and he emptied my letter

> rack the other day and he'd cut everything up . . . he gets a plastic bag, cuts everything up into tiny pieces and piles them into the bag.   (1981)

> His bedroom – I don't know how he gets it so – he carries two carrier bags around with him – he won't go anywhere without them. I bought him a bag but he didn't want that, he wants the carriers and they're full of junk . . . . He has a bath every night and if I'd let him he'd take all the pots and pans in – he'll stay in there for an hour or so.   (1981)

Another boy spent much of his time changing his clothes and two were constantly moving furniture around.

A minority of mothers – unfortunately not quantified – reported that their children were constantly demanding attention and, particularly when visitors were present, monopolised proceedings. In some instances a relaxed lifestyle was only possible because parents organised their own lives around that of the Down's syndrome teenager in order to reduce friction to a minimum. As one mother remarked, quite without complaint or bitterness, her son demanded a certain routine. 'Charles controls us, you see.' This insistence on set routine was not uncommon. One very personable boy had developed his own routine when he came home from school:

> He's no problem – he comes in, puts his bag down, goes upstairs, changes into his jeans, picks up the newspaper and reads every story on the front page of the newspaper. He'll then make himself a drink. He's a creature of habit, then, that's what he is.   (1981)

Sadly, quite unexpectedly, and very much at odds with the stereotype attributed to Down's syndrome children of being loving, affectionate and rewarding to bring up, a handful of mothers felt that their Down's syndrome teenagers were quite unaware of the attention that had been lavished upon them (and the sacrifices that had been made for them) and indeed were almost indifferent towards their mothers. One father was not even sure if his severely retarded daughter recognised them, although his wife was convinced she did. There were very few mothers who mentioned this problem yet it obviously has an important bearing on the satisfaction mothers feel. Mothers made the following comments (which are, of course, subjective reports; how far they would correlate with an objective assessment of behaviour cannot be judged here).

> I think, well, my God, here's me, I've given my life for 17 years to him and he couldn't care that much about me. He obviously likes to know I'm around.   (1981)

> He's more attached to my husband now. I've been – he's thrown me aside like a rag doll now. I did mind in the beginning – I don't now though – because I felt 'God, I've looked after this one for all these years – 16 years – and look . . . ' Well the thing with me is – as long as he's happy I don't really care, to be truthful.   (1981)

> He's never been close, he hasn't seemed to want me. He always seemed to want the men. Now and then he'll put his arms round me and kiss me and say he loves me, you know, but not very often. I'd like it because I'd have a feeling that I was – well, appreciated then. I don't think I am appreciated really. I suppose if I went he would – he would miss me then, he certainly would.   (1981)

Three more teenagers were described as very close to their fathers, e.g. 'she's more for her daddy than me.' Needless to say, other mothers mentioned how affectionate their children were.

SUMMARY

A fairly low level of independence had been achieved by the teenagers overall. Since the youngsters were in a somewhat transitional state – neither child nor adult – parental expectations for some were low and could be expected to increase in the following years. It cannot be overstressed that guidance to parents had been extremely limited and such gains as the teenagers had made were usually the result of parents' own efforts and initiatives. New service provisions in Wales (Welsh Office, 1983) may ensure a greater level of help will reach parents during the next decade.

Part 2
Variations in the Emotional and
Practical Responses of Parents

3 How Mothers Respond to Having a Down's Syndrome Child

Over the years there has been widespread discussion about the emotional response parents make to the birth of a disabled child (e.g. Rosen, 1954; Holt, 1957; Cohen, 1962; Michaels and Schucman, 1962; Schaffer, 1964; Sheridan, 1965; Pringle and Fiddes, 1970; Kennedy, 1970). It can be argued that this trend did little service to parents as it diverted discussion away from identifying the kinds of practical help parents certainly needed and sometimes, indeed, it seemed to be implied that the major problem parents encountered was their own inability to 'adjust'. As a reaction to this approach some writers attempted to show that parents' responses were entirely natural (Olshansky, 1962), or not particularly extreme (Roith, 1963), or did not differ substantially from the rest of the population (Boles, 1959; Hewett, 1970). Parents, too, began to point out that discussion of the practical problems was more relevant to them than endless counselling (Younghusband, 1970). Others asked pertinently what parents could do that could be construed as 'right' (Roith, 1963; Hewett, 1970; Carr, 1975). It is possible to criticise many of the earliest studies on the grounds that they are self-selected samples, lack control groups or clear definitions of the terms used. Hewett (1970) and Carr (1975) have useful discussions on the limitations of the research in this area.

Although it can be argued that undue emphasis was placed on parents' feelings in the past, nowadays it may be that concentration on the practical problems of mothers has gone a litle too far to help the minority of mothers who are unable to become quickly reconciled to the birth. It is obvious that parents – even with the improved services available today – can still encounter emotional difficulties at the birth of a disabled child and indeed extreme problems arising at the birth of a Down's syndrome child have been the subject of legal proceedings in recent years. In *Re B (minor)* (1981), the parents refused permission for a life-saving operation on Alexandra, a Down's syndrome baby. The child was made a ward of court. In *R. v. Arthur* (1981), a doctor was acquitted of murdering a 3-day-old Down's syndrome baby, and in *R. v. Brown* (1985) a father was convicted of the manslaughter of his Down's syndrome baby. A mother's emotional response is crucial, not only for her own happiness, but also because it is likely to affect all family functioning. Moreover, 'chronic sorrow', as Olshansky (1962) puts it, is likely to affect adversely a mother's perception of her situation. Gath's work (1978) nicely illustrates this point: mothers with normal babies were losing more sleep than those who had Down's syndrome babies of the same age but it was the latter who felt more tired and irritable.

A major problem is concerned with the difficulty of measuring 'acceptance' and 'unhappiness', essentially subjective states that mean different things to different people, with an objective index. It is also hard to determine how far the stress some mothers undoubtedly feel is purely emotional in origin and how far it stems from the spiritual and physical exhaustion that can result from the large claims made by their children on their time and energy. However, just because the topic is complex, this does not mean that it can be ignored.

It was decided in these studies, despite the naivety of the approach (which was certainly recognised), to rely on what mothers said themselves in order to illustrate the range of responses they made and, except where statements were blatantly inconsistent with each other or the known facts, to avoid imputing hidden motives and emotions to their behaviour. MacKeith (1973) states that 'Whatever the handicap, the reactions of parents to all the varieties of handicapped children have much that is similar.' Although this is possibly so, it is equally true that there are parental reactions that are very different, even when the disability is the same. The South Wales study shows that mothers exhibit a complete range of responses, even though the disabilities of their children are ostensibly similar. This variation is of interest in itself but, in addition to this, it was felt to be important to attempt a classification of responses so that an assessment could be made of the proportions of mothers who responded 'well' or 'badly', and to attempt an estimate of changes over time. However, the use of such classifications may give an impression of certainty that is not intended. The classifications have been explained by reference to the words of the mothers, but ambiguities are inevitable. The alternative strategy, however, of presenting the range of opinions alone, without suggesting proportions, was felt to be the less desirable option. It is relatively easy to classify mothers at each end of the range – that is those who were very positive and those who were very negative – but problems obviously arose where feelings were less straightforward.

There are serious problems with attempting to classify responses. One is that feelings change and fluctuate, as the mothers themselves recognised. One mother, in 1972, asked to postpone her interview since, immediately after the half-term holiday, she would not want to talk about the child. Another said:

> I've never rejected her, never resented her in any way. I might have *said* it, but I never meant it. When you're in a temper – we're all human and we all say terrible things and I'm no better than anybody else.
>
> (1972)

More than this, feelings are not always clear-cut. Not only do they change over time but they are usually mixed.

> I could say that if anything happened to her tomorrow, we'd be very distressed, but on the other hand we'd be able to say 'Well, this is for the best.' But we can't help loving her, can we? She is our own child.
>
> (1972)

Again, reliance on comments that mothers make does bring problems when statements are very inconsistent. For instance, one mother said she had derived more pleasure out of the handicapped child than out of her other children. This could have indicated a positive or at least midway feeling towards her situation. However, this mother was in tears for much of the interview, emphasised that family life and her own mental health had been ruined since the birth of the child, that she was cross with him for most of the day and thankful to get him into bed as early as possible at night, and so it was hardly possible to accept that this one statement was correct or gave an entirely true picture. Similarly, in 1972, school staff and other parents had said, before a particular home was visited, that the parents in question had rejected their Down's syndrome child. Although the interview was not wholly relaxed and answers were guarded rather than expansive, there was no spoken evidence of rejection. Consequently, it would have been impossible to justify placing the parents in either a negative or positive category. The midway position which was chosen to resolve the indecision implied a non-extreme response and was possibly completely misleading. In fact, in 1981 this mother was more expansive and relaxed, and was reclassified as positive.

A further and obvious complication is that it is highly probable that mothers are reluctant to admit to hostile feelings about their child both to themselves and particularly to a stranger, not least one who is intruding on possible 'private grief'.

Yet more difficulties arise when classifying the inarticulate or reticent mother. Such mothers were assumed to be positive, in the absence of any evidence to the contrary. In other words, they were assumed not to find the situation appalling, if they did not say so. The problems that arise with classification in these circumstances are illustrated by the following extract from a 1972 interview with the mother of a severely disabled child. In the absence of any flow of spontaneous words, it was difficult to feel that her comments were always a genuine reflection of her feelings. Nor was it always possible to see what was meant by her words. In these circumstances, it was very hard to avoid leading questions. Possibly the grossly stilted English used in the following extract lacked fluency because the mother's first language was Welsh. There may well, also, have been an element of Welsh reserve towards an English speaker, although the interview in 1981 with the same mother flowed more easily.

Interviewer: How did you first find out something was wrong with Arthur?
Mother: Well, I don't know.
I: Did anybody say anything in the hospital?
M: No, nothing at all.
I: No one said anything in the hospital?
M: Yes – they never told me nothing. Nothing at all. No, no.
I: What happened after he left hospital?
M: The doctor came out. When he came out of hospital the second time, he [the doctor] came to No. 30 and told me, 'He'll come' he said, 'he won't come very good now', he said, 'but he'll come in a year's time', he said. Yes. 'And his eyes is different', he said. That's all he said.
I: How did you feel?
M: Well, I felt awful, yes.
I: Did he give you any advice?
M: No, nothing at all, no.
I: What did you do?
M: I told my husband, you see. 'There's nothing wrong with his eyes', I said.
I: Did you believe what the doctor had told you?
M: Well, I could see nothing wrong with his eyes. I didn't realise nothing.
I: When did you begin to realise?
M: Well, now lately, I realise that.
I: Do you think the doctor was right?
M: I don't now. Well, he's grand now, isn't he? I felt very embarrassed at that time.
I: How do you feel about it now?
M: Oh, I feel pretty good now anyway . . . Oh yes, he's come quite good. Yes . . . he's a normal child, isn't he? He's coming on good *now*, anyway. I feel better now anyway.   (1972)

Luckily, interviews of such difficulty were not common. Most mothers were much easier than this to interview and so to classify. They usually showed that they had thought out their feelings and were well able to discuss them. Just one question would generally produce a flow of spontaneous comment.

The responses of the mothers for three different periods of their child's life – birth, early childhood and mid teens – were classified as follows:

1. *Positive response.* Responses here were mainly clear. Mothers either fulsomely, or quietly accepted their situation: 'No, we just treat him normally, perhaps I forget sometimes'.

2. *Ambivalent response.* These were the most difficult responses to classify and there was certainly overlap with the positively graded mothers and, possibly, with the negative. These were mothers who largely accepted their situation, could see the disadvantages but were not overwhelmed by them. Some still felt a pang when they compared their child with what he might have been but could none the less have enjoy-

ment from him. The reservations these ambivalent women expressed could be interpreted as entirely natural and understandable even in the context of complete 'adjustment'.

3. *Negative response*. These responses were the least difficult to classify in that statements lacked ambiguity. These were mothers who were constantly aware of the disadvantages of their situation and any compensations were outweighed by their problems and feelings. Mothers who spoke in similar ways to the following were fairly easily classified:

> It's parenthood without joy. I don't think there are any compensations, quite honestly. I don't know why these little children live. I feel very strongly about it. I can see no point in their life at all. (1972)

Since this account is concerned with change, the discussion centres on those mothers who were seen in both 1972 and 1981. There is some emphasis in the text on negative responses, not because such responses were more numerous (which they were not) but because parenthood is not commonly spoken of as a negative experience and such classifications consequently need justification. On a practical note, it is those who are unhappy about the situation who may need most help and so information about such parents is useful.

BIRTH RESPONSES OF MOTHERS (RETROSPECTIVE)

In 1972 mothers were asked about events surrounding the birth of their handicapped child. Clearly dealing with events that are several years old demands caution. The advantage that, by 1972, mothers could place events in perspective and give a coherent account must be balanced against a possible lack of accuracy and the danger that the memory of earlier responses will be coloured by subsequent feelings. An example of this sort of difficulty can be illustrated by quoting what a mother said in 1981 about her earlier response in 1972. She had, with confidence, been classified as negative in 1972 but she made mainly positive comments in 1981 and when she was asked if her feelings had changed she replied 'I can't remember what I felt at that time but I don't think I've changed'. Asked about how far she had come to terms with having a handicapped child, she answered 'I think I came to terms with that about 15 years ago. I imagine when you were here last I must have said the same thing'. When the inconsistency between the 1981 and 1972 responses was pointed out, she gave this response: 'It did upset me for several years. Oh yes, that's true, I was very upset in the beginning for years – several years – but no, it doesn't bother me now.'

Of course, classifying mothers on the basis of one meeting on one day can be very misleading but the contrast here was very marked and it does illustrate the difficulty of dealing with retrospective opinions. Considerable caution should therefore be shown when discussing the mothers' birth responses. The event itself, however, is so important that it cannot be ignored and indeed, in 1972, some parents were still suffering from that shock. Also, for those who argue that even the first few days of life play an important part in the mother–child relationship, this initial response cannot be dismissed. It is important to remember that this relationship is not fixed only by the mother's lead: the response of the child also plays a part. Even a potentially accepting mother could be daunted in the face of a continuing lack of response or progress. The child failing to live up to expectations can possibly set a pattern or begin a process of deterioration that is accelerated when the mother finds her worst fears confirmed. With children who are handicapped from birth, active response on the part of the child is not necessary to start a bad relationship – the child is wrong from the beginning and cannot be fitted into the role of 'new baby' from the start, or as Elizabeth Jenkins (1954) says in another context it is 'Not that she *does* wrong but that she *is* wrong.' (See Hewett, 1970, pp. 67–68 for a discussion of the part a child can play in the mother–child relationship.)

Since the early response can perhaps colour the later one, it seems relevant to discover who these mothers are who report they react well or badly to the news. It is not possible to assess the subtleties of any damage done to the child, the mother or the relationship by any initial reaction (or any advantage gained where things go well), but it is possible to see whether this reported initial reaction is related in any way to how mothers feel about their situation a few years later.

Positive birth response

Positive mothers were in a minority but, even so, nine (24%) mothers – almost one-quarter – could be placed in this category.

The following quotations, from mothers classified as positive, illustrate that not all were devastated by the news:

> Two days and I'd accepted it . . . There's nothing you can do about it and you just have to accept – naturally I was upset – no one wants a child who isn't normal but at the same time – it's something that you've got to accept. (1972)

> It was only that day. (1972)

> Well, horrible really, terrible. Now when I look back and think how upset I was about it all, I think – well, silly really, because you get quite hardened to it as time goes on, or you get used to it or something – I don't know quite. But we don't think about it very much now, do we? . . . We were never in such a terrible state about it. (1972)

> Well, I was relieved more than anything, because I knew there was something the matter with him, but it wasn't as bad – well – as I thought it might have been. I thought he might have been mental or something – like – you know. (1972)

A mother's response could be influenced by her familiarity with, or feelings about, handicap. One mother explained her lack of concern by saying she was used to handicap because her own mother had a brain tumour. Others explained that they had always felt they would like to care for the old or handicapped and so were not unhappy to have to do this. One mother was able to regard it as a challenge and made a rapid recovery:

> I felt cheated somehow – you know – why did it happen to me – at that moment, but coming home in the car I thought 'Is he hell going to be in a corner' – I was all right by the time I got to the house. (1972)

Ambivalent birth response

At the time of the birth most women – 15 (41%) – fell into this category. These mothers were clearly upset by the news but were able to come to terms with the situation within months rather than years and were able to respond with affection to their new babies.

Negative birth response

Thirteen (35%) mothers were classified as responding negatively at the birth. Primarily, to be classified as negative, mothers must have *said* that they had difficulty adjusting to the situation. They spoke in the following ways:

I just felt nothing – I didn't want to look after her like – you know. I suppose it took a long time – my husband would come in [to hospital] and I'd say I'd look after her, then I'd say I couldn't . . . I was sort of undecided for quite a while.   (1972)

I was very bitter for four-and-a-half years . . . I didn't want him out of hospital. I didn't care what they did with him then . . . My sister-in-law – she had him for a fortnight. I just didn't want to see him or do anything for him . . . she stayed with me for three months. I wouldn't let her go home. It was well over three months, and then I used to do it with a grudge. But I used to go up there [to my sister-in-law's]every day. I wouldn't bath him. She had to bath him at her house.   (1972)

I often think the worst time of my life was those two years when he was a baby.   (1972)

Mothers who looked ahead and it must be difficult not to, often worried about the future and this made the present situation worse.

I was looking too far ahead – what's going to happen when it comes to school and what's going to happen when she's older, what's going to happen after us, sort of thing – you know. You go ahead of yourself.   (1972)

Not all mothers would agree that the situation got better.

I could imagine what it would be like . . . I know this is something that happens – and it gets worse. I was telling the doctor 'I'm sorry I'm like this, but it's just that this is something that's going to get worse as he gets older – it's not something that's going to get better'. I realised that at the time – and of course it has got worse. It was all right when he was a baby.   (1972)

Most mothers classified here gave other information that tended to support their words: mild or more severe mental illness (4 mothers), rejection of the child (6 mothers and 3 who were doubtful), institutional care considered (4 mothers and 2 who were doubtful) or initial negative feelings persisting for over two years (10 mothers).

How the mothers adjusted

Most children were born in hospital and all mothers in the original sample did have to adjust sufficiently to take their children home. Usually they were not given any option about taking the child home, though nowadays reluctant mothers may be offered foster care for the child (see Appendix 2).

They couldn't do anything about it – they couldn't murder her, could they? They didn't give me the choice of a home – they didn't say, 'Are you going to keep her?' [What would you have said if asked?] Well, I couldn't have answered because I didn't know what a mongol was going to be like.   (1972)

I said I didn't want to stay any longer [in the maternity hospital]. They said, 'Well, you can't leave the baby'. I didn't feel anything towards him [but] I wouldn't leave him in any circumstances.   (1972)

I can't remember what I was feeling . . . I know I left the hospital next day. I couldn't stay there any longer. And I wanted to leave the baby. I didn't tell anybody this, but when they put him in the carrycot, I was a bit distressed. I don't know what I expected – I was so ignorant of everything you know – and when I got out – I don't know if I thought they'd keep him a bit longer or what . . . I didn't say anything but that was the first feeling, I suppose. A feeling of rejection.   (1972)

Several mothers mentioned a wish to leave the hospital – hardly a surprising reaction to the general euphoria of the maternity wards. A similar reaction was a wish to hide the child:

I was in two minds – I was, in a way, ashamed to see him at that moment . . . what will people think? – [but] I wanted to keep him. I didn't care what they thought.   (1972)

Oh, I cried – a whole fortnight I cried – until all [my eyes] were black. If anybody came in, I'd take the baby out into the back kitchen or the front room. (1972)

The reaction of others did affect a mother's own feelings. One way was by encouragement:

My sister came down that day . . . and I was crying – she was in a high chair there and I was looking at her . . . She said 'Well, I don't know, she looks lovely' she said. And she tried to pacify me in every way, you know. 'Oh, she looks lovely. You'll have to love her just the same', she said. I couldn't *not* love her, see what I mean, I'd had her for five or six months. 'We'll all bear it together then', she said. I had plenty of encouragement. (1972)

With some mothers the negative reaction of others made them feel more positively about the child:

Well, I realised if I didn't love her nobody else would – I did realise that. (1972)

One woman, later divorced, explained how her husband's attitude to the child affected her own.

Oh, where Dennis [her child] was concerned, I never wasted my time. After that my attention was turned towards the kids . . . Where Dennis was concerned, I hardened towards him. But where the others were – I mean – it was just one of those things . . . As far as he [my husband] was concerned, Dennis wasn't there. When he took that attitude I went more less to Dennis so I could give him that bit more attention. I mean, he needed it. (1972)

With mothers who failed to make an adjustment that was satisfactory to themselves the attitudes and responses of the other family members sometimes played a crucial part.

Mothers were asked who helped them most at the time (see Table 3.1). The most disturbing finding is that nearly one-third of the mothers felt that they had to meet the trouble on their own without any help. Not surprisingly, a woman's husband and own family played a major role (51% of help came from this source). The help given by these sources was both emotional support and practical help. No one mentioned a professional worker as their main source of help.

Table 3.1 *People from whom mothers received most help*

	n	(%)
Husband	10	(27)
Mother's kin	7	(19)
Father's kin	1	(3)
Children	1	(3)
Friends	3	(8)
Priest	1	(3)
NAMHC	1	(3)
No one	11	(30)
No need of help	2	(5)
Total	37	(100)

Mothers frequently mentioned that the beginning of an upward change in attitudes to the child came when they found the child was doing more than they had expected – when their blighted expectations were proved wrong and the child showed some promise. One mother spoke of her feelings 12 months after the birth:

Well, I could see her coming on so well. She started walking, started talking. She had clean habits – telling me she wanted to go to the toilet and that. Well, then she was like – well, like any of my other children you can say . . . I'm different altogether now. (1972)

Another said:

I didn't neglect him but I couldn't love him – not for – oh, about six months, I should think – until he started to behave like a 6-week-old baby does . . . When he started to smile, you got something out of it. But imagine having a 6-month-old baby who does nothing . . . it just came gradually as he began to develop and got his own personality.   (1972)

However, for at least one mother the child's almost normal early development prevented her coming to terms with the situation, especially when her doctor had painted a very different picture:

Well, after 6 weeks Donald began to move round, to kick and jump around. He was terribly active and this convinced me [that there wasn't much wrong] – not only that, he seemed to be developing normally and at 6 weeks he began to take notice and smile. And I was thinking there must be something wrong and the health visitor said he was developing normally – he began to sit up at 5 months and began to feed himself – well, almost younger [than normal]. [His brother] was a little younger but there's such a wide range when you talk about normal. And anyway . . . he started to crawl round at about a year and he was getting into everthing. And I just couldn't believe there was going to be very much wrong with him. He started to say a few words – 'Mam' and 'Dad' and he seemed to be – well – a pretty little baby I remember, and I remember the doctor saying to me 'Oh, mongol children are lovely children – they look worse, that's the worst thing about them.' Well, Donald looked all right. There can't be anything wrong with him, I thought. I'm glad this happened – it kept this hope . . . so I think he was about 2 when I realised that, although he was doing things I didn't expect him to – or other people didn't expect, because I did – [he wasn't like the other children] . . . and then when he was 3 I noticed he started to slip behind . . . What I meant by saying I didn't accept it was – because I *wanted* to think they were wrong. I mean I knew his cells were abnormal at a year old . . . but even then I kept thinking, well, perhaps there were a lot of people with abnormal cells walking about and we think they're normal. That's the way I wanted to think. I don't say I didn't believe it entirely, I *did* believe it really.   (1972)

For most mothers, however, the child's progress, after a long period when there had been none, made them feel better. Possibly one sort of adjustment involves the child progressing towards expected norms together with a lowering of the parent's own expectations to a point they could not imagine earlier. Change is needed on both sides (in the behaviour of the child and the expectations of the parents) so that behaviour and expectations coincide and some adjustment becomes possible. A consistent failure to accept lower standards or unavoidable inconvenience prevents enjoyment of what there is to enjoy. Tizard and Grad (1961) point out that those parents in their study who made the best adjustment were those who were able to give the child a realistic role to play, that is, their preconceived role had to change.

Another means of recovery parents mentioned came when they began to look outside their own family and found others in a similar or worse position. The role of the National Association for Mentally Handicapped Children (NAMHC) cannot be over-estimated here. Although not all parents wanted to join, and not all parents agreed with its aims or found help from it, for the few who did become involved, it was very important. Simply meeting mothers and being able to find they were not alone helped emotionally. No doubt, too, practical advice was also available from other mothers and this had often been lacking before. Again, seeing other children with greater problems made parents thankful that their own position was not worse. For others, starting school was a major step forward, once mothers had recovered from the traumatic experience of seeing the school that was thought to be appropriate for their child. Here again, they found others in a similar or worse position and they also were given a few hours break from the child every day.

For many recovery was a long, slow healing process with no single thing helping:

Well, we accepted it from the start, you know. We never thought there was a mistake or anything like that. I think really it was about two years before – well, whenever I'd think of him my tummy would absolutely just turn over, you know – just the thought of it. But eventually, it passed. I would say it did take a long time.   (1972)

In fact, 14 (38%) of the mothers had made an improved adjustment by 1972.

CHILDHOOD RESPONSES OF MOTHERS (1972)

Perhaps a more important response than that made initially is the response made by the mother as the child grows up. By 5, 6, 7, and 8 years attitudes have probably hardened, changes in the child are less dramatic and changes in parental attitudes are probably less likely after this time.

Mothers were again divided into three categories. Once more this was largely based on what mothers said they felt. It is encouraging to note that, by the time the children were between 5 and 8 most mothers were positive in their responses.

Positive childhood response

A large number of mothers – 18 (49%) – seemed to have come to terms with the situation and were rated as positive. Typical comments were as follows:

> Afterwards, I just lived with it – well, not that – I enjoy his company. (1972)

> It's not nearly as bad as I expected. There's a tremendous amount of pleasure to be had . . . there's nice parts to it as well. All you can see in the beginning is blackness. (1972)

> We love her so much, don't we. That's how we catch all our colds, cuddling her, and when she gets a cold we get it . . . she's ruined in a way and yet we're strict with her . . . oh, she's marvellous. We don't know she's around. (1972)

As was stated earlier, mothers who did not qualify their feelings were assumed to find life bearable. A few of these parents, no doubt, had not given much thought to their position. They had had the child, he was theirs, they loved him, he joined in with their lives and they would not really have thought of anything else. One woman explained she had not bothered to find out the results of tests carried out on the child:

> Well, I don't see it makes much difference now – she's here, she's ours, whatever she is. (1972)

It seems likely, however, that those who unthinkingly accept their child are making a positive response. No one was so inarticulate that they could not have voiced a complaint had they wished to do so.

Ambivalent childhood response

In 1972 nine mothers (24%) were classified as ambivalent. These were mothers who were not, unlike the negative mothers, constantly aware of the disadvantages of their situation. They could see the problems involved (present and future) but they did not allow themselves constantly to be overcome by them. They did not find the situation intolerable, but at times would be depressed and unhappy about it. They could also see the brighter side of things. One mother, who had few problems with her child, said:

> I mean, there are worse things in life than that.

But later in the interview she also said:

> It's always there, it never goes completely. We're lucky to have her as she is, but if we could have her different we would have her different, you know? (1972)

Negative childhood response

Ten (27%) mothers had failed to adjust satisfactorily and were constantly aware of the disadvantages of their situation. Any small compensations were far outweighed by the problems and feelings they had now, and expected to have in the future. Mothers who spoke in the following ways were fairly confidently placed in this category:

> I haven't got over it today – never will, in fact. You have to accept these things, you have to live with it, but I don't think I'll ever get over it . . . I wish it wasn't really, but there you are, I'll never accept it. I mean I've got to face up to it and it's there, we know, but you know it's always on my mind – it worries me and there it is. Some people are that way – others . . .   (1972)

> [I feel] trapped. It's a dreadful feeling. You know it's inevitable, you know there's nothing you can do about it, and you know that sooner or later you've got to come to terms with it, but you feel so absolutely helpless.   (1972)

This category also includes one mother who did not really fit into any category. She is placed here since she refused to accept the diagnosis of Down's syndrome. Although she thoroughly enjoyed her child and found nothing irksome in his management, it cannot be said that she had 'adjusted' or come to terms with the handicap: she attempted to adjust by disbelieving the true situation. She is in marked contrast to the other mothers in this category, who were very clear-sighted about the true situation. With hindsight, in 1981, it was possible to see that her rejection of the diagnosis was more extreme than had been suspected in 1972 and the negative classification possibly was justified (see below).

MID-TEEN RESPONSES OF MOTHERS (1981)

In 1981 mothers were again classified according to how they spoke about their feelings, their children and their own level of contentment. Only 31 mothers could be followed up. Table 3.2 shows the mothers who were lost to the study in 1981 and the responses they had made in 1972.

Table 3.2 *Mothers not interviewed in 1981*

Reason for loss	Number of mothers	1972 Response
Refused to take part in 1981	2	1 Negative 1 Ambivalent
Child died	1	Positive
Mother died	2	Both positive
Mothers left household	1	Negative

The mother who had left the family household had been the one who was doubtfully categorised as negative in 1972, since her only apparent problem was her strong refusal to accept the diagnosis of Down's syndrome for her son. In that year the only obvious influence of this on her behaviour was her unwillingness to accept an ESN(S) school placement for the boy. In fact several parents showed disquiet over such placements for their children and, indeed, the modern trend is to avoid such early decisions. Consequently, her behaviour was not considered to be excessively unusual and by 1973, at the father's insistence, he did attend the ESN(S) school. The mother was not British and it was known in 1972 that many foreign medical specialists had been consulted and that the mother was spending money on medicines sent from abroad for the boy, but the extent and nature of this expenditure was not appreciated. In fact the sums were substantial and medicine included twice daily injections, antibiotics and creams intended to soothe the boy's fissured tongue. In all, with specialist consultations and medicines, the father calculated he had spent £7000 to £8000. The conflict this produced in the family eventually erupted in 1978 and the mother returned to her own country leaving the boy in the care of his father. This was the situation in 1981.

Positive teenage response

Eighteen mothers (68%) were classified as responding positively. They made comments of the sort recorded below:

> Oh, yes [the pleasure from him] has increased. Malcolm gets better each year – he's a humorous little boy . . . we're very proud of Malcolm. (1981)

> I wasn't worried if I had another one because Terry was so good that I thought . . . 'Well, if he comes like Terry is, I've got nothing to worry about.' (1981)

> It's never bothered me. (1981)

> I feel marvellous – I'd have ten of them. They're so lovable, aren't they, and can do things you don't realise they could. They're not as handicapped as a lot of people put them down to be. He comes out with things you'd never realise he could say or do, like. I'd never part with him. (1981)

> You get to love them more and more all the time and it doesn't bother you now as it did. In the beginning it was very upsetting and horrible. As time goes on you get to love them so much . . . (1981)

Ambivalent teenage response

Six mothers (19%) were classified as having more ambivalent feelings about their situation. Again, these are the most difficult mothers to classify and the line between the ambivalent and the positive is difficult to draw. These mothers spoke in the following ways:

> I think I am quite used to it now, though I look at him and still can't believe it's happened . . . I still mind although I feel as long as I can look after him and he's happy . . . (1981)

> Oh, I wouldn't swap Kevin for the world you know – but he still breaks my heart, you know – I still get upset about it. I suppose I have in a way [come to terms with it] but, as I say, I still get very depressed about it – you know. (1981)

The following quotation is from a mother who was coping well in 1972 and indeed rejoiced at having a little girl to care for after two boys but, in 1981, she was not in good health herself and was coping alone with a very severely disabled daughter. She was obviously finding increasing problems.

> Well, you can't say – you can only say you wish she wasn't, but you can't alter anything can you? – it's an experience but I wouldn't like to see anyone else having one and wouldn't like to see my [other] children having one. It's uphill all the time, it's hard work. No matter how good friends are, when you really need them they don't want to know. (1981)

Negative teenage response

Classifying mothers became more difficult in 1981. Even the seven (23%) mothers who were classified as negative in 1981 had, for the most part, learned how to cope with problems. Three said that caring for the child had become easier, but none of the three was still caring for the child at home full time. The other four said life had become more difficult. All were extremely conscientious mothers.

Quotations from the seven mothers are given liberally so that explanation of their feelings is clearer. While most children became easier to manage, one girl had deteriorated substantially from 1972 to 1981 leaving the mother with an even greater problem and even less heart to cope.

You're tied. You've got to be on beck and call the whole time. It's not eight hours – you haven't got a job eight hours – it's 24 . . . You've got no life of your own, that's the thing, and the attention that they need that you're too old to give . . . Sometimes some say 'Oh, she's company for you' . . . Well, she's here, sitting down there like an old woman, you can't talk to her, she's just someone in the house with you, that's all – because I've got to be here, haven't I? If I didn't have her I could go out, couldn't I? I'd have more time and less tension – I'd be able to have the energy then to go out . . . And she makes these funny noises, like a dog, like an animal you know, and she sits like a monkey – she doesn't sit like – she's got her feet all curled up underneath.   (1981)

Two other mothers, though at the same time they reported that caring for the child had become more difficult, seemed less stressed than in 1972, or become more resigned, but not sufficiently so to be reclassified. Asked if her feelings had changed since 1972 one mother replied:

Well, no, [I haven't got over it] not really. I accept it now and I think we've got him here and he's like a normal child you know – when we're all together I just don't think of him as mentally handicapped, you know, on my own. I just try to lead as normal a life as I can. [Does it still upset you?] Oh, yes, often I feel upset. I still get very emotional about it. Not as much as I used to be. I was upset when he started his epilepsy [at 12 years]. I'm afraid now when he's out in case something's going to happen – have a turn. I couldn't talk about that for a bit – it's one of those things. If you cry it out of your system it's better. I found I was bottling it in and it was making me feel worse.   (1981)

Another mother, who coped extremely well, but whose husband had responded very badly and unremittingly at the birth of the child said:

No, I don't think I'll ever feel differently for the reason that it's spoiled my life with my husband, but I don't have it out on [the boy] . . . Well yes I do [feel resentful], I think I do, to be honest. What it amounts to is that we'd planned we'd have a little bit of a life once the children were grown up, instead of that we're tied worse. Oh yes, I think I feel – definitely I feel –

Asked if she thought she had come to terms with the practical and emotional problems she said:

I do, I do. I accept him as he is and I don't look for any big improvements, but I do worry as things come up, obviously.   (1981)

Only one mother had become negative since 1972. Her modest aim in life was a settled and happy marriage and she had been thwarted in this throughout her son's 17 years. Although her Down's syndrome son was not responsible for all her misfortunes his presence had undoubtedly played a part and was implicated in all her relationship breakdowns. When the child was born her husband had responded very badly and the marriage ended in divorce for reasons she attributed to his response at the birth of the child. By 1972 she had remarried and her new husband was extremely supportive and all seemed set fair at the first interview. Her new husband became less involved with the Down's syndrome boy when his own child was born and he later developed psychological problems himself, there were severe difficulties and the couple separated. Later she was widowed. A third relationship deteriorated, again when the man's own child was born, and in 1981 this woman was left coping alone with the Down's syndrome teenager, a daughter of 15, a son of 8 and the part-time care of her 5-year-old son. Furthermore her determined efforts to support herself in business had ended in failure and she had considerable financial worries. All told, in 1981 she was at a low ebb and was desperately seeking residential care for her son. Despite the fact that she spoke of him with affection, she found his presence a barrier both to finding work and a chance of 'a settled relationship'. As she said:

If their own parents can't accept them, they're very few and far between the men who can accept a [Down's syndrome] man like that.   (1981)

As well as this there was friction in the home between her Down's syndrome teenager and her other young sons. Her comments on the situation were as follows:

> Maybe a little bit [resentful] now, yes. I think looking back, how things have turned out – I think things would have been a lot different if he'd been normal and I don't seem to have the same patience with him as I had before – you tend to get a bit cross with him. When he was little you accepted him as a little boy – now he's a man – your feelings have got to change towards him, you know . . . I think you have to try to adapt yourself to coping with a male adult, mentally handicapped – rather than a little boy . . . with Roger you've got a boy who's still a baby so you're muddled in your feelings. You keep thinking to yourself – he's a young man but he's not . . . nine years ago [in 1972] I was married and I hadn't gone through the problems I've explained – I'd every reason to hope we'd be together as a family . . . but of course things have happened in the last eight years, they've become tougher . . . maybe over the years, as things have gone, I've resented him a little bit. (1981)

Two mothers spoke in ways that showed a remarkable improvement from their 1972 position. They are not reclassified because their greater contentment was due to a large extent to their children's admission to boarding school and residential care. In both cases pressure had been reduced but neither felt they could cope with the child at home on a full-time basis. The following quotations illustrate the strength of improvement. Both mothers showed the relief that came from reduced responsibilities but also, most importantly, they displayed a new warmth and affection towards their children.

In 1972 one of these mothers had claimed to have no strong feelings towards her child and yet the following quotation shows how instinctive and strong her feelings in fact were.

> A lot [of the difficulty] is my attitude. I often find her repulsive – you know – her table manners, this sort of thing. She always has a runny nose, she's always dribbling. I'm not exactly house-proud – I believe in them living in a house and if they make a mess – well – but with her, I don't know. There are times when I don't want to pick her up and I feel I . . . with the others, if they've eaten something and leave it, you wouldn't mind picking it up and having it yourself – but with her – no. It's this awful revulsion . . . I feel extremely guilty about it. (1972)

In 1981 she said:

> I don't feel the same [as in 1972] – I feel far more affection for her simply because she's not suffocating me. I can enjoy her in a way I couldn't do at any time before because she's not always there, you know, making me feel almost panicky because I'm so much tied . . . and there's not so much of the unpleasant things you have to do for her such as taking her to the toilet and the bath, changing wet or dirty beds and less dribbling and runny noses which used to turn my stomach when I had to do them, especially as she got older . . . at 10 or 11 she was developing into a young woman, it was very unpleasant . . . I mean she's very loving and now I look forward to her coming home which I've never done before . . . and we often keep her for the extra week . . . Yes, it has been hard – it would have made so much difference if we hadn't had her, we still suffer from repercussions. (1981)

In fact, the daughter was cared for at school during the week in 1972 but the parents were never allowed to feel the arrangement was permanent and consequently the pressure was still there. In 1981 residential arrangements were very satisfactory and she came home at least every third weekend.

Again, the second mother showed a change in the feeling she had for her child.

> I think there was a change when he was ill and I thought he might die [two years earlier]. Before that I felt that I didn't feel the same about him, you know. I knew I cared for him and wanted to look after him but I just didn't feel I had this emotional bond – you can't communicate – but then, when he was so ill, I realised how much I did care – just the same, [as the others] . . . I think I began to value his good points and sort of reassessed things.

Asked how she would cope with him at home if her plans for extended residential education did not succeed, she replied,

> Apprehensive . . . I know I wouldn't cope much being tied to him all the time. Once the children grow up and become independent the fact that I'd have to be – *with* him and responsible all the time. I know I wouldn't like that.   (1981)

In contrast, another mother who had responded similarly to this mother in 1972 and who had also received a boarding-school place for her child did not fundamentally change her view, although undoubtedly she benefited enormously with the relief from the strain. She compared the difference between her life during the holidays and term time as 'the difference between living and existing'. Nevertheless, when her daughter was at home she made every effort to provide her with an enjoyable and stimulating holiday, arguably to a standard she could not have maintained if she had been under constant stress. Her underlying unhappiness, which is described below, makes her conscientious efforts at holiday times all the more commendable.

> There's a lot of personal distress that comes into it. She's the major cause of any unhappiness there is in the family. There's an awful lot of resentment on my part – there was that I was pregnant at 40 . . . it's there all the time . . . I still feel it's a thing no one should have to endure . . . I think I'd have coped better with it if it had been a planned pregnancy.

Asked about her feelings towards her daughter, she said,

> Not as I feel towards the boys – I do what I do because I have to – it sounds very brutal doesn't it . . . there's not the warmth, not the depth of feeling that there is towards the boys. Oh, yes, of course I do [feel guilty about it] . . . when I see contemporaries of mine with daughters – they have such wonderful relationships – there's a certain amount of jealousy there, or deprivation . . . I see 14- or 15-year-old girls going to school, it's a knife in the wound.   (1981)

The Malaise Inventory

As a further measure of the emotional state of mothers the Malaise Inventory was administered to each carer in 1981, with one exception. A score of over 5 or 6 implies possible emotional stress. Bradshaw's (1980) sample scored an average of 9.2, which is perhaps not surprising since his respondents were all seeking help from the Family

Table 3.3 *Responses of mothers 1981 and their scores on the Malaise Inventory (Max. score 20)*

Mothers' responses	n	Average score	Range
Negative	7	10.2	2–17
Ambivalent	6	9.2	7–13
Positive	17	6.5	0–14
Total	30	7.9	0–17

Fund and so are likely to have encountered stress. Carers in Pahl and Quine's (1985) study scored an average of 5.8. Scores for families without handicapped children are much lower. Table 3.3 shows the difference in scores for mothers in this sample. The difference in average scores for positive and negative mothers lends some reassurance to the subjective classification given to mothers.

Changes in responses

Looking at responses over the period since birth, it can be seen that overall there was a steady improvement with the most major adjustments and reconciliations taking place in the early years (Table 3.4).

Whereas at the birth a minority of mothers were wholly happy with their situation, by the time their Down's child reached his teens the majority were reconciled and content. Even for the seven who were classified as negative most were coping with the situation, albeit because, in some cases, they did not care for the child on a full-time basis.

Table 3.4 *Mothers' responses from birth to teens (% in brackets)*

Response	Birth (1964–6) (Retrospective)	Childhood (1972)	Teenage (1981)
Negative	13 (35)	10 (27)	7 (23)
Ambivalent	15 (41)	9 (24)	6 (19)
Positive	9 (24)	18 (49)	18 (58)
Total	37 (100)	37 (100)	31 (100)

Changes in mothers' responses from birth to teens (excluding childhood) can be summarised as follows:

3 (10%) deteriorated: all ambivalent to negative.
16 (52%) remained the same.
12 (39%) improved: 3 negative to ambivalent; 4 negative to positive; 5 ambivalent to positive.

Possible explanations of mothers' responses

Why did certain mothers respond in certain ways and why did they change their responses over time?

Obviously, the kind of stress a family and its members can tolerate is to some extent specific to that family and the kind of stress each handicapped child brings will vary. Some families can tolerate a physical handicap more than a mental handicap, and so on. Farber *et al.* (1960) found fathers were more affected by having a handicapped son and mothers initially more affected if the child was a daughter. Moreover actual stress and perceived stress are not always the same. The age of the child will also make a difference. Some parents will be gratified as the child increasingly makes small achievements, but others will feel the problem increases as the achievements lag further and further behind those of his peers.

Social class explanation

Whilst there was some reluctance to engage in further analysis of data that, because of its subjective nature, may be suspect, an attempt was made to see if mothers who responded in similar ways had other characteristics in common. The most important characteristic of parents in this sample related to response seemed to be social class (see Table 3.5).

Table 3.5 *Mothers' responses and social class 1972 and 1981 (% in brackets)*

	Childhood and teenage responses							
	Negative		Ambivalent		Positive		Total	
Social class	1972	1981	1972	1981	1972	1981	1972	1981
I and II	4 (50)	5 (71)	1 (13)	–	3 (38)	2 (29)	8	7
III	5 (26)	2 (12)	7 (37)	5 (29)	7 (37)	10 (59)	19	17
IV and V	1 (10)	–	1 (10)	1 (14)	8 (80)	6 (86)	10	7
Total	10 (27)	7 (23)	9 (24)	6 (19)	18 (49)	18 (58)	37	31

1972: Goodman and Kruskal's $\gamma = 0.45$. This produces a standardised normal deviate of 1.99 (significant at 5% level).
1981: (Ambivalent response grouped with positive response) Goodman and Kruskal's $\gamma = 0.938$. This produces a standardised normal deviate of 3.14 (significant at 1% level).

Several writers have found that the birth of a handicapped child has a greater impact on parents of high social class. At first sight this might seem surprising in view of the fact that some part of the hardships of handicap (e.g. extra work, extra clothing, special schooling) could be mitigated by extra expenditure. Several similar explanations are offered. Tizard and Grad (1961, p. 84) found 'the best adjustments' were made by parents who 'replaced their perceived role by a realistic one'. They suggest this is more likely to be found in working-class households and in large families because – 'those who have been buffeted by life may find it easier to restructure their expectations, and to face hardships as they come'. They also suggest there is support from 'solidarity of the social group' in working-class districts. Similarly, in large families (possibly found more in working-class districts in those days when there was a higher birth rate and lower geographical mobility) the burden can be shared.

Baylcy (1973, p. 242) also found differences in families' responses and likewise emphasises the importance of the mother's expectations. He gives one example:

> The mother of a severely disabled man in a pit village on the outskirts of Sheffield was prepared to tolerate an apparently joyless life of undiluted slog in a way few, if any, mothers from a professional background would.

A further example of the part expectations may play in determining how a person copes with unexpected hardships can be found in another context. Coxon (1985), during a conference on AIDS, reported that mothers of the proportion of haemophiliac children who are at risk of contracting AIDS seem to cope with this potential hazard better than homosexuals. He suggested that this may be because of the different expectations of good health held by the two groups.

Farber (1968) suggests it is the hard work that is the main problem for working-class families in contrast to the middle-class families where the problems centre around frustrated family aims and aspirations. Unless there are large problems of care, the 'label' of mental retardation is a less severe shock for working-class families since the labels usually ascribed to them (e.g. 'unemployed', 'poor', 'uneducated') often also carry low status ('a multiplicity of stigma'). For the middle-class family, however, there will be a severe contrast between the retardation label and labels (e.g. 'professional', 'affluent', 'well-educated') usually given to the family (see, too, Gath, 1972).

All these explanations hint at the high expectations middle-class parents have for themselves and for their children. A handicapped child can easily be seen as imposing limitations on the lives of the parents and new long-term obligations (e.g. freedom of movement, use of resources, retirement plans). The life of the child himself will be restricted when compared with the expected achievements of normal children. These are to some extent practical difficulties. Farber, discussing 'stigma', perhaps also implies that the impact on the middle-class parents' feelings is also likely to be greater. Certainly, information from the South Wales study would support some of these explanations. Numbers are small but mothers of high social class who responded negatively tended to have high expectations for themselves and their children. Children were expected to 'do well' at school; mothers were not content with a life of housework and childminding but felt the need of some life of their own that did not involve children. A Down's syndrome child was seen as an automatic 'low achiever': to do well in the context of the ESN(S) school was not enough since the point of reference for these parents was always the average (or above average) child. More than this even, the Down's child was felt to be imposing restrictions on parents and to act as a source of deprivation for both them and his siblings. Because of him the parents were not to have the freedom from child-care duties they would otherwise have anticipated and their other, potentially high-achieving children could lack necessary parental attention.

A further point may be that those of high social class are assumed to plan for the future, defer immediate gratification of wishes for later rewards and to protect and insure themselves against misfortune. The birth of a handicapped child cannot be insured against and the characteristic of planning for the future may be the very thing that is of least service to these parents. Very many parents mentioned the importance of not looking ahead and 'living from day to day'. It may be particularly difficult for middle-class parents not to concern themselves with the future.

Mothers' own explanations

A more subjective approach is to see why parents themselves said they felt negatively about their situation. Table 3.6 gives details of mothers who responded negatively in 1972 and the reasons they gave for their feelings. Examining the statements of those mothers whose responses deteriorated, similar reasons emerge (Tables 3.7a and 3.7b).

Table 3.6 *Reasons mothers gave in 1972 for their negative response (excluding doubtful inclusion)*

	Sex of child, social class and mother's age								
	Girl,[a] II, 53[b]	Girl,[a] II, 32	Girl, II, 46	Girl, III, 41	Boy, III, 41	Boy[a], III, 49[b]	Boy, III, 39	Boy,[a] III, 57[b]	Boy, I, 38
Work complaints	+	Large young family	Hired help in past	+	+	+	+	+	Hired help
Other family members									
Negative response	–	?	–	–	+	–	+	+	?
Presenting problems	+[c]	+	–	–	+	–	+	+	–
Spoilt family life	–	+	+	?	+	–	+	+	?
Restrictions imposed	+	+	+	–	?	+	?embarrassed	+	+
Isolation	?	–	–	–	–	+	–	?	–
Some negative feelings to child	Behaviour problems	+	+	Behaviour problems	Behaviour problems	–	Behaviour problems	?	+
Relationship with husband	Some problems	Some early problems	–	–	Some problems	Separated[c]	–	Some problems	Some early problems
1981 response	Negative	Negative	Negative	Not available	Positive	Positive	Negative	Negative	Negative

+ , characteristic present; –, characteristic absent.
[a] Ambivalent birth response.
[b] Five mothers were over 49. Three responded negatively.
[c] Problems not connected with or caused by Down's syndrome child.

Some of the reasons given here for negative or deteriorating responses are difficult to assess objectively (for example, work involved, restrictions imposed, destruction of family life). As a consequence, it is difficult to say a certain family is under strain because it has a heavier burden to bear than another family, or because its members are unable to withstand stress to the same degree. The reason for strain is of some importance since to ease the situation it must be decided which issues are most fundamental.

Multiple problems explanation

Leaving aside the type of problems mothers encountered, one of the things most families had in common was the clustering or presence of a number of adverse factors, any of which possibly could have been tackled had it arisen on its own. For example, where a family member responds negatively but the child itself is a little problem a mother can possibly cope – or vice versa. However, when the family is non-supportive, the child is demanding and the mother herself older (and less energetic), then the situation can become impossible. In such situations it is important to consider the combination of events as a whole in order to understand the response of one particular mother. It is not possible to predict the response any individual mother will make when she gives birth to a Down's syndrome child, but it is possible to speculate that, where these

Table 3.7a *Factors contributing to deteriorating responses of mothers in 1972*

	Ambivalent to negative				Positive to ambivalent
Sex	Girl	Girl	Boy	Boy	Boy
Response					
Birth	Ambivalent	Ambivalent	Ambivalent	Ambivalent	Positive
Childhood	Negative	Negative	Negative	Negative	Ambivalent
Teenage	(Negative)	(Negative)	(Positive)	(Negative)	(Positive)
Social class	II	II	III	III	III
Age of mother	53[a]	32	49	57[b]	27
Work with child	Behaviour problems	Very close in age to sibling	Mother reported hard work	Severely ill	Some behaviour problems
Other family members					
Negative response	–	+	–	+	–
Presenting problems	+[c]	+	–	–	–
Isolation	+	–	+	–	–
Restriction of mother by child	+	+	+	+	–
Feelings towards child	Irritation	Repulsion	–	–	–
Less support from child's father	Invalid	–	Separated[c] 1981 – dead	Very strong negative response	Worked away 1981 – divorced (about to remarry)
Other	–	4 children under 9	–	7 children	–

+, characteristic present; –, characteristic absent.
[a] Second oldest mother
[b] Oldest mother
[c] Not connected with Down's syndrome

Table 3.7b *Factors contributing to deteriorating responses of mothers in 1981*

	Positive to negative	Positive to ambivalent	
Sex	Boy	Girl	Boy
Response			
Birth	(Negative)	(Ambivalent)	(Ambivalent)
Childhood	Positive	Positive	Positive
Teenage	Negative	Ambivalent	Ambivalent
Social class	II	IV	III
Age of mother	38	44	40
Work with child	–	Severely disabled	–
Other family members			
Negative response	+	–	–
Isolation	?	+	–
Restriction of mother by child	+	+	–
Feelings towards child	–	–	–
Less support from child's father	Divorced – later relationships suffered	Divorced[a] – later relationships suffered	–
Other	–	Mother unwell	–

+, characteristic present; –, characteristic absent.
[a] Not connected with Down's syndrome.

clusters of problems or negative indicators occur, a woman may be 'at risk' of making a negative response, rather than because of any single factor. The absence of such indicators would augur well for a positive response. From the South Wales study the following indicators have been drawn which, if present in any numbers, would seem to be predictive of a mother making a negative response. The list can only be tentative since not all factors could be fully assessed and numbers in the study were small. Certain indicators cannot be detected at birth but become apparent only with time.

Mothers of high social class
The fact that mothers in high social classes are more likely to make a negative response, for whatever reason, has been discussed at some length. There was a significant relationship between social class and response for all except the responses made at birth.

Mothers who have a negative birth response
It has been shown that most mothers do recover from the initial shock, but not all do so. For those who respond negatively it should not be assumed, as it may be tempting to do, that they will 'get over it'. All mothers who were positive at the birth were positive a decade and a half later.

Mothers whose relationships with others are seriously distorted by the presence of the Down's syndrome child or where another member of the nuclear family makes an unambiguously negative response
The exception to this seemed to be where a father responded negatively and left the family. In the three cases where this occurred in this sample the mother responded positively (although they were more vulnerable as a one-parent family). Where the fathers stayed the mothers did not respond positively.

A household with an abnormal amount of work for the mother (e.g. because of the child's ill health or behaviour, or because of another family member) or where she is less able to cope with such work (e.g. because of her own ill-health or commitments outside the home)
In fact, by 1981 some mothers who had had excessive domestic burdens in 1972 were no longer in this position. It may be that early heavy workloads take their toll in the future also: some mothers in South Wales remained negative in 1981 despite reduced work loads.

Lack of a supportive mate for whatever reason (divorce, husband's illness, absence from home, lack of interest, etc.)

The following factors involved very small numbers and so are very tentative:

Mothers who find the child distasteful
This was not common in the sample.

Mothers who would not want a child in any case even if it were normal
Although an obvious means of assessment for this factor is to ask which mothers had considered abortion, Jolly (1975) suggests that a mother's likely relationship with her child can be predicted in pregnancy by such signs as the presence of the father at ante-natal visits, the reaction of the mother to the confirmation of her pregnancy, her willingness to wear maternity clothes, and whether she has chosen a name for the child before the birth. Such predictions are likely to be more complex than this but

presumably the danger of a damaged relationship between mother and child would be increased for such women should the outcome of the unwanted pregnancy be a disabled child. Certainly in South Wales both of the women who had wanted an abortion responded negatively.

Mothers who are well over normal child-bearing age
It seems likely that amongst mothers who are well over the normal child-bearing age at the time of birth there is a greater likelihood of their making a negative response.

When these criteria were applied to the mothers in this sample, it was seen that negative mothers had a higher average score of these negative indicators than had others (Table 3.8).

Table 3.8 *Responses of mothers and presence of negative indicators (1981)*

Responses of mothers	n	Average number of indicators	Range of indicators
Negative	7	3.7	2–5
Ambivalent	6	1.3	0–3
Positive	18	1.2	0–3
Total	31	1.8	0–5

Other studies find that it is the combination of factors which contributes to stress. Pahl and Quine (1985) have constructed an 'adversity score' for families with mentally handicapped children. In families with a high adversity score, carers had higher malaise scores. Malaise scores became even higher when the child was multiply impaired or had severe behaviour problems. Gath (1987) also suggests that it is the *total* family situation that determines the mental health of a mother of a Down's syndrome child. (See, too, Byrne and Cunningham, 1985.)

The new sample

The new sample of mothers in 1981 did not display the negative responses of the original sample. Two mothers could be classified as ambivalent, but all the others were positive. It was obvious that some mothers had encountered severe problems in the past; however, these had been overcome. One mother with a severely disabled, incontinent and disturbed daughter and a husband who worked away from home suffered from arthritis. Eventually her daughter had been taken into residential care and visited her home only for holidays; the relief from strain for the mother was substantial. Her score on the Malaise Inventory was 10, the second highest for the new sample.

> Oh I never really did [get over it] – never ever. Well, it's always on your mind – even though, she's away we think about her a lot . . . for a long time I thought '*why*?' You know, 'Why Joanna?', and I don't think it ever leaves you, you still think about it.   (1981)

A non-British mother could only be interviewed through her son who acted as an interpreter. Her answers were very bland, in spite of the major problems he outlined and, consequently, accurate classification here was deemed to be impossible. Her Malaise score of 15 was the highest recorded for the new sample. The average score for the new sample as a whole was 6.4 (range 0–15), which is lower than the average for the original sample and on a par with that of the positive mothers in the original sample.

SUMMARY

This chapter has attempted to give a flavour of how mothers feel about having a Down's syndrome child. Accounts are given with some diffidence, because of the problems of method discussed at the beginning of the chapter. However, it is possible to say with confidence that there are variations in how mothers respond emotionally to this event. It seems likely that at any one time, the response a mother makes is not purely dependent upon her own emotional psychological make-up, but will be influenced by other external factors in her life. Possible factors that may contribute to a woman's perception of the situation have been identified.

Over all, the mothers' responses appeared to improve rather than deteriorate. Most change took place in the early years of childhood. Although evidence from this study was slight there was some indication that services that did relieve pressure on very stressed mothers did more than simply avoid the worst consequence of stress (e.g. family breakdown, mental illness or, very speculatively, child abuse) but, more positively, helped mothers to achieve actual happiness and enjoyment from their Down's children.

4 How Others Respond to a Down's Syndrome Child in the Family

THE FATHER

The problems of classifying parental responses were increased when dealing with fathers. The biggest difficulty lay in the fact that the mothers were often interviewed alone, and the fathers not even met. The mother was focused upon since she was thought likely to be the most closely involved with the child and so the more important figure in the family. It was recognised, however, that a father's own response was likely to affect the child and also to influence his wife's response (with a further indirect impact on the child) and, because of this, efforts were made to find out the father's reaction to the situation. The answers were not wholly satisfactory for comparison since many questions were answered by the mother on behalf of her husband.

Information through a third party is never satisfactory, and there was evidence that wives were not always able to give confident or accurate answers about their husbands. For example, in one instance the interview was the means of the wife's discovering information she had suspected, but had never directly asked her husband about before. She discovered that her husband had known the child had Down's syndrome at birth although she herself only found this out at 6 months. One father, met for the first time in 1981, revealed that at the outset he had wanted institutional care for his son.

> My first reaction – though I've never said it to her – but my own thoughts were perhaps it would be better if he went into a home and was cared for there. She [his wife] was suffering a hell of a lot with asthma. But, looking back now I'm glad I never – I accepted it I suppose when he started school at two-and-a-half, and within 6 months they got him moving about, but it was a while before I *inwardly* accepted it – outwardly I did – I had a bit of a façade and found it hard to accept. But now – great.   (1981)

There seemed to be a lack of discussion between husband and wife in many cases, and wives made assumptions about their husbands' attitudes that were not necessarily true. A common and unsatisfactory reply was the glib 'he feels the same as me', sometimes given even in the face of evidence that he did not. Other wives readily assumed he must feel as they did themselves. The reasons for this lack of discussion varied. In some cases it was believed that there was no problem to discuss, in other instances one or both parents were clearly avoiding the problem.

> ... and for years my husband wouldn't talk about it – he wouldn't even say 'mongol' at all – for years he never mentioned him, until one day – well, I said I would leave him. Well, if you don't talk about it you just can't get through. You must talk about these things. I mean once you talk about it, and accept it, and you know you've got a mongol – you can't push him in a corner and forget about him.   (1972)

In other cases wives did not accept what their husbands said. 'He pretends he doesn't worry but he does.' What a man tells his wife, or does not tell her, perhaps gives as much information about the relationship between them as about his feelings on the subject. Other wives obviously thought they knew their husbands' attitudes themselves but were not able to explain them satisfactorily to others. In 1972 one mother kept repeating what she thought her husband's feelings were, but it was not at all clear what she meant:

> ... every now and again my husband's trying to treat him – well – like a mongol child like. [Repeated many times but with no explanation of how a mongol child should be treated.] He'd just love to have a go at him . . . . You know, he just wants him to be treated different, because he's different, treat him different . . . let him get on with what he's doing like . . . he'd give in to him more if I didn't have my say about it, like.   (1972) (By 1981 this couple was divorced.)

The difficulty here was reconciling 'he'd love to have a go at him' – it was impossible to get an explanation of this – with 'giving in to him more'.

Mothers felt that their problem was not the same as their husband's. Often they felt their own response was the important one:

> He didn't mind if I didn't . . . men, they're not the same as women – I mean, they don't feel as much as a woman do – at least I don't think so – there are a few, I suppose, but the majority of men don't feel like a woman towards a child.   (1972)

Many women were ready to assume this and consequently to assume and assert that their husbands felt less than they did. Other women saw their own strongly negative response partly as being linked to the maternal situation of responsibility for child-rearing: given the same role as their husbands had with the child, their own response could have been less intense. They could account for their husbands' more detached responses by the fact that they *were* more detached:

> Well, this is it, they're out at work, you see. They get the break, don't they? I mean it wasn't until . . . he was with her all day [that] after a few weeks he said to me he realised for the first time what a tremendous strain it was having her here all day. She's very demanding.   (1972)

> ... he's less resentful [than me] but he has less to do – *he's* still free.   (1972)

To these difficulties was added the further problem that, in any case, feelings often fluctuated. In view of these complications, fathers' responses have not been analysed to the extent of those of the mothers. For some fathers, of course, mothers were able to give clear, well-thought-out (and, it is to be hoped, accurate) accounts of their husband's feelings. Also, where husbands had responded very unambiguously, mothers were generally able to convey this. However, in other instances, either the father's feelings, or the mother's answers, were not clear cut and attempts to classify them could imply a certainty and precision that was in fact lacking. Consequently, an attempt will be made to give a range of responses made by fathers, but the classifications are very tentative. As with mothers, this report relies on fathers whose families were seen in 1972 and 1981.

Birth responses of fathers (retrospective)

Fathers' initial responses were fairly evenly divided between negative, ambivalent and positive. This is unlike the mothers, amongst whom 24% initially responded positively.

About a third of the fathers, according to their wives, were inclined to make light of the situation: 'He never said nothing. He said Doctor – had told him. "But", he said, "It don't matter, do it?" he said. "She's lovely" – you know – like that, and it didn't make any difference.' Where husbands were able to do more than this and be really supportive wives found it a great help: 'He was very good. He was very shocked, but the next day he said to me "Now, whatever happens this is our child and we'll keep him." And that, I thought, was excellent – he was so positive.'

Another father himself described how his own, rather casual feelings changed when he heard the news. Far from rejecting the child, he felt more involved and protective:

No, I think when we found out he was a mongol that – this is what I think about them – when they're small, little babies like that – when they're small, let them lie in the carrycot or the cot or whatever – give them their feed, keep them dry and they're happy and I'm happy like – you know. But once I found out – I wanted to – I don't know how to explain it, but you wanted to – to catch hold of him and nurse him, poor dab that he was, like. That didn't affect me with [elder brother] – as long as he was in his cot – and with Edmund as well until I found out, but after that then – I don't know what to say – I had more feeling I suppose then because he was handicapped, although he was the same little baby – I seemed to be more *for* him then.   (1972)

A similar number of fathers could not be classified in either extreme. Wives reported they were 'terrible upset' and 'upset like', but they seemed able to cope: 'He was very disappointed and shocked but very realistic and he accepted it. He was a very, very big comfort.'

About a third of the fathers responded negatively. With three fathers there was a dramatic change in their attitudes, which eventually led to divorce. The wives were sure that the birth of the Down's child and the later divorce were closely linked. These three mothers emphasised the lack of the normal interaction that usually takes place between father and child:

All those two years he never handled her except when I actually put her on his lap and then he just wanted to get rid of her as quickly as possible. Well, I did ask him one day if Carole repelled him and he took a long time to answer and said 'No, I don't think so', – but it was the long hesitation in between.   (1972)

Well, he was shocked and as soon as he got back in the house he said, 'That's it' and I said 'What's what?'. 'No good', he said, 'He'll have to go. We'll just have to put him in a home' and that was it. I said I wasn't going through all that to have him and then give him up just like that and he said 'Think it over' . . . . He didn't like to see anything that wasn't perfect, no matter what came into the house he'd got to take it apart to see what it was made of and put it together again, and I think that was what was wrong with Dennis – he wasn't perfect and because he wasn't perfect he didn't want it.   (1972)

These husbands' responses were as extreme as any recorded for the mothers – so extreme that they resolved the situation eventually by leaving – probably an easier solution for them than would have been possible for their wives. Other husbands responded equally badly but did not leave home:

Oh, he was dreadful, he was terrible. My children said they'd never seen him cry – well, he didn't cry very often – he's a big man. But they said he was terrible, really terrible . . . he went into a shell, my husband, like that, and he never came out. He slept, he came home from work, he'd have his food and he slept and he slept and slept and slept. And the doctor said this was the one way he could cope with it – so I had him, the baby and a family of six.   (1972)

Only one husband had an undoubtedly negative response that (after quite a short while) changed unreservedly to positive.

F.   I must admit for a while I couldn't stand her. [I wanted to] do something to get rid of her – put her in some place.

M.   If she'd cry for a drink he wouldn't pick her up . . . and he's so good as a rule, he's always so good, but he wouldn't, he just couldn't somehow.

F.   Then I came round and I wouldn't swap her for anything now.   (1972)

Childhood responses of fathers

As with the mothers, most fathers seemed able to come to terms with the situation and accept their Down's syndrome children. Over half were able to do this without reservation. In these cases the wives were in no doubt about their husband's feelings saying for instance: 'Oh, he thinks she's wonderful' and 'He's more for her than any of them.'

Other husbands, although accepting the child and situation, had a more considered approach:

> Up till now he's been a bit wary of him – you know – he's accepted him just as I have, but he's – I think what it was with him – he used to work with other men and their children were all right. He was a little bit – what do you call it – about taking Hafryn with him up to the site or something, you know. I don't know what it is – he's very deep, you know, so you can't get to his feelings all that . . . and I used to quarrel with him that he – you know, but how can I expect him to feel like me? But I couldn't understand when he didn't. But he's wonderful with the children, mind.   (1972)

> F. The thing is you've got to help yourself. You're waking up in the mornings and the first thing that was coming across your mind like 'Edmund's a mongol, the baby's a mongol.' But there you are, you've got to adjust, haven't you . . . . I don't suppose *now* we've got over it in that respect. You see them running round and you think he can't enjoy himself to that extent . . . . You're not relaxed any hour out of the twenty-four really. And silly things they may sound to you perhaps, but I'm thinking like this – that Christmas time, Father Christmas, he can always come to this house and that's sad, like, isn't it? Because as far as [elder brother] is concerned, he realises there is no Father Christmas and that phase of his life has passed and he's grown up, but Edmund will never reach that stage. We can *tell* him there's no Father Christmas but whether he'll realise it – I don't know – and that's a sad thing, see. And the fact that we realise it makes it worse then. It's on you all the time . . .   (1972)

In 1972 about a quarter of fathers could be said not fully to have come to terms with the situation. This, however, includes three fathers whose wives felt their husbands did not fully accept the situation and one case in which neither parent accepted the diagnosis of Down's syndrome. These fathers cannot be said to be wholly negative since they were quite happy with their children, but, in their wives' estimation, did not really understand the situation:

> Really, to this day, he doesn't see anything wrong with her. He knows she's slow, like.   (1972)

> Well, now, this is the point. My husband is dramatic about everything. This was if a big drama had happened to him. This is how I felt he never really appreciated the situation. He rushed up to the church and he rushed up to the convent and he came back with a medal for the child to wear from the priest. [Laughed] It didn't cut any ice with me, I'm afraid, but it comforted him at the time. I thought he was very lucky to be able to comfort himself like that. I could find no comfort in the situation. After he'd been to the convent he said: 'Everything's going to be all right' – great. Oh, he's had to realise a lot but I don't think it's completely gone from him. I don't know if it will . . . . To be quite honest, he doesn't look at him anything other than normal, you know. I think he enjoys him as he is and he's not going to think any further than that.   (1972)

> I don't think he mentioned it afterwards – he just said 'Oh, he's going to be all right, there's not going to be anything wrong with him.' He does now, you know – he keeps saying 'Wait till he's older, he'll get better, he'll be able to do things.' My father said this as well: 'There's not going to be much wrong with him.' They tried to convince me – they think what they want to think.   (1972)

Of the five husbands who appreciated the problem and responded negatively only two were still living with their wives. One of these two responded wholly negatively and this affected his relationship with the child and his wife. For the other, while his wife felt 'The shock is as much now as it has ever been', he still did his very best for the child and was able to be supportive to his wife.

Mid-teen responses of fathers

There were no dramatic changes in responses by 1981. The three fathers who had divorced their wives at the birth of their Down's syndrome children continued to take little interest. In one case the relationship with the normal sibling would have been maintained, but because the Down's syndrome teenager was shunned, the father had little contact with either of his children. Since 1972 there were two more divorces, neither of which was directly attributed to the presence in the family of a Down's syndrome child. Two fathers were dead by 1972 and, by 1981, two more had died. As a result, there were only 24 fathers remaining with their wives by 1981. Two fathers had been left, through death and separation, with the responsibility for the Down's syndrome teenager, but both children were in residential schools and a major part of their care was taken over by their normal sisters when the teenagers were at home.

In 1972, only 6 fathers (19% of those living at home) were not working and at home for most of the day but by 1981 as many as 11 fathers (42% of those at home) were not working. Consequently, fewer mothers were in a position to claim their husbands were unavoidably more detached from the situation because they were out at work. For those who were not at work interaction with their offspring necessarily increased, but in fact their role did not seem substantially to change because of this. Indeed, rather more of the fathers in work helped regularly with their Down's teenagers than did those out of work. Where husbands were supportive it was not taken for granted and women were full of gratitude, as if expectations of the average father were low:

> I mean a lot of men would just say 'It's your responsibility, you get on with it.' (1981)

> He [father] does a lot of work with our children at the club – he's a great father to them all and I think he's been really great to what some husbands have been. A lot of the marriages have broken up through this you know – and it's – er – frightening. You see it happening. (1981)

Several fathers did, however, mention their responsibility towards their children even if this did not always result in day-to-day involvement.

> It has worried me more in the past that it does now. It took me 18 months to accept it when she was born. Once I'd accepted it we realised then that the responsibility of looking after the child was ours in any case, whether we wanted the child or not. She's got her own little personality now. (1981)

This overall responsibility led to a protective spirit. Shyer men could wish to avoid conflict but a few others seemed almost to seek out opportunities to fly to the teenager's defence. One father described an incident on a caravan holiday:

> A gentleman came down and his son came down to our caravan to play and he told us, 'My father says he should be in a home.' So I thought I wouldn't go there now, I'd wait. So we both called in the same pub and we were there one evening and who was there but this chap – tall fellow, mind, made two of me – and I had him at the bar. I told him what I thought of him, see. I told him he had no right to say what he had said and he was talking a load of nonsense. 'The sooner that type mix with your boy the better it is all round. And you.' 'Oh, I didn't mean it', he said. (1981)

Not unlike mothers, there was evidence that fathers were increasingly coming to terms with disability and its implications. Those who had possessed unrealistically high notions about their children had gained greater insight into their children's potential.

> He loves Malcolm – he does now realise, living with him, the slowness of his achievements – a slow acceptance. It's brought out something better in both of us, I think. (1981)

Several fathers also described the process of becoming 'wise' (using Goffman's (1963) term).

> Well, I don't feel so bad now . . . . I think the fact that he's mentally [rather than physically] handicapped – if you haven't got your reason you've got nothing . . . . When he was born it was a bit of a bang, you know – if I'd known what I know now I wouldn't have worried so much . . . it's the same when you're injured, [until] you get into hospital you don't realise people *are* ill when you're walking about healthy. If you've not seen handicapped people, you don't realise. (1981)

Most fathers who had stayed at home had, from their own and their wives' accounts, come to accept the position with very minor and entirely understandable reservations. 'He loves him. Sometimes I think he wishes he was all right.' One father described his own acceptance in this way: 'If you see someone, a friend with children more or less the same age, then you think how he could be. And then, on the other hand, he could be much worse . . . ' This father, reminded of his position in 1972, which had emphasised a more constant awareness of distress, said:

> Well, you get more used to it, I suppose. He's there with us and there he is to stay and – that's it, isn't it? . . . I'm not unhappy about it all the time, no. Well you can't be, can you? Well, it's the same if somebody dies – you can't be unhappy about that all the time, you've got to face the facts.   (1981)

In a minority of cases mothers felt that the father had more affection for the child than they themselves had: 'He's got a great deal of love for her – more than I have.'

Only two women expressed real reservations about their husband's feelings though both emphasised that the fathers still cared for their children. Just one of the two had been rated as negative in 1972.

> He doesn't want to know. He's ashamed of her really in a way but he won't say it. He loves her mind – he thinks a lot of her – but he doesn't want to take her, he'd rather be at home with her than take her to things. But he won't admit it, see, he won't say.

> He never talks about it, he never talks to *me* about it. It's just the same [as in 1972]. He never says 'What will happen to him', he never ever talks about it, he doesn't want to know. He wouldn't let anyone hurt him mind – I don't mean that, I don't mean he doesn't like him, or anything like that.   (1981)

The new sample

The new sample of 19 teenagers contained families in which one father was dead and one was living apart from his wife and son. A third father, a widower, did not live with his Down's syndrome daughter but visited her weekly, since she was cared for by his mother-in-law.

Four fathers in the new sample had responded very badly when their Down's syndrome children were born. One – who was completely reconciled to the child by 1981 – had gone so far, by the mother's account, as to ask the specialist to 'put him down' after the child's disability was revealed to him when the boy was 3 months old. As in the original sample a few fathers were apt to close their minds to a realisation of the full extent of the problem:

> When they told me that day I was bawling my eyes out and my husband said 'What are you crying for – there's nothing wrong with Frank, don't worry about it, he's fine. No matter what they say, we know there's nothing wrong with him.' And he never saw it – he was quite – er – it was me, I knew, I was worried, I knew what was to come, you know, but he didn't. [Does he appreciate the true situation now?] Yes, but he's proud of him, see. He thinks he's clever, you know.   (1981)

By 1981 all fathers in the new sample were reported as feeling positively about their situation.

THE SIBLINGS

Most writers (e.g. Gath (1978), Farber (1968), Kew, 1975) suggest that brothers and sisters of disabled children take their 'cue' on attitudes from their parents, and certainly, in this study, mothers who reported major problems with their normal siblings were more likely to find that they themselves had response problems with the

Down's syndrome child. It is impossible to say, though, whether this is because a mother who finds a situation difficult or intolerable will assume others find it the same and therefore report this as a fact, or whether these siblings were experiencing difficulties because they took the lead from the adults' own attitudes and so encountered problems. As well as this it is unlikely that a mother, however much goodwill there is for her Down's syndrome child, will remain unmoved herself if she sees her other children suffering because of the child. Consequently, it is not surprising if there is a 'match' between a mother's attitudes and her children's.

Mothers could also make assumptions that were perhaps unfounded; certainly some mothers were very ready to believe that the normal children *must* be affected by the presence of a disabled sibling. They believed that the children could not fail to be influenced by the mother's own response to the event, and that the complex situations that arose simply from the birth of the Down's syndrome child must affect the other children:

> She's a different person [than she would have been]. Knowing the fundamental change it had on me at 23, it *must* have [affected her sister]. There's no way she couldn't have been affected.   (1981)

> I think they've all been affected by the effect it had on me and my reaction to it. It's not made life very easy for them in many cases.   (1981)

> All of them [have been affected]. Any child from any broken marriage is affected but in these circumstances it's worse because it's depressed me an awful lot – er – you find – I'm very unsettled now . . . it affects you and consequently the children.   (1981)

A full study of the effect of a Down's syndrome child on his siblings was beyond the scope of this work and was not attempted. A subjective account given from the mother's point of view is included, however, both to illustrate how mothers perceive the events taking place in their families and to give a fuller picture of the lives of families with a Down's syndrome member. Table 4.1 shows the number of siblings, and their ages, in 1972 and 1981.

Table 4.1 *Age distribution and sex of siblings (% in brackets)*

	No. of siblings			
	Original sample		New sample (1981)	Total population (1981)
	(1972)	(1981)		
Number of families	37	34	19	53
Ages				
40+	–	2 (3)	–	2 (2)
30–39	2 (2)	12 (15)	5 (11)	17 (14)
20–29	22 (26)	31 (39)	24 (52)	55 (44)
10–19	36 (43)	28 (35)	15 (33)	43 (34)
6–9	10 (12)	6 (8)	1 (2)	7 (6)
Under 5	14 (17)	1 (1)	1 (2)	2 (2)
Total	84	80	46	126
Boys	45 (54)	47 (59)	24 (52)	71 (56)
Girls	39 (46)	33 (41)	22 (48)	55 (44)

The following information is based on what mothers said and is unsatisfactory both because there is no control group and because mothers themselves were often not privy to their children's own thoughts on the matter. Mothers had often not discussed the position in detail with their children and their opinions were usually based on observation rather than on what the children had said. On both sides there was a lack of frankness in case feelings were hurt:

> The poor boy, he doesn't say a lot because he knows we wouldn't like it, but I think the older one is a bit ashamed of her, though he doesn't say.   (1972)

I think – if she thought I'd told you she'd be bothered about it because she's very sensitive – but I *do* think she minds a bit, you know – when we all go out together. When he's in the house that's all right . . . . I've noticed it the last couple of years. I wouldn't mention it to her but if I had to admit the truth [I'd say she minded].   (1972)

So ready were mothers to assume effects on the children (and in this context it was usually assumed to be a harmful rather than beneficial experience) that they were aware of the possibility even though no actual injury had been detected.

Well, this one here – it's nearly spoiled her life. Well, I didn't have time for her. If she wanted anything she just had to get it and get out.   (1972)

And of course the dreadful thing was [elder sister]. I'd so much wanted another child so that she could have some company . . . for when we [died]. And then this came. Well, now, we were not halving her loneliness, we were *adding* to it really . . . so really I suppose it was feeling what we had done to this child as much as anything.   (1972)

The young children

The fact that when the population was born, more Down's syndrome children were born to older mothers meant that these children were often the youngest in a family and more likely to have older siblings than younger ones. In 1972 only 27% of the sample were of a similar age to their siblings (i.e. under 10 years), and this must affect inter- action between them and the type of problems siblings encounter. According to their mothers, about one-third of the normal siblings in the original sample expressed minor degrees of dissatisfaction with their disabled sibling. Apart from feelings of embarrass- ment and having to tolerate teasing from unsympathetic 'friends', the major difficulties for siblings arose from the Down's syndrome child interfering in games, destroying precious possessions, monopolising parental attention and, as a younger and less competent companion, limiting many activities. The sort of irritation and jealousy expressed in these situations is possibly no more than many experience who share a house with a young and active child, but the daily irritations for a child should not be discounted or underestimated. A mother from the new sample in 1981 described her daughter's situation:

You *had* to put a lot on the older child – say 'Grab her and hold her while I shut the gate, etc.' . . . she's been affected in all kinds of things – every aspect of life – eating around a table, sloppy eating habits, sharing a bedroom with someone who would destroy everything you had. She's destroyed tons of pre- cious things for [her sister] over the years.   (1981)

Other children avoided irritation by simply ignoring the Down's sibling or limiting interaction:

He hasn't much time for him.   (1972)

Some mothers stressed the restrictions their Down's syndrome sibling placed upon the other children.

[They mind] only inasmuch as it restricts them. They know that when Janet comes home there are certain things they can and can't do . . . they know they can't go out as much as when Janet isn't there . . . . She's inclined to poke her nose in everywhere. She doesn't want to play with her things, she wants to go right in the middle of what everyone's doing. This caused a lot of dissension at one time. Now they seem to be growing up more. She still does get on their nerves but it's not quite so pronounced as it was at one time. I think they go off on their own downstairs and they get on with what they want to do and she can't inter- fere quite as much as she did.   (1972)

Jealousy in varying degrees was mentioned quite frequently and the mother's behaviour must, in several instances, have justified the accusation of favouritism. Usually, the closer the age of the children the more favouritism was resented. Adult children would often comment on the difference in treatment they had received but without any real appearance of minding it. With one 13-year-old boy, however, the effects persisted: 'The boy felt pushed out . . . he still resents her in little ways.'

In 1972 only three children showed more severe problems, and here the whole web of relationships between parents, children and the Down's syndrome child had been adversely affected. It was only for the sibling in the first quotation below that effects were felt to persist until 1981 and, indeed, relationships between the parents and the normal child had deteriorated rather than improved at the time of the second interview.

> [The sister] is very much of a problem. Admittedly she's had very little attention when she was a baby . . . and she's always been very much the underdog and very, very put upon in many ways and she's very sorry for herself and now she's got to the stage that she enjoys it unfortunately. And if you treat her like the others she'll get herself in such a position that you've got to get annoyed with her . . . then she enjoys a sorrowful couple of days . . . . She demands your attention by being naughty now (since she wasn't able to get it before). I blame myself to a certain extent – not that I know what I could have done.
> (1972)

By 1981 the brother mentioned here had married and the situation had cleared:

> We found [the brother] was playing truant and this started trouble with my husband and [the brother] and he said he had to leave school at fourteen. When he used to bring friends to the house he'd say 'Don't let Donald come in'. I could understand – Donald broke everything – but my husband couldn't understand. He thought he was ashamed. This is what started the trouble between my husband and myself – basically it has to do with Donald. Now [the brother] is nervous and upset and has asthma attacks . . . . Now my husband and [the brother] quarrel all the time.'
> (1972)

At the other end of the scale almost two-thirds of the siblings were reported by their mothers to have wholly positive relationships with the Down's syndrome child as the following typical quotations show:

> He makes a big fuss of her . . . . I sometimes think, well honestly, does he realise what sort of a child she is because he's *so* unconcerned about it.
> (1972)

> I used to think they'd [mind] but they take her everywhere.
> (1972)

The teenagers

By 1981 there were even fewer siblings at home and those who were still at home had gradually begun to organise their own social lives outside the home and away from their Down's sibling. Parents could, consequently – as they were more detached from the daily interaction between their children – be more evaluative about the position. Whereas in 1972 the main problems centred around the nuisance value of the Down's syndrome child to his siblings, by 1981 mothers were regretting the lack of companionship for the normal siblings. Even where the children had played together when younger, understandably, the siblings developed other interests and the Down's syndrome child became a less acceptable companion. One mother pointed out this inevitable consequence of one sibling being mentally disabled:

> The lack of companionship which two sisters only two years apart might have developed if she'd been normal.
> (1981)

> I feel sometimes that [younger brother] really is like an older child. Although he's got Kevin [Down's child] he can't really play with him, play the games, you know – and now perhaps if [brother] wants to go fishing, well if Kevin was all right he'd be able to go along but of course they can't really go just the both of them – not fishing . . . . Oh, [brother] is very good to him, he's marvellous in fact, everyone says how

good he is, you know, but sometimes if he wants Kevin to do something – like at the moment he wants to have the layout for a railway and he wants to get Kevin involved and Kevin just isn't interested and [brother] gets so annoyed . . . and perhaps if he wants to play games – well Kevin can't really concentrate for long and he gets a bit annoyed then, you know, and he says 'I've got no one to play with' but on the whole they get on very well.   (1981)

Oh, they love him. I find now that [sister] – often in the holidays she'd take him down to the Sports Centre to play badminton but now, with her own friends, she doesn't take him anywhere. Well, I suppose he's a bit of a drag, isn't he.   (1981)

Other problems of childhood – e.g. destructiveness and jealousy – were diminishing, although in some instances this was probably only because the siblings were not there or were involved in their own lives. The embarrassment siblings felt varied:

If [brother] came in and saw him sitting outside in his wheelchair he used to bundle him in quick. Oh, yes, he wouldn't have him outside, you know. And yet the girls weren't like that, they didn't mind at all.
                                                        (1981)

In some cases embarrassment persisted even when the siblings left home; one brother had not invited his handicapped sibling to his wedding.

McAllister *et al.* (1973) found that for parents with a 'behaviourally retarded child' formal activities and interaction with close kin were little different from parents with normal children, but informal contacts were restricted. The authors explained this in terms of the 'visibility' of the child. Joining formal organisations does not necessarily involve the child and concealment is impossible with close relations, so in these two areas where he is 'visible' there is no restriction. The notion of 'visibility' receives some support if it is applied to some siblings in this study. Those of their acquaintances who were sufficiently distant to be kept in ignorance were not told of the Down's syndrome child at home:

Well, yes, I think they're bound to have been affected. I think they like to be proud of their brothers and sisters and the way she [sister] talks about it and she laughs she finds him entertaining, but she is still embarrassed by him, by some of the things he does – it can happen in families where they've got intelligent children and brothers and sisters who are less intelligent, I mean they don't like to talk about it, to admit they are. She used to try to pretend he was quite normal and better than he was in fact. I've seen her do this, so she wouldn't take the trouble if she was entirely unaffected by it. She used to talk about him to other people 'My brother does this', 'Oh, yes, my brother does that' . . . where in fact he couldn't possibly have done the things she said he was doing . . . . Generally I think she accepts things very well . . . she accepts him and she talks about him to people – she doesn't mind too much. She won't bring her friends home sometimes, unless they know him, she's hesitant about asking people up – because her friends are in T – quite a long way away. I say, 'Well, ring them up', and she won't and I think this is why – she doesn't say so – I think this is probably why, she's afraid he won't behave himself. She doesn't mind the people who – her best friend has got a handicapped brother – so they're all right. She comes here to stay the night. [More distant friends don't?] Mmmm.   (1981)

Oh, [elder brother] was affected – very much so. It affected his school life. He used to say he could never have friends here and very, very bitter he was, you know. You know he used to say he'd like the boys to come and play music in his bedroom and 'I can't because *he* won't stay out of the bedroom' – things like this, you know. And I used to do my best to keep him out but he wouldn't bring them here. And he'd never talk to his friends, you know. Once he started the Tech he never spoke to his friends about him 'cos his best man didn't know we had a handicapped child until he got to the wedding – so strange . . . the best man said he'd talked about his brothers, John and Peter, but he'd never said one was handicapped.(1981)

They haven't shown they were embarrassed to me but it's often crossed my mind. They don't bring their young ladies home and I've wondered if it was because of Joan. They do bring their boyfriends home. Not the girls, they did.   (1981)

Other mothers emphasised that their problems of embarrassment ended when the siblings became adult.

Not unnaturally, perhaps, mothers were alert to the possibility of more serious effects on the siblings. There was speculation about the causes of unexplained illnesses and three mothers mentioned problems with school work. One mother felt her younger child had been slow talking and another that the Down's teenager had set a bad example of behaviour to her younger sons. In addition, several mothers hinted that some siblings had experienced a limited or shortened childhood and they had had to 'grow up too quick.'

In 1981, a minority of the siblings of the Down's syndrome population were being affected in a more lasting way. The effect on one sibling's relationships with her parents has been mentioned (p.64). Other siblings were to become more affected when they reached adulthood because they became involved in providing care. One married woman had taken over the full-time care of her Down's syndrome sister when her parents died and was bringing her up with her own, much younger, normal children. Another sister, who was divorced herself and whose mother had left the family home, was ready to give up her own job to devote herself to the care of her Down's syndrome brother when he left residential school. She already undertook a substantial part of his care and claimed she would only consider marriage to a man who would accommodate himself to her responsibilities. Her normal brother had already given up one job when he was needed at home and now he was engaged he planned to live in the house next door with his future wife who fully realised she had 'also married his Down's syndrome brother.' A sister, in a third family, was given less choice in the matter. When her mother died her father called the siblings together and, by his own account, said:

> Are you going to change or get out? . . . What are you going to do with Lisa? So naturally, fair enough, she'd [sister] see to Lisa . . . it's not a lot of work . . . . As I explained, we've accepted it, it's natural, isn't it?   (1981)

In fact the Down's syndrome teenager was only at home three days a week, but during that time, the 18-year-old was left caring totally for this very severely retarded and incontinent 16-year-old. The older girl's own background had hardly been settled and arguably she was not a sufficiently mature and stable candidate for this work, quite apart from the effect it was having on her. A final example of a more lasting influence on siblings was one brother who, his mother felt, had refused a university place because of the expense and because he felt the trouble involved in bringing up his young Down's syndrome sister required him to be at home.

The negative effects on a minority of brothers and sisters have been outlined, but the opposite view should be also stressed. Some mothers spoke, not only of the absence of any *harm* to the normal siblings, but of the benefits that accrued to them. At the very lowest level, some mothers felt that siblings benefited from the insights into the world of disability in that it showed them how lucky they were themselves and made them more understanding of the situation and hardships of others. More positively still, mothers spoke of the character-building that had resulted so that the siblings were, in effect, better adults themselves because of their experiences.

Counselling for families

Chapters 3 and 4 outlined the impact the Down's syndrome child had on family members. Most responded well, some did not. It has been said that in the 1960s most professional interest in families with a handicapped child centred on the emotional (especially morbid or abnormal) responses of parents. In spite of this there was little help with these problems for families in the population. The general lack of practical services at that time is well known, but it is particularly to be regretted that even the need of families for counselling was neglected. It was not that services failed to identify the need: there were several families who repeatedly told professionals of their emotional problems. Since the 1981 study it is possible to predict that one young girl at least will carry the scars arising from her sibling's disability into her adult life and a mother commented about the neglect of her husband's problems in this way:

> I would have liked them to speak to my husband more – not *me* so much, my husband. My husband should have had – well, being as [paediatrician] *knew* how my husband took it, they should have helped him more – at least, they should have tried.   (1972)

Counselling for these problems is a minority need but, where the need exists and remains unmet, the cost for families is likely to be high.

SUMMARY

As with mothers, there were variations in the way fathers and siblings responded to the birth of a Down's syndrome child in the family. Fewer fathers than mothers responded negatively and, as with the mothers, their responses tended to improve rather than deteriorate.

Few siblings, objectively, were harmed by the presence of a Down's child in the family. The situation for those siblings for whom there were more severe conflicts was improved when they grew up and left home. Subjectively, mothers sometimes felt that siblings were disadvantaged and, to an extent, neglected because they had a Down's syndrome brother or sister. A minority emphasised the advantages of the experience for siblings.

5 How Down's Syndrome Children Influence Their Parents' Lives

A Down's syndrome person in a family will affect other family members' lives because of a number of interrelated reasons. The additional work, which inevitably leads to changes and shifts in routine, has already been discussed, and so too have the emotional reactions of parents. The insidious and debilitating influence on day-to-day life that results from chronic unhappiness, experienced by a minority of family members, but that can affect all activities and relationships, should not be underestimated. A third influence for change arises, not from the child, but from the parents themselves and their understanding of what is wrong with their child, how they perceive that condition, and what they consider to be the needs arising from it. The changes they make in their lives will, in part, be a response to these perceptions: a mother who perceives Down's syndrome to be a very slight disability will not feel it necessary to make the same adjustments as a mother who sees it as a more crippling condition. This Chapter outlines how a mother changes her own life to fit into this perception and the following Chapter discusses the upbringing she considers appropriate for a Down's syndrome child. Both aspects are influenced by her attitudes towards, and understanding of, the needs of a Down's child and, later, teenager and how she reconciles this with the competing needs of herself and the rest of the family.

ATTITUDES UNDERLYING CHANGES IN THE LIVES OF FAMILIES

Carers' perceptions of their child's condition

Almost all parents knew that their children had Down's syndrome, but there were exceptions. In 1972 a father made the following comment:

> What's wrong with Simon now? Oh, well, he's spastic isn't he. He can't hold things properly, his hands aren't right, see.   (1972)

Similarly, in 1981, it was suspected that the mother of one of the teenagers in the new sample did not know the diagnosis given to her child. One mother knew the name of her child's condition but felt the label 'mongol' was so terrible that she avoided using it.

> I was saying to myself 'he's the best of the mongols'. I cheered myself up that way. [You knew he was a mongol although you hadn't been told?] I knew the word and I just had it in myself because the children wouldn't hear of it. ... My husband didn't say nothing, we all seemed just to keep it to ourselves and just said 'Little Raymond needs more attention than other children' perhaps he would say. But we all knew each other what we meant. We wouldn't say 'he's a mongol' – direct.   (1972)

Similarly, for the majority of parents the causes of Down's syndrome did not worry them. Most mothers were ready to accept they had simply been 'unlucky'. As one woman said, laughing, 'I don't blame my husband and he doesn't blame me', but, again there were differences. One young mother admitted she felt she 'deserved' the child since she had been a wayward teenager and the child had been conceived out of wedlock. Another complained because she 'hadn't done anything'. One father, revealing his own prejudices, felt that outsiders thought the family must have something wrong with it: 'I see people look – "Oh", they say, "he's got a mongol" – almost as if we were coloured.' Such feelings cannot be expected to help the adjustment process.

For the majority of parents neither the label nor the cause of Down's syndrome presented undue problems. What the implications of the label meant for parents did, in practice, vary. In 1981, carers of the teenagers were asked how severely handicapped they considered their Down's syndrome teenagers to be. Table 5.1 shows that the majority of carers thought the handicap was only slight, but examination of the range of the Gunzburg scores of the teenagers shows that this parental assessment was not invariably related to the abilities of the child and there was considerable overlap. (See Shepperdson, 1985b, for a fuller discussion.)

Table 5.1 *Carers' assessment of the severity of their teenager's handicap*

Carers' assessment of handicap	n (%)	Gunzburg score	
		Average	Range
Severe	13 (25)	35.3	0–93
Moderate	18 (34)	65.2	17–95
Slight	22 (42)	74.3	24–107
Total	53 (100)	61.6	0–107

Carers' perceptions of the needs of a Down's syndrome child

Most parents in 1972 perceived their Down's syndrome child's physical and emotional needs to be little different from those of their other children. These needs they were, on the whole, happy to meet. In fact a minority of parents did not think their child was other than completely normal and so vast changes would have been considered totally inappropriate. One mother showed that she thought her son was suffering from a very minor disability: 'He's only backward. If he was mental he would be dependent on me.' (What do mean, "mental"?) 'Well, retarded.'

Others were confident in their new task:

I can't do no more for her. I baths her, feeds her, puts her to bed, sends her to school. (1972)

She's in the right school, I give her all I can, I love her all I can. I don't think you can go much wrong there. (1972)

By placing school in this context the implication was that all educational needs had been taken care of. Other parents were very aware that there were educational requirements that had to be met out of school, although whether they were prepared to meet all these needs was a separate issue.

Carers' perceptions of the needs of a Down's syndrome teenager

As the children grew into adults parents were faced with new adjustments and their perception of what a Down's syndrome person needed had to be accommodated to their perception of the needs of a teenager. Different parents made different decisions about which 'label' ('Down's syndrome' or 'teenager') was paramount. A minority resolved the dilemma by denying the teenage status altogether – aided no doubt by the teenagers' small stature and their childish ways – and it was clear that they regarded this as a hurdle for the future. Others were becoming increasingly aware of the approach of adulthood and indeed stressed it to their offspring as encouragement. One or two mothers took a delight in the physical maturity of their sons and daughters – 'he's got a body on him'. For others adolescence was less happily welcomed as it heralded the loss of their own physical control over their children (especially the sons) and the advent of such antisocial acts as public masturbation.

Also, there were fewer guidelines for parents of teenagers to call upon. In 1972, though the Down's syndrome child could be more difficult than a normal child (although not invariably so) and could present more physical problems and more uncertainty about upbringing, the differences between the Down's children and their normal peers were then often ones of scale and intensity rather than presenting a novel set of problems. This parallel with normal children was less marked as the children grew up. Parents pointed out the contrast between their Down's teenager and their other teenage children. When siblings reached their teens they began to take control of their own lives: friends, activities and clothes were more of their own choice and they could sample new experiences without the initiative and guidance of parents. In contrast, the Down's teenager could indulge in little of normal teenage life unless his parents made active efforts to involve him. 'I wouldn't have had to be a companion as well as a mother to him', said one mother of an only child in 1981, explaining how other siblings would have made a difference to her.

As an indication of how far they did feel adjustments were necessary, 48 carers were asked if they tried to 'make it up' to the Down's teenager because he was handicapped. Of that number 23 (48%) said they did and 25 (52%) said they did not. There were no significant differences between the carers who did try to compensate the teenagers, and those who did not, either in social class or age of other siblings.

Some parents themselves believed their Down's teenagers were leading abnormal and circumscribed lives for youngsters of their age but felt that it scarcely mattered since, from the teenagers' own subjective points of view, they suffered little and had few of the more subtle and sophisticated worries that come from greater intelligence and insight. There were also responsibilities from which they were excused. Besides, some parents felt that their teenagers' own desires and aspirations were so few and simple and that they could be made happy relatively easily.

> Oh no I don't make it up to her. No, because on the whole she has a happy little life really – she is loved, she's well fed, she's spoilt in the shops around here – she goes in and looks pathetic and is given an apple or an orange. She has quite a happy little life really.   (1981)

> F. But parents should want their children to be happy and they don't come any happier than our Katy. She hasn't the trauma of O-levels.   (1981)

Carers' perceptions of changes in caring for their Down's syndrome teenagers

In spite of the problems, only a quarter of carers viewed their task as having increased over the years and half the carers felt that things had become easier (see Table 5.2).

A greater number of carers with boys found the task more difficult as the children reached their teens, 9 (32%) compared with 5 (20%) who had girls. More with daughters reported that things had improved (15 (60%) girls compared with 12 (43%) boys), but differences were not significant.

Changes over the years in the parents themselves combined with those in the children to give an improved or deteriorating situation.

Table 5.2 *Carers' perceptions of changes in caring for their Down's syndrome teenagers (% in brackets)*

Changes in task	Original sample		New sample		Total population	
Easier	18	(53)	9	(47)	27	(51)
No change	4	(12)	3	(16)	7	(13)
Mixture	2	(6)	3	(16)	5	(9)
Harder	10	(29)	4	(21)	14	(26)
Total	34	(100)	19	(100)	53	(99)

Aspects that made life easier were predictable: parents became accustomed to the task ('Practice makes perfect' said one mother) and the teenagers, in spite of needing the considerable help outlined in Chapter 2, were for the most part still a great deal more independent than they had been as children. There was satisfaction, too, for those parents who had brought about these changes by their own efforts.

> [It is easier] – simply because she's so good that – I mean it's taken a long time to teach her to do these things, obviously – it took me four years to teach her to walk for instance, it took a couple of years to teach her to feed herself, it took hours and hours – it's been a long, hard haul but now that she does things for herself, yes, it is definitely easier. She can dress herself and go to the toilet – I acknowledge the fact that it could be far worse. She could be incontinent, all sorts of things. There are so many who are worse off.   (1981)

> There's more satisfaction – to see her doing something – sitting quietly turning a page. As a small baby she did *nothing*. I used to have to prop her up on pillows, and to think she's got to this stage. She can walk, and talk in a fashion, and eat and understand most things. I didn't think she'd ever get to this stage.   (1981)

Most mothers found the teenagers easier to control: they were less active, less naughty and most were more responsive to reason. One mother who had expected in 1972 that life would grow steadily worse was greatly surprised.

> Yes I remember saying that when he was born [that the situation would get worse and worse] – I said it to the doctor and in some ways they will because when I'm too old to look after him then this is the biggest problem, but as far as being able to cope with him, he is easier to cope with now than he was – three or four years ago even. He's bigger but he's more reasonable. If he'd been as active and as wild now as when he was young I'd never have coped with him – he was a tiny little thing so really I could physically handle him. Now I couldn't but I haven't got the same problem – you couldn't grab hold of him and hold him down. It would take four men to hold him down at the moment because he's quite a big boy.
>   (1981)

There were a number of reasons for life becoming more difficult. Parents who found their offspring were 'improving all the time' were offset by others who felt that the major gains had already been made and there were fewer advances to enjoy and look forward to.

> When they're younger they're learning to do things and every little step that he took forward we thought was wonderful.   (1981)

About a fifth of the mothers spoke not only of a lack of improvement but of an actual deterioration in their children's behaviour that added to the difficulties. Some problems were specifically mentioned: increased stubbornness, moodiness, naughtiness and tantrums. If behaviour did not improve mothers who had resorted largely to physical control of their children in the past found it increasingly difficult to cope as the teenagers gained in size. Those who remained heavily dependent for physical care also presented increasing problems: one mother who had been able to use a pushchair in earlier days now found going out practically impossible. Several mothers spoke of 'a whole new set of problems with a Down's syndrome adult'. One problem was that what outsiders had found acceptable behaviour in a child, was no longer acceptable in an adult. Furthermore, families who had other children of a similar age found that the Down's teenager, who had once been integrated into the siblings' activities, could no longer participate and so the divisions between them were widening.

The children themselves were not the only ones subject to change – another crucial factor was the age of the parents, older on average in any case than most parents of teenagers. Several spoke of having less patience and less will to make the constant effort necessary to train their teenagers. 'Your mind might be young but your body isn't', said one mother, and another, 'Your brain is tired and your body's tired.' Although only one mother had become so physically ill that she could no longer cope with her child at home, there were early signs that parents were no longer so fit or energetic as in younger days. Three mothers had very poor health and as many as 15 had some minor problems. One grandmother of 78 had almost sole charge of her Down's syndrome grand-daughter. There were health problems for 30% of the fathers too, including two who had very poor health.

Carers' perceptions of competing family needs

How parents view the needs of their Down's syndrome children, and how easy they find it to satisfy these needs, is not, of course, the whole story. Most parents, from both the 1972 and 1981 studies agreed that a Down's syndrome child needed more attention than a normal child, and it was at this point that decisions had to be made between what they saw as the needs of the Down's syndrome child, what they saw as the needs of the siblings and what they saw as their own needs.

In 1972 choices of this nature were greatly influenced by the mother's feelings about whether she had to recompense the Down's child because he was handicapped, or whether she had to compensate the siblings because their brother or sister was not normal. Despite the fact that many parents heroically made efforts to do their best by everyone and were not always aware of their motives, it was possible to sense that underlying decisions on priorities had been made. Sometimes these were made explicit.

In 1972 several parents felt the handicapped child was the unfortunate one and so needed special treatment. Explaining the slight resentment towards her Down's syndrome brother by a sister two years older, one mother said:

> Perhaps it's nothing really – I had boxes of chocolates for Mother's day and I naturally gave one to Ronald – he always takes the best . . . I'd have either a lollipop or an Easter Egg in the drawer and she wanted to know 'whose was that?' Oh yes, he always gets things, so I had to give her half.   (1972)

One mother could see that later on needs would change and she would then perhaps give preference to the Down's child in order to 'make it up' to her. For the time that the needs of the children were similar and all could take pleasure in childish pursuits, the Down's syndrome child missed nothing. When the others began to enjoy more adult activities, then the Down's child would begin to be left out and would need to be compensated and indeed, in 1981, this mother was making efforts in this direction.

> Not when she's little – I thinks she gets enough pleasures out of life. Maybe later on I'll feel that way inclined because I think they do miss more when they get older. Although I mean, as people have said to me, *they* don't know. No, fair enough, they don't, but I know what she's missing, you see.   (1972)

Attitudes amongst mothers ranged from the feeling that the normal children would develop in any case whereas the handicapped child needed special help, to the feeling (current in a minority) that even though the handicapped child would improve with special help this use of time and energy would be something of a waste. Not only would the mother suffer according to this view, but time spent with siblings could produce more results than it could with the Down's syndrome child, who would always have a low ceiling in achievements.

The concern to make the most profitable use of resources was also shown in attitudes to money. Although in 1972 some families were thinking seriously about boarding school for the Down's syndrome child, it was felt that to spend the money on schooling for the siblings would be more sensible since they make better use of it. The parents who emphasised that siblings should not suffer were inclined to make sure that they had special times and outings with their mother on her own, such as swimming and holidays.

Another important area of decision making that parents have to tackle is how much of their own needs and lives they are prepared to subjugate to the needs of the Down's child. In 1972 the paramount conflict was between meeting the Down's child's needs and those of his siblings. In 1981 the conflict had shifted to decisions about meeting the Down's teenager's needs and their own. Many mothers made extreme accommodation to their children, and indeed sacrifice on their part was often seen to be the 'correct' decision. A doctor who said to one mother, 'How is Ronald to manage if you go ill like this?' was seen to be presenting a reasonable argument that would indeed encourage the mother to rally her own strength. Those who baulked against this approach were inclined to accuse themselves of selfishness. In 1981, one mother, divorced and working, who devoted every weekend and most of her holidays to her child admitted to wishing not to resume full-time care but kept saying 'I suppose it's selfish.' Others put forward similar points of view. The mother in the following quotation had, in particular, devoted herself to caring for her child.

> Whatever I've done with Charles, this I can honestly say and I think it's what helps me to cope, I did it for Charles' benefit – not for myself, completely and solely for Charles. Whatever I've done wrong or right – I didn't even consider my husband.

Although parents were prepared to make adjustments and sacrifices when the child was young, and child-care was their chosen employment, the disparity between expected and actual lifestyles became greater as the generation moved on. Parents found their contemporaries had left child-care behind and were moving on to new life-styles – a second honeymoon as one put it.

> You think things, as the years go on, they'll get better but they've gone worse, you know. You're getting older and getting too old to do the things you normally do every day and take it in your stride – an ordinary housewife. People in their 40s now have a good life, their children all grown up and married and out of the way. (1981)

> I didn't have a job – I was a housewife and a mother so [it was] not so much then, but *now* I'm tied. In the beginning it didn't make any difference. A normal mother and housewife would be relaxing more now with her husband, you've brought the family up and you can get together again, can't you? (1981)

> I can go over my friend's, I could take him but it's two of us going everywhere, you know. Now at my age I should be free and just going anywhere – not with a boy of 17. I don't mind, no ... I think we go out more [because of him]. Many a night we say we'd like to stay in tonight but he will go, 'Mam, it's my night tonight.' Many a Sunday we think 'Oh I'd like to stay in and watch that film' and he says 'Mam it's my night' and I think 'Oh God, let's go. It's his night, let him have it.' (1981)

Parents were not only affected in their activities – being in when they wanted to go out and forcing themselves out when they wanted to stay in – but everyday life could also be affected. One mother described why she would not like her other children to take on her Down's syndrome daughter and the disruptive effect was presumably what she herself experienced:

> I wouldn't expect it. A. [daughter] has always said 'Oh, Joan will never have to go anywhere, Mam, while I've got a home.' But then I don't think it would be fair – she's looking at Joan now. What is Joan

going to be like in 20 years' time – will there be an improvement, will she get worse, with her tantrums and her shouting? I don't think it would be fair to her – any of them. I wouldn't expect them to do it . . . it wouldn't be fair to her marriage or her home, or her husband. I couldn't expect the boys to do it – it would be their wives who'd have to look after her – and she does need looking after, their lives would be entirely disrupted and they wouldn't have the same life. They don't realise that, they just come visiting now – they don't realise how different their lives would be if Joan was living with them . . . I don't see they should be burdened with her and it would be a burden. They say no it wouldn't, Joan is their sister but – we'll see, she'll probably improve. I hope she will.   (1981)

Others spoke of the complete reorganisation needed in their lives and the way in which the teenagers' wishes were paramount. This is a situation that is acceptable with a young baby when an end is in sight, but no doubt becomes more irksome when this is not the case.

He controls us, you see, this is the thing. I know it's a hard thing to say but once you start doing something for him it's in that routine and that's it, you see . . . when you get in a way of life you don't stop to question it, you just accept it.   (1981)

Brother: If he feels like doing it he will do it, if he don't you've got no chance . . . eventually you just have to accept it. If there's sport on the television he'll change it just to spite you. [What do you do?] Ask him again nicely. Sometimes you give him a little tap on his hand, not hard. He'll lose his temper with us 'I'm the boss', he says. We leave him alone then and have to accept it'.   (1981)

One mother in the new sample described the relief she felt when she eventually accepted full-time care for her daughter and illustrates how the care of a severely disabled child, combined with ill health, can become to much to cope with.

Yes, I'll be honest – you're free – you haven't got to think 'Is Joanna all right?' or 'How long is it going to be?' or anything like that now, that's done. When she was at home you had to be around – you wouldn't be missing for very long – any period, no way. Looking back I wonder now how I really did cope, you know, 'til she was 14, I . . . it was getting to be a real burden to me, taking my whole life over. I couldn't think straight then. Everything was centred on Joanna and this was it. I thought there was more I could do and I used to get worried that I wasn't doing the right sort of thing. Up to then I thought I'd coped pretty well you know and it suddenly became – I couldn't see Joanna getting any better and I think it all jumbled up in your mind that you weren't doing the right things.   (1981)

A minority of parents spoke of the ways in which they did keep some life of their own. Some insisted on their evenings out alone, one or two took up jobs to avoid too exclusive an involvement with the teenager, three or four took holidays away, but only if the teenager tolerated this. One mother occasionally gave her teenager drugs if he became too difficult 'for us to have some life' and others resolved some of the problems by sending the teenager to boarding school so that the total commitment was reduced.

Yet another potential area of loyalty conflict lay with the grandchildren. Six mothers said that their Down's syndrome teenagers were actively hostile to the grandchildren and jealous of the attention paid to them.

He causes more trouble with my grandchildren [than with the siblings]. That is the biggest problem, he just resents them terribly. We found that harder to bear than any single thing since he has been born. He just won't allow them near him. He'll come in and just give them a kiss – you know – duty, then walk out. But if they go into his room he gets really violent – he just throws things, not at them, but say he goes by the sideboard he'll knock a vase off and throw the wine glasses into the room . . . Well, the grandchildren are frightened . . . it's since they're toddling around. The trouble is with him – he – with little children, he doesn't know what they're going to do, you know, they're unpredictable – he expresses his fright with – er – aggression. [Is he jealous?] No, he just doesn't like them interrupting him and intruding, you know, in his room . . . he just stays in his room. Well, it's shortened [my daughter's] visits very often. Whereas she would have stayed a couple of hours she'd have to go home within half an hour and in that half hour we'd have a few upsets, you know. That's been the most difficult thing to cope with.   (1981)

[The grandchildren] don't bother with her, and she doesn't bother with them. They just look at her, you know, she sits there like an old woman and they just look at her. She won't do anything – she used to, mind. She'd catch hold of their hair and pull them and, oh gosh, yes, I've had to smack her a lot, mind, because when they were small one chance she'd have and she'd hit them, or pull their hair. I've had to check her, that's the only way I've stopped her.   (1981)

Most grandchildren enjoyed good relations with the teenagers, although sadly, like their own parents, they too began to outstrip the teenagers in a few years and they could then grow apart. Some quite tiny grandchildren adopted a protective attitude towards their Down's syndrome uncles and aunts, but others teased them for being unable to read or rejected them as 'dull'. Two mothers said their daughters-in-law discouraged interaction between their children and the teenager. Some parents said they were too exhausted themselves to carry out what they would normally consider their duties as grandparents (e.g. baby-sitting).

CHANGES IN FAMILY LIFE

Voluntary changes

Now that the background against which changes take place has been discussed at some length it becomes necessary to consider the actual changes that occurred, some of which were based on assumptions and decisions that had been made about the child's needs and the family's needs.

In 1972 12 mothers (32%) considered they had made many changes when their children were born. Not surprisingly, all except three were amongst those who had been rated as making a negative response. Of these three, two had rated positive and one of them considered the change in circumstances was for the better. Since the 25 mothers who minimised the changes included the three divorced mothers, the question 'Have you had to make many changes in your life since X was born?' was perhaps badly phrased. Another fault was that most equated 'change' with deterioration.

In 1981 only 9 (17%) of those caring for the teenagers thought they had made major changes, 13 (25%) some change and 31 (59%) felt it had made little difference to them. Changes that were frequently mentioned were restrictions, loss of freedom, isolation, extra work and the spoiling of family life. Occasionally small but distinct changes were made, such as giving up smoking in order to buy a car to make hospital visits easier. Surprisingly, those who had made changes that seemed quite major (for example giving up a job or house, or having a divorce) were not always those mothers who said they had made a lot of changes. It may be that it is easier to adjust to one major change than to a number of minor changes made all day and every day. A few specific areas of change will be looked at in detail.

Parents' jobs

Not unexpectedly it was mothers rather than fathers whose jobs were most frequently affected because they had a Down's child. Table 1.8 (p.10) gives the employment status of women in 1972 and 1981. The proportion of women employed in 1972 was lower than the proportion of women as a whole in England and Wales (27% compared with 43.9% nationally), but this difference was reduced in 1981 (45% compared with 47.5% nationally). It is likely that the difference for mothers of Down's teenagers lay in the hours of work and type of employment rather than in whether or not they were working at all.

In 1972 five women were in full-time employment at the time of the interview and five were in part-time work. Only two women could be said to have given up work because of the child's handicap (as opposed to giving up because of the demands of a baby). Both had had fairly demanding jobs and had made arrangements that would allow them to continue after the baby's birth. Three others with similar arrangements had kept on working. One mother was possibly influenced to keep her job because she felt the child would perhaps need expensive schooling later on, although, by 1981, she said it had not been necessary because everything had been provided by the school. Of the mothers who were in full-time work (including two who had shops on the home premises), two relied heavily on the extended family and two had hired help.

By 1981 the proportion of women in the original sample who worked full-time had fallen very slightly but there were a few more mothers in part-time work. Half of all mothers who were not in work said this was because of the Down's teenager and 11 of the 17 who worked part-time said they would prefer to work full-time if they did not have other responsibilities. One mother in full-time work felt she would have to give it up both because day care arrangements were not entirely satisfactory and also because she felt that, since residential care would one day be essential for her daughter, she wanted to give her 'something to remember us by'. In all, 48% of women were affected in their working arrangements because of their Down's syndrome teenagers.

The influence on jobs, however, was not limited to the hours women were able to work. They were also restricted in their choice of employment and their opportunity to pursue careers rather than simply take the jobs that were offered. Six women worked in schools (only one as a teacher and the rest as auxiliaries or part-time staff) because the hours and holidays made such jobs possible. Similarly shops that could offer flexible hours or tolerated the teenager on the premises afforded work for eight women. Two who had been trained for work before marriage were able to find part-time work in their own fields. Only one woman had embarked on training (as a nurse) since her child was born, but there was another who had planned to begin a full-time degree course in 1981. The lack of a control group makes it impossible to say if the women suffered more in this sphere than all women who give up work to have children. Only three women actually worked *because* of the Down's teenager: two for financial, and one for emotional reasons. One mother had left her own job and bought a shop with a view to employing her daughter later but, by 1981, the plan had been abandoned as unsuitable.

Fathers were affected in the area of work less frequently and less fundamentally than mothers, but did not always remain untouched by circumstances. Only one father had changed his job because it had involved moving the family quite often. It was felt that even more than a normal one a handicapped child needed a settled home and school. This was perhaps only one of the factors influencing the decision. Very often reasons of handicap were given for courses of action for which other 'good' reasons would have been found had the child not been handicapped. Three husbands changed jobs because of the strains at home although, again, in one case there were other problems influencing this decision. Two fathers had, in the past, missed work, one of them because the Down's child was ill and his wife was working and the other because his wife left home. Luckily both men had understanding employers.

Two professional men were influenced in the job market by having to consider facilities for Down's syndrome children in the areas where promotion was available. One moved to South Wales to avoid poor services and another man who had left South Wales after 1972 was reluctant to apply for promotion elsewhere since services were so good in his own area.

Houses and accommodation

In 1972 23 (62%) parents had moved house since the birth of the Down's syndrome child. In at least 10 families (27%) the fact that they had the child influenced the decision although in some cases they would possibly have moved anyway. The reasons were not always clear cut:

> Oh, I think it was mostly for Jill. We wanted to get away [but] it was hard to sell the house and as years went on we might have stayed. She had to have somewhere – to try and advance her as much as we could.
> (1972)

One mother felt she had been allocated a council house because of her child's handicap. One family perhaps delayed moving to their own house, which was ready to be occupied, since arrangements were so simple while they lived with the wife's family.

Reasons for moving were similar whether the child was involved or not. These were usually 'more space', 'more freedom' (i.e. a garden), usually, in other words, 'a better house'. Four of those who changed house did it in conjunction with other changes in their lives: two parents had jobs that had houses attached and two mothers were divorced.

Since 1972 seven families in the original sample had moved house and one other girl had gone to her sister's home when her parents died. Only one mother explained the move as directly concerned with the Down's child saying it was because she felt neighbours and relatives were 'picking on' her daughter and calling her 'mentally handicapped' in an abusive fashion. She also found difficulty keeping her daughter off the roads.

Of the new sample four (21%) had moved during the lifetime of their Down's children for reasons connected with those children. One to seek better services, another to buy a farm in order to give the child more freedom, another for a safer home without a balcony and one that was nearer her in-laws, and one woman with a severely disabled son was given a purpose-built ground-floor flat by the council. When a move was inevitable for other reasons, choices of a home were influenced by services in the area, privacy (one mother avoided council estates fearing the children would tease her son) and safety.

Instead of moving house others altered their existing homes by making concrete play areas, paths and ramps and erecting secure fencing. Two mothers wanted downstairs lavatories installed, one because her son was incontinent and the other because her daughter still needed help with periods and the mother found it tiring going up and down stairs.

Social life

Tables 5.3a and b show that patterns of going out had not changed substantially over the years except that fewer mothers now went out alone. There were 10 women who less often went out alone or with husbands but, with one exception, they did not complain.

Table 5.3a *How often parents went out in 1972 (% in brackets)*

	Mother	Father	Together
Weekly	15 (41)	17 (57)	9 (30)
Monthly	7 (19)	2 (7)	4 (13)
Less often	10 (27)	6 (20)	11 (37)
Never	5 (13)	5 (16)	6 (20)
Not known or absent[a]	–	7	7
Total	37 (100)	30 (100)	30 (100)

[a] Not included in total

Table 5.3b   *How often parents went out in 1981 (% in brackets)*

	Mother		Father		Together	
	Original sample	New sample	Original sample	New sample	Original sample	New sample
Weekly	14 (44)	8 (42)	12 (48)	12 (80)	8 (33)	9 (56)
Monthly	6 (19)	0 (0)	2 (8)	0 (0)	1 (4)	2 (13)
Less often	3 (9)	2 (11)	4 (16)	1 (7)	8 (33)	1 (6)
Never	9 (28)	9 (47)	7 (28)	2 (13)	7 (29)	4 (25)
Not known or absent[a]	2	–	9	4	10	3
Total	32 (100)	19 (100)	25 (100)	15 (100)	24 (99)	16 (100)

[a] Not included in total

In 1972 families varied greatly in how far they allowed the Down's syndrome child to restrict them as a family. One mother, when she spoke of the impossibility of going to hotels and eating out with the child, seemed to think this needed no explanation. Other mothers made a special point of taking the child to such places so that he could learn to behave acceptably in public. Sometimes time and trouble turned an occasion that was planned for enjoyment into a hardship and the effort was dropped, and it is impossible to say if persistence would have made the problem any easier. Many who made the effort were constantly ready for rebuffs:

> If I go to a hotel or anywhere I always say, 'Well, we have a mongol child'. I always *do* say it so if they want to say, 'No', well, they can say 'No'. No-one has said 'No' yet, no. But I mean when we book I say, 'I have a daughter of so and so and the little boy is a mongol.' I always say it . . . It's a job to say, I hate having to say it. (1972)

> She's never stopped us going anywhere. She's been abroad and to Ireland twice with my mother and father. Wherever we go she goes with us and that's it. (1972)

Although several mothers said, or implied, that by the time the child was born they had made their friends and that these did not change, others, for various reasons, felt that their lives had changed socially.

    4 (11%) felt that their social lives had improved;
   21 (57%) felt there had been little change;
   12 (32%) felt their social lives had become more limited.

Explanations given by the 12 with reduced social lives varied and there was often a combination of reasons. Four mothers gave their own feelings as the main reason:

> I got to the stage when I avoided everybody – I still get a bit peculiar at times – you just don't want to talk to anyone or go out and see anyone. This is when I get tired. (1972)

> It's made me different. It's made me more within myself. Well – I don't know –you think everyone's against the child. People generally make a big fuss of her but there are one or two you get hurt very badly with and then you shut the door, then if you don't bother with people then they can't hurt you . . . I've stopped speaking to three neighbours because of Helen. You see, that's where I've changed. (1972)

Six mothers gave as the main reason the trouble involved in making arrangements, or lack of time and energy. Parents mentioned the difficulties of taking the child to other people's houses. Some simply did not bother and preferred to have friends to their own home or not to see people. One father and a mother gave examples of the problems:

> A lot of people will say, 'Oh, let him do this, let him do that', and really speaking they're thinking to themselves, 'Why don't they stop that kid'; but they *say*, 'Oh, it's all right, it's all right'. He's just

smashed ten pounds' worth of china – 'Oh, it's all right, leave him alone'. Well, I know for a fact it *can't* be all right. They must be annoyed about it. It's common sense. (1972)

Well, it's obvious that when you've got one of these the family just breaks up and you haven't got time to – well – I've lost most of my friends because I haven't got time to go out. And I mean when they were coming to the house he was having heart attacks and one thing and another – well – I couldn't be *bothered* with them then, there you are. (1972)

Embarrassment was only mentioned by six mothers (16%). One mother wished her child looked *more* handicapped since then his bizarre behaviour would be easily accounted for and excused. Another said she pretended the child was much younger (about 3) to avoid explaining his lack of speech. Only two mothers specifically mentioned baby sitters as a problem.

In 1981, oddly enough in view of the fact that parents on the whole were happier, found their task easier as the years went by and did not go out substantially less than they had in 1972, more carers were inclined to say that their social lives were restricted by their children than was so in 1972 (see Table 5.4).

Table 5.4 *Changes in social lives of carers (1972 and 1981) (% in brackets)*

Social lives	Original sample		New sample	Total population
	(1972)	(1981)	(1981)	(1981)
Improved	4 (11)	1 (3)	1 (5)	2 (4)
Without change	21 (57)	17 (50)	8 (42)	25 (47)
Restricted	12 (32)	16 (47)	10 (53)	26 (49)
Total	37 (100)	34 (100)	19 (100)	53 (100)

The anomaly that carers felt more restricted in 1981 when in fact their position had not changed in this respect since 1972 may perhaps be explained by the change in expectations discussed earlier: parents whose children are in their teens *expect* to be fairly free to come and go as they please whereas parents of young children do not. Some mothers were very conscious of the changed pattern of their lives:

Now and again I feel a bit bitter – I'd like to go out because we're very fond of dancing – I'd like to go to dances and you know you can't go. But now we've sort of – got a different life. We've just accepted it. We have people in, you know, and it's . . . so really we don't mind. (1981)

The mothers were asked about making friends. Eleven (21%) of them found some problems making friends, three (6%) had formed new friendships, thirty-eight (72%) found no problems and one mother felt she had more friends because of her son. Four mothers in 1981 (two from the original sample and two from the new) stressed the initial impact handicap had made on their own personalities making them more withdrawn and less ready to socialise. Two pointed out that by the time they had made some recovery they had lost contact with their old friends and had to find new. The barriers between the 'in group' and the 'out group' to use Oswin's (1971) terms or 'the wise' and the rest of society, to use Goffman's (1963) terms, were illustrated by what mothers said about the barriers they sensed between themselves and others.

A lot of people haven't realised I've got him, you know, they know me and – it's not because I've hidden him away – it's just because – 'Oh I didn't know you had a boy like that' you know. There again they don't seem as *nice* as they were about him – I don't know – perhaps it's just me, my imagination. (1981)

You lose your friends, you know, if they've all normal children you've got nothing in common, we seem to have drifted away like, you know. We're more friendly now with people like ourselves and we make our own life. I get bitter about it now and again but – it's just one of those things. We used to go to the park and all that, but I never wanted to do that with Pete. Nobody seemed to ask me – we've gone to the park for a picnic and you could feel yourself getting cut off. In the beginning I know I didn't want to – I'm to blame a little bit – but when I got to accept it I felt – I used to say to the girls 'let's go out' and they said they'd made arrangements and you could read between the lines like, you know. And then you compare children, and Pete was that much slower, that's why I never went to the clinics, I just couldn't cope with it, you know.   (1981)

Although the modern publicity on television and in magazines may help to break down barriers, for one mother the interest her daughter aroused seemed to her more impertinent than helpful:

Some people, yes, you do avoid – they're very morbid. 'Are you going to teach her?' Some people make it worse than it is, always telling a story about somebody else's baby and what happened to them. You learn who your friends are . . . It did make a difference to my sister-in-law when I took Pat at 6 months old. Her husband had got a book – he's one of those people who likes to know everything – to read about Pat's condition. So when I took her there he was pointing out the characteristics, eyes, high cheekbones, which I didn't like. He was studying her to see how different she was from a normal child. This is one reason I've never been again for 15 years. I was very sensitive at the time. You do get this sort of thing with these children – on a bus you see someone nudge someone. They see these programmes on TV and they look out for it. It's not always a help – a little knowledge is a dangerous thing.   (1981)

In order to avoid having to make explanations and face unwelcome comparisons, four or five mothers said they sought friends from among those in a similar position. Four other mothers blamed, not themselves, but others for creating barriers and avoiding them and their Down's children. One mother felt her own sister arranged visits when her daughter was at school. Others found their handicapped children were 'picked on' by children and this created friction between the parents. One mother, in her late 40s, unable to join the life of her contemporaries, had plenty of friends but explained they were all much younger than herself:

They're all younger than me – well my oldest is 23. They're all women in their 20s and 30s. One, she has two children – 7 or 8 – I used to go down if it was raining and mind one so she didn't have to dress two to go up to the school. She's a nice girl but she's only 26, see – I'm old to them, really, even though they don't notice that I am.   (1981)

Only three mothers mentioned disruptive behaviour of their children as a barrier to going out, but other mothers, who did not make a specific point about it, in another context described behaviour that must have produced difficulties:

I ignore some behaviour when I am out to avoid a performance. I think she realises she gets away with more outside. My aunt on Sundays says 'She needs a hiding', but if I did and they saw the chaos it can cause they wouldn't say it, so I give in a bit. She screams and shouts and kicks so I avoid it in someone's house. If she says 'I want to go home' I give it eight minutes and home we come. We do or she nags and gives you your handbag and coat. She very often does that. Once she's had her tea she thinks she's ready to go. I say 'I'm sorry but it's better to go'. They understand.   (1981)

To tell you the truth I haven't the confidence to take her to a guest house – I don't know how she'd be. I'd find myself coming home after two days.   (1981)

Embarrassment was experienced by 16 (30%) mothers (almost twice the proportion who mentioned it in 1972), although only four were restricted by it and one other forced herself to ignore it. Embarrassment was more often the result of the actions of the teenager rather than his appearance. Past embarrassment now overcome was spoken of by seven mothers and eight mothers said their husbands felt embarrassed when out with their child. Problem-behaviour included 'kissing ladies', 'shouting and bawling', 'scratching in embarrassing places', pulling children's hair and being 'full of himself' with visitors. Mothers said 'I'm not relaxed' and another 'I'm on pins with her the whole time'. One mother of an epileptic boy said they did not go out much in case he had a convulsion; she would be embarrassed 'for him'.

In spite of the problems two mothers found their social lives greatly improved because of their children. One mother put it this way:

Judy has enriched our lives. Perhaps we wouldn't have been going out and about – we'd have been sat here probably on a nice day wondering where to go. I know you've got grandchildren but we wouldn't have had quite the same life as we've had with her. (1981)

The use of babysitters

Table 5.5 shows the type of babysitters used in 1972 and 1981.

Table 5.5 *Use of babysitters 1972 and 1981 (% in brackets)*

	Original sample (1972)	Original sample (1981)	New sample (1981)	Total population (1981)
Babysitters }	15 (41)	4 (12)	2 (11)	6 (11)
Friends or neighbours }		5 (15)	1 (5)	6 (11)
Relatives only }	11 (30)	4 (12)	2 (11)	6 (11)
Siblings }		15 (41)	10 (23)	25 (47)
No one	11 (30)	6 (18)	4 (21)	10 (19)
Total	37 (101)	34 (101)	19 (101)	53 (99)

Even in 1972 the question of babysitters hardly arose in some families because the older children were able to babysit for parents (obviously this was a more common situation for older parents). Similarly, those with relatives living very near could say firmly, 'only relatives', where they might have been prepared to reconsider this decision in other circumstances. A few parents certainly mentioned that the child's handicap forced them to consider only having relatives or having no one. Sometimes this was because it was thought to be too much for the babysitter and sometimes because they were not happy to leave the child. (People qualified to work with handicapped children would probably have been welcomed.)

But I'll be honest ... I'm not keen on leaving him with other people personally. That's my feeling on it ... I don't think they can look after him as well as what we do ... I see people looking after their own children and I think, well, if they look after their own like that they're not looking after mine. (1972)

In 1972 nine women over 40 years had no babysitters at all, but only two women under that age refused to use anyone.

By 1981 almost half of the baby sitting was being done by siblings of the teenagers and other carers relied on relatives, friends and neighbours rather than paid baby-sitters. Just six people used a babysitter whose only real connection with the family was through this function. One of these was a 'county sitter', paid by the local authority. Since she lived next door to the mother in question she could be most useful collecting the teenager from the school bus and so on, although the mother rarely used the whole eight hours a week to which she was entitled. Hers was the only example of this service in the whole population but it would undoubtedly have been valued by others. By 1981 there were fewer parents who had no one to whom they could turn; five of those who had been in that position in 1972 could now use siblings and two others used friends.

There were two teenagers who were extremely troublesome if their mothers left them; they would throw tantrums and be generally unmanageable, and so outings for these mothers were extremely difficult.

Family planning

One fundamental influence a Down's syndrome child can have on a family is its size.

For the parents a vital factor in this decision can be the advice given on the chances of having a second Down's baby. This aspect will be dealt with in Chapter 8 but since very few parents had had any advice, or seemed to know what it meant when they were given it, this aspect can play little part here. The results of the study shown here use details from the original sample collected in 1972, and information on the new sample which has been added where appropriate and relates to what was said in 1981. In the original sample, 17 mothers (average age, 29.1 years) had planned the Down's syndrome child, 10 (average age, 38.0 years) had not and 10 (average age, 38.1 years) did not care whether or not they had another child.

Not surprisingly, there was some relationship between family planning attitudes, age of the mother and the number of children. Older mothers who either wanted further children, or at least did not mind if they had more were generally those mothers who had small families. Those who were younger and did not want more children generally had larger families. Since so few women had actually wanted more children even before the Down's syndrome child was born, after that birth, quite apart from the issue of handicap, even more of them could be assumed to have reached their chosen family size, meaning that even fewer would be likely to be wanting more children.

Of the original sample 13 mothers (35%) went on to have more children after the Down's syndrome birth, as did 4 (21%) of the new sample. Far from preventing some mothers, the fact of having a handicapped child encouraged them to have more, sometimes for the sake of the Down's syndrome child (an extreme case of giving priority to the handicapped child, where the new child is born to be of service) and sometimes for the existing children. Both the following quotations are from one mother:

> Oh, I wanted more for his sake . . . I mean he teaches from his sister . . . I'd like another boy . . . for him you know . . . to have the same interests as him.

Asked whether she would expect the children to take care of the Down's child later on, she said:

> Oh, yes. That's why we had them. We had [sister] and we didn't feel it was fair for her to shoulder the responsibility of him so we went in for another child and luckily we had a daughter, because women are more apt to be able to cope with somebody like that.   (1972)

It should be said that this woman would probably have wanted a large family in any case. One other, who had two Down's syndrome children, wanted company for her normal child; two others made their choice because they felt that the Down's syndrome child might not survive.

It should not be assumed that parents limited their families only because they were afraid they would have another Down's syndrome baby. The dominant factor was sometimes that the child they had was so demanding that they did not feel they could cope with a new baby.

> (Pilot Study) Well, we've got to be fair now. There's Amanda. How would she be now with another child coming? She needs all the attention we can give her. Well, you can't be fair to two children when one needs all that she's getting.   (1972)

Of the 13 in the original sample who had more children, 4 seemed to have been taken by surprise, 1 did not know the child was handicapped and so was not influenced by this, and 8 mothers wanted more. Only 4 mothers either checked about the possibility of having more Down's syndrome children or had already been told there was no danger (or so they thought). One mother alone was so concerned that she decided to have another baby only when she heard of the amniocentesis test and was given written assurance she could have it. All 4 mothers in the new sample who increased their families did so intentionally. Two had been given tests and advice, two had not and this includes the woman who had two Down's children.

Table 5.6 *Children born after the Down's syndrome child and mother's age at birth (whole population)*

	Additional children			
Mother's age at the birth	0	1	2 or more[a]	Total
Under 29	5	7	6	18
30–39	15	3	0	18
40–49	15	–	1[b]	16
Over 50	2	–	–	2
Total	37	10	7	54

Excludes two mothers whose ages were not known; includes three mothers seen only in 1972.
[a]2 mothers had 3 more children.
[b]Mother asked to be sterilised after Down's syndrome birth but was refused because 'it was only the third birth'.
Mothers 29 years and under compared with the rest, mothers without additional children compared with the rest: $\chi^2 = 18.04$; df = 1; p < 0.001.

Of the 48 natural mothers interviewed 18 (38%) mothers specifically mentioned that the Down's syndrome child would be a factor in decisions about having more children. This attitude deterred them from having more, or made them check (not always very well, however) on the possibility of recurrence before enlarging their families. Twenty-one (44%) other mothers probably did not want more in any case, but it cannot be assumed that had they wanted them they would have been uninfluenced by the handicap of their Down's syndrome child. (Two more had children anyway.) Of the nine (19%) who did not know about the child's condition, or simply wanted more children regardless of the handicap issue, only four had had a child in 1981.

Fourteen mothers had been sterilised – 9 immediately after the birth of the Down's syndrome child. In only one instance was there an indication that this drastic method of birth control was adopted because the mother felt very strongly against having more children because of the Down's syndrome child. Two more women asked for sterilisation but were refused it. Only three husbands in the sample had been sterilised and in two cases this was because of the fear of having another Down's child. Two women had had amniocentesis tests – one at her own request when the test first became available.

For the 39 who did not add to their families, then, many of the mothers were of an age, or with the size of family, to make them unlikely to want more children in any case. Possibly about eight or nine mothers were stopped from having more children because of the handicap issue. A sample which was not biased towards older mothers would be likely to produce different results.

One sad result of the decision not to enlarge a family was the mother who died in hospital after an abortion. It was not entirely clear if it was the fact that she had a Down's child that made her choose an abortion rather than proceed with the pregnancy.

The changes that have been discussed so far have been changes over which the parents have had some measure of control and some choice, but other major changes also took place in families. These were involuntary changes brought about by the complex situation that arose at the birth of the child and linked to some extent to the response and feelings parents experienced at the birth of the child. Only two such changes will be dealt with here: the mental health of the mother and changes in the relationship between husband and wife. The importance of these two factors for the welfare of the family as a whole does not need stressing.

Involuntary changes

Mental stress

Mothers were asked in 1972 and 1981 whether any illness had resulted from, or worsened since, the birth of the child. Mental stress or illness is notoriously difficult to assess and the label is often only formally applied when someone goes to a doctor and the doctor recognises it in the surgery. The decision to visit a doctor and the doctor's recognition of a psychiatric problem do not necessarily distinguish between people who suffer high or low degrees of mental stress (Goldberg and Huxley, 1980). Mothers were asked about 'nervous illnesses' and, as a rough indication of those who felt themselves to be subject to some sort of mental stress, this was adequate, but the purely subjective nature of the account should be borne in mind.

Three mothers from the study are not included here as suffering stress from the birth of their Down's child. One had epileptic attacks, one had had 'bouts of depression' and another had had psychiatric treatment. The last two mothers are not included because they claimed these symptoms had nothing to do with the handicapped child. It should be pointed out that psychiatric disorder is extremely common (especially in women) and that conservative estimates place the one-year prevalence rate as high as 140 per 1000 of the population (Shepherd *et al.*, 1966).

Table 5.7 shows the self-reported mental stress of mothers in 1972 and 1981.

Table 5.7 *Mental stress of mothers 1972 and 1981 (% in brackets)*

	Original sample (1972)	(1981)	New sample (1981)	Total population (1981)
Problems	19 (51)	14 (44)	7 (37)	21 (41)
No problems	18 (49)	18 (55)	12 (63)	30 (59)
Total	37 (100)	32 (99)	19 (100)	51 (100)

Figures include women carers but exclude two fathers.

In 1972, of the 19 (51%) mothers who complained of suffering some form of stress, four reported that their doctors had said a physical condition (loss of weight, shingles, psoriasis, and 'nervous rash') was the result of stress. At least 10 of the 19 mothers had had medication of some sort. Six did not speak of medication, but in any case an absence of medication does not necessarily imply a less serious condition. At least one mother in this category was having constant visits from her general practitioner. On a conservative estimate three (8%) mothers could be said to have experienced severe mental health problems after the birth of their babies. All were classified as negative mothers. Troubles experienced by the other mothers included 'depression' and threatened or actual 'nervous breakdowns', because of the problem of living with constant stress.

As the table shows, by 1981 a rather lower proportion of women were experiencing problems. Fifteen of those who complained of mental stress in 1981 gave such symptoms as depression, bouts of crying, and feelings of stress that resulted in taking tablets, or feeling the need of medication – although two women avoided its use. Other women spoke of physical symptoms: loss of weight, asthma attacks, blood pressure and three women had had thyroidectomies, although only two gave stress as the cause. The following quotation shows the kind of link women made between physical complaints and their lifestyles:

> I don't want to wrong him but I think he's brought the blood pressure with the frights I've had with him and the rushing around because of the running out. He used to run away a lot a few years ago. Once he would go out from here goodness knows where you'd find him and the police would bring him back and it would worry me so much that he'd be knocked down or somebody would take him and I think that Raymond has upset me so much that I've had the blood pressure – perhaps it was normal that I would have it but I think Raymond has done a lot for it. He would go, you see, and I was crying my eyes out. I wouldn't come back to normal for a month or so after.   (1981)

Five women who had felt under some stress in 1972 had no complaints in 1981 but for four women the reverse was true. There was no obvious difference between the two groups, except that the former had more capable children. The average score of their teenagers on the Gunzburg PAC was 79.6 compared with an average of 54.0 for the children whose mothers complained of more stress in 1981.

Conflict between husband and wife

Mothers were asked in 1972 and 1981 if their relationship with their husband had changed since the birth of the Down's child. Obviously a question of this nature is open to evasive replies but mothers seemed to answer frankly on the whole and, when they spoke of deterioration, there was generally other supporting evidence from the rest of the interview.

This section is primarily concerned with deterioration. Where parents spoke of improvement there was no attempt to see if 'too cohesive' (see Schaffer, 1964) would have been an apt description because it seemed impertinent and unnecessary to try to detect a morbid aspect of a relationship which was satisfying to the people concerned. Details of actual divorces have been given earlier in this book and details of relationships in 1972 and 1981 are given in Table 5.8.

Table 5.8 *Relationships between fathers and mothers, 1972 and 1981 (% in brackets)*

| | Original sample | | New sample | Total population |
	(1972)	(1981)	(1981)	(1981)
Closer				
Closer relationship	12 (32)	11 (32)	6 (32)	17 (32)
No change				
No change in relationship	15 (41)	8 (24)	7 (37)	15 (28)
Widowed/separated not directly because of child	3 (8)	5 (15)	4 (21)	9 (17)
Divorced – not directly because of child	1 (3)	3 (9)	–	3 (6)
Deteriorated				
Deteriorated relationship because of child	3 (8)	3 (9)	–	3 (6)
Divorced because of child	3 (8)	3 (9)	–	3 (6)
Separated because of child	–	1 (3)	–	1 (2)
Not available	–	–	2 (11)	2 (4)
Total	37 (100)	34 (101)	19 (101)	53 (101)

The 'no change' category in Table 5.8 is not always very revealing in terms of the state of the relationship. It contains both mothers who said, 'We were very close, anyway', and mothers whose relationship was poor in any case. Since the concern here is with changes that took place because of the child, the often dramatic conflicts that took place before and after the birth will be ignored, although in such circumstances the child's environment was probably far from ideal. Whether a poor relationship can remain completely untouched by potentially stressful events is another matter (see Gath, 1978; Farber, 1968). One divorced mother who claimed the child was not concerned in the conflict said: 'I was up ten weeks without sleep. One night he offered to help and let me sleep. Things like that, they put you off.' Another woman, who had gone through a divorce in 1981 in which the child was not the only cause, described her situation as follows:

> Well I think it was a lot to do with Adrian. I think Adrian actually *being* there, I think my husband would have liked to have me put him away. He never actually said it, but it was the way he was acting – you know – towards Adrian. He ignored him and he'd be telling him off for doing things – well – that I wouldn't have thought was wrong like, you know – well playing with his toys – he couldn't play with his flaming toys. Children should be seen and not heard, that was it. The same with the others, but it was a bit worse with Adrian.   (1981)

Divorced fathers could – hurtfully – perpetuate the distinction between their children after the divorce. They welcomed contact with the normal children but not the one with Down's syndrome. One did not welcome any of his children.

The 'no change' category for 1972 includes two mothers who reported that initially their marriages were under stress but had improved by 1972. Both in fact reported a closer relationship in 1981. In the new sample three mothers similarly reported initial problems because they were under stress themselves because of the birth and one because of the discrepancy between the rate of adjustment to the birth by the husband and wife.

No more than two relationships showed any additional strain in the original sample in 1981 and in only one case was this severe. For the others one father claimed that their child had brought him and his wife closer together (as indeed the wife had said in 1972), but later in the interview the wife privately disagreed with this and said 'it divides you'. In her case one manifestation of this was her husband's reluctance to attend any functions to do with the handicapped and, since she felt obliged to attend, she had to go alone.

Three who had said the Down's syndrome child brought them closer in 1972 said 'no change' in 1981, but this could simply be a change in emphasis – although one did say she wished her husband would do a little more to help. Two women who had felt the child was a divisive influence in 1972 actually reported closer relationships in 1981 and four who said in 1972 it made no difference decided by 1981 that they were closer.

It is scarcely necessary to go into detail over the various conflicts between husband and wife, but it is perhaps worth mentioning that a relationship that was acceptable before the child was born could be found wanting when the wife had extra stress laid on her. One woman, in 1972, described how she had always been the partner to take over the practical aspects of life (tax returns, house repairs and so on) and had been content to do this. She had been happily married, she said, 'with no rows at all' for 25 years. However, when the child was born her own needs changed and she would have welcomed help and support, but her husband did not change, and this led to considerable unhappiness that persisted to 1981. It should also be said that even though wives were quite happy with their marriages, the Down's child could still cause disagreements of a minor nature.

> The fact that he's hard work – mentally hard work – and I get tired and irritable and my husband comes home and out it all comes. I pick at him, I suppose, because of it and of course he's tired himself.   (1972)

Another very common form of minor disagreement was over discipline – most often because the husband thought the wife was too strict and the wife thought the husband too lenient.

In fact, the reasons for stress in a relationship are all too easy to identify, but perhaps less easy to understand are the reasons for the closer relationships reported by a third of the families. One mother felt the whole experience had 'brought out the best in both of us' and three mothers illustrated the sort of mechanisms that could throw a couple together and make them interact and cooperate more than might have been the case in other circumstances.

> Yes, it probably does bring you closer because you deal more together, you know, with – perhaps I'd be out with the girls, I'd be with my sisters but you're more together because you've got to be.   (1981)

I think we're closer than we would have been. We've pulled ourselves out of some scrapes where if we hadn't him perhaps we would have said 'You can go your way, I'll go mine.'   (1981)

Over the years we talk things out. Not so much now, but when we were younger we would discuss everything, you know, but we do try to be of one mind on what's best for her. At times we both had a different opinion – the main thing was going away to school . . .   (1981)

This section has dealt so far with relationships between the natural parents of the child, but there are other circumstances to be considered and those who were divorced or widowed were asked how the presence of the Down's syndrome child affected their chances of remarriage. Six women were divorced and two had already attempted remarriage but both remarriages had failed (twice for one women) with the Down's child being implicated in all cases. For the remaining four women, one woman did not want to remarry and risk another trauma of divorce for her children, another felt men she had known were 'put off', another was engaged and the last was too recently divorced to have any experience of these matters. Of the four widowed and separated women, one had remarried but the three others (all over 50) had not given it much thought. One father was divorced, one separated and two were widowed. The divorced man had remarried and had a new family, and both the widowers had prospects of remarriage.

SUMMARY

How parents viewed their Down's syndrome children and their needs varied, as did the priority they put on meeting these needs along with the competing needs of other family members. Consequently there were differences between families and the changes they made in their lives as a response to these perceptions. For instance, at the extremes, the same event – the birth of a Down's syndrome child – made some parents actively want another baby while the reverse was true for others. A few mothers chose to work *because* they had a Down's child, others decided to stay at home for the very same reason. For some the event drew husbands and wives together but, for others, it increased marital disharmony.

6 How Parents Influence Their Down's Syndrome Child

UPBRINGING

Parents vary considerably in how they tackle the upbringing of their children and something that is allowed in one family will be forbidden in another. With Down's syndrome children, with their wide range of abilities, there is equal scope for variation in upbringing but, as will be seen, differences in upbringing of the study population were not invariably related to the abilities and competence of the children.

Not only does upbringing differ considerably, but Down's children are particularly vulnerable to the decisions their parents make about this. Discipline and rules for normal children are often a subject of negotiation between them and their parents, but this is less likely to be true for Down's syndrome children. Other children are more able to interact with their peers and can attempt to change home rules that seem inappropriate, or out of touch, by use of arguments about what happens in other families; Down's syndrome children are often much more isolated from friends and may, in any case, be unable to discuss such issues in an articulate fashion. In short, they are more likely to have to accept what their parents see as natural and right for them.

A particular difficulty for loving and caring parents of Down's children is to decide at what age they can discontinue or modify their protective stance. It is all too easy to cast a Down's syndrome teenager, with his limited abilities, into the role of a much younger child. Whereas the average teenager would rebel against this, a youngster with Down's syndrome may passively accept it. In addition to lack of feedback, parents may also lack direct advice. There are fewer books, television programmes and articles on the subject and, because children tend to be transported to school by bus, contact with parents in the same position may be limited. The situation is improving but professional advice can still be inadequate, or even conflicting. A parent may therefore be left to make his or her own rules in something of a vacuum.

This chapter sets out to describe the decisions made by parents who have Down's syndrome children.

Attitudes to discipline

In 1972 and 1981 carers were asked how far they considered themselves to be 'strict', 'average', or 'lenient' compared with others. Their replies are shown in Table 6.1.

Variations in approaches to upbringing were immediately apparent in 1972 and mothers were fairly evenly divided between the three categories. The following quotations illustrate the differences in approaches to upbringing amongst the mothers in the 1972 study.

One mother was asked how many sweets the child was allowed and said:

Table 6.1 *Carers' self-classification of strictness 1972 and 1981 (% in brackets)*

Upbringing	Original sample (1972)	(1981)	New sample (1981)	Total (1981)
Strict	11 (30)	6 (18)	4 (21)	10 (19)
Average	12 (32)	11 (32)	6 (32)	17 (32)
Lenient	11 (30)	14 (41)	7 (37)	21 (40)
Vary	3 (8)	3 (9)	2 (11)	5 (9)
Total	37 (100)	34 (100)	19 (101)	53 (100)

> We let her have that because she don't eat food so good as all that so we let her have sweets and choco-
> lates – and cream Easter eggs. (1972)

Other mothers had an entirely different policy:

> I make him do things all the time the right way. People might think I'm hard but that's the only way I
> think I could get through to him. (1972)

Several parents were at pains to point out that they treated the child as normally as possible:

> You shouldn't pamper – over-pamper them. She's always been slapped and checked. I don't say we hit
> hell out of her but she's been stopped when she's deserved it. I don't think, 'Oh, pity, poor Clare.' Clare
> is an ordinary child and if she does anything naughty she's promised a slap or a treat – and she'll get it.
> (1972)

In 1981 there was a slight tendency for more mothers to adopt a lenient approach to their teenagers than when the children were younger.

The level of strictness adopted was the balance struck between how they viewed their teenager's ability to tolerate correction ('What they can take') and their own view of what was acceptable behaviour. Changes in fashion were apparent. One mother said her own views on discipline 'would be considered strict today but we've always been very free – the children have always known the rules.' Another described the very great variation in the way mentally handicapped children were brought up:

> They see me as easy going, the other mothers. I see them as very easy going, one as simple. 'Come here,
> Sugar' and this sort of thing – that gets under my skin . . . . I see another one who's far too strict about the
> child's appearance – I say boy, he's six foot six – and he's very awkward – if he ambles through a pool of
> mud as he did the other day she leathers hell out of him. No, we're all different and react differently. And
> I say 'For God's sake, Jane, he can't help that' – but to her it's so important that he keeps himself clean
> and tidy and I couldn't give a damn. You know, we've all got different ways and no one would dare tell
> me how to bring mine up – they have tried. But I don't tell them either – I just think 'Well, that's your
> problem' . . . we've all got our own ways and all think we're right. At least I hope I know my mistakes but
> I don't want to be told what they are. (1981)

Fifty-two carers of teenagers were asked what they felt to be the ideal approach to Down's teenagers. There were 22 (42%) in favour of a strict approach, 8 (15%) an average regime, and 16 (30%) favoured leniency. Six (11%) felt that different circumstances called for different approaches. So, in spite of a slight move towards leniency in actual behaviour as the children grew up, most mothers clearly did not consider it an ideal approach, and this was confirmed by comments that arose in the interviews in 1981. Those mothers who had been strict over the years felt the good behaviour of their teenagers entirely vindicated their policy and others, who had been lenient, now attributed problems they experienced with their teenagers to their own past approach. No one who had taken a lenient stance pointed out the benefits of this regime. The relationship between those who felt they were lenient in 1972 and who reported problems of obedience in 1981 fell just short of significance. There was no difference between boys and girls and obedience problems.

Table 6.2 *Upbringing and obedience problems 1981 (% in brackets)*

Upbringing	Obedience problems			
	Many	Few	None	Total
Strict	2 (18)	1 (9)	8 (73)	11
Average	6 (38)	6 (38)	4 (25)	16
Lenient	9 (43)	7 (33)	5 (24)	21
Total	17 (35)	14 (29)	17 (35)	48

Figures exclude those whose upbringing varied.
Those with 'many' and 'few' obedience problems compared with those with 'none': $\chi^2 = 8.34$; df = 2; p < 0.02.

Upbringing in 1981 was significantly related to the reported obedience problems of that year – strict mothers being less likely to experience obedience problems than those who said they were average or lenient (Table 6.2).

Some of the emphasis on strictness was a reflection of the mothers' insistence on normal behaviour. Those who were determined to make their children as normal as possible were inclined to direct efforts to removing any behaviour that drew critical attention to their children. Consequently, good manners were considered more obligatory for the Down's syndrome child than for the normal. Again, one mother curbed the over-boisterous play of her son in the swimming pool, one stamped out any feminine activities for her son and very many mothers considered clean and tidy dress mandatory for their Down's syndrome children in order to avoid any additional stigma. The trend for modern children to be encouraged to express themselves and reject stereotyped attitudes and roles was not reflected in the population: the parents of Down's syndrome teenagers were anxious to make them conform to a narrower and less flexible range of behaviour based on what others expected rather than on the teenagers' own choices. Similarly, there was less concentration on internalised standards of behaviour and more emphasis on externally imposed rules.

The need some mothers felt for definite and inflexible rules of behaviour can be illustrated by the mother in the first of the following quotations; she argued that a normal child may have the adaptability to adjust his behaviour in varying circumstances, but the Down's syndrome child may not be able to distinguish so easily between the circumstances in which a certain behaviour is acceptable and those in which the same behaviour is wrong or inappropriate. Not only this, she expected the public to be less tolerant.

We went to [hotel] one night and there was a fellow singing and another chap in the middle and this chap started stripping off – showing off. Frank had gone and was sitting by this man so I said, 'Excuse me, back to your seat. Let me tell you one thing, you can sit by me or you can go home and get a baby sitter – I'm still coming out. You choose'. So he sat back in his seat straight away, no messing. And the man said to me, 'I think you're very hard, he hadn't done anything.' So I was mad, and I said 'I don't know you, I don't remember asking your advice how to bring my son up. Until I do, love, mind your own bloody business.' I was fuming, see. And he said, 'I'm awfully sorry I've upset you.' I said 'No, you haven't upset me, love, not one bit. When I knew what I had to put into life I put a big barrier up against interfering people like you, just leave it there, OK?' And ever since then I say, 'Frank' and that's it, no way he's going to get out of that seat if I say no. He *hadn't* done anything, but next time *he* could have gone in and started stripping and 'There's a stupid child', but with that fellow 'Oh, pity, he's drunk' but they wouldn't have said that to Frank if he'd done it. So I thought I'd stop that before it starts. I won't have it. There was another woman always kissing him. I said, 'Look, love, if you don't mind, please don't kiss Frank. I don't want it. Kiss him on the cheek if you like by all means but he's a young man and one day he's going to kiss someone's girlfriend and the fellow's not going to appreciate that very much, so let's get things in their right prospect [sic].' 'I'm sorry' she said, I said 'That's all right, but I've got to look for all these things.' I'm ahead. My husband would say 'There's nice, they're being kind to him' but I don't, see – no way, he's got to live, he's a man. I said 'Do you see your father kissing women?' He said 'No.' 'Well, he's a man', I said. 'Oh, yes.' Then he realises, so he won't do it now, he knows now, but these are all things that people will do, you know.'   (1981)

As an example of a contrasting approach, the following mother, who had been lenient, noticed the change in her daughter's behaviour when she went into full-time residential care:

M. She's made progress in another direction now – you couldn't put anything up there [on the mantel-piece] – whoosh – it would just go – Christmas tree, cups, anything, she'd knock it down!

F. She don't do that now.

M. Since she's been in B. [residential hostel]. When she went to school she did the same but in B. I noticed the first Christmas she was home – she went in in August and came home at Christmas – she didn't go near the Christmas tree – I told the warden he said 'Well, it's simple when you know how, you know.' This is it, the know how. [What used you to do?] We just used to go and put everything back up – what could you do, really – say 'It's naughty'? You couldn't smack her very well. The warden said 'When they're naughty they're sent to their rooms and they know the difference between right and wrong – don't tell me they don't, [even] the [most severely handicapped] they know what they're doing'. As far as Joanna was concerned I could see he was right.

F. Mr. J. was very good with Joanna. Of course, since he left they haven't had a regular warden – he was very good.

M. Knowing what I know now it would never have been that way. I'd have tried to make her more independent – you fed her yourself so that you knew she'd had something and you knew she was all right. Up there they say 'Come on Joanna, come and sit down,' and she sits. (1981)

An important facet of upbringing for the mentally handicapped child that is not always found with normal children, was the link mothers made between the abilities and progress of the child and discipline. For mothers who have to make decisions about not only whether a child *will* do a task but also whether he is *able* to do it the situation obviously becomes difficult. For the teenagers too, the connection between over-indulgence and poor development was inextricably made in some mothers' minds.

Yes, she's stubborn and gone lazy and doesn't want to bother, you know. Sitting down here for years she's gone lazy. There's no one to take her in hand, no one got time to bother with her. (1981)

S. We pushed him to do things in the house – before he was all toys and things. [My mother] would tell him to clear up but when he didn't she wouldn't push him – if he didn't want to do it, 'well leave him', which is wrong. And he had an awful habit – he used to spend a lot of time under the table with a cushion and playing with his – er – willie, and she never used to say nothing to him. She didn't realise the effect that it could have on him and he's never done it since she's gone. And she used to let him walk around with nothing on, you know, but he won't do it now.

F. When I was coming home from work nearly every day he was naked by here, no clothes on him. As soon as he heard me at the front door he would rush to put his trousers on. (1981)

Strictness, carried to the extreme, however, was unlikely to be popular with parents. Behaviour modification techniques, so popular at present for use with the mentally handicapped, could be regarded as an extreme example of a natural progression from this link between strict training and progress, but parents made little reference to the technique. One boy had had actual experience of it when his parents, acting on professional advice tried toilet training him using grapes as a reward. This had been discontinued. Another mother had seen an extreme training method on television but was hardly enthusiastic:

I saw it on television about a little mongolian [*sic*] or spastic girl and they had her and had to teach her – learn her to do things. And she took her away to this little cottage and she wouldn't give her anything to eat, not until she said something. And I felt ever so sorry for her, you know – I could have cried. I thought 'Poor little bugger', you know – giving her nothing to eat – it's cruel, you know. Probably that's the only way to do it. Like if he throws his food he should do without it. (1981)

Factors influencing the strictness of carers

Carers' reported approaches to upbringing depended, to some extent, on their own

Table 6.3 *Social class and carers' own classification of strictness in 1981 (% in brackets)*

| Social classes | Carers' classification | | | | |
	Strict	Average	Lenient	Varies	Total
I & II	6 (50)	3 (25)	3 (25)	–	12
III	4 (14)	9 (32)	12 (43)	3 (11)	28
IV & V	1 (8)	4 (31)	6 (46)	2 (15)	13
Total	11 (21)	16 (30)	21 (40)	5 (9)	53

Excluding 'varies'.
Social classes I and II compared with the rest, 'Strict' carers compared with the rest: $\chi^2 = 4.76$; df = 2; p < 0.05.

characteristics, but also on how they perceived their offspring. Carers who said they were strict were significantly more likely to be younger and of high social class. (See Tables 6.3 and 6.4.)

Table 6.4 *Age of mothers and own classification of strictness (1981)*

| Age of mother | Carers' classification | | | | |
	Strict	Average	Lenient	Varies	Total
Under 49	9 (36)	8 (32)	7 (28)	1 (4)	25
50 and over	1 (5)	5 (23)	12 (18)	4 (18)	22
Total	10 (21)	13 (28)	19 (40)	5 (11)	47

Excluding 'varies'.
'Strict' carers compared with the rest: $\chi^2 = 4.16$; df = 1; p < 0.05.

It was not only characteristics of the carers themselves, however, that influenced upbringing. Characteristics – actual or perceived – of the children frequently militated against a firm unyielding approach. A very big problem was the lack of understanding of the children, particularly so for the more retarded, whose parents were gratified if their offspring simply could distinguish between right and wrong.

> Since she can't speak it is very difficult – you bend a lot of rules. It's the natural thing to do.   (1981)

> I don't think they entirely know – they know right from wrong – if it's really wrong then you must be firm but you can't treat them exactly as a normal child – you've got to bend the rules a little.   (1981)

One or two mothers found their children forgot any rebukes or corrections very quickly. Three others said that relatives had spoiled their children all their lives and this created problems and one mother admitted that she herself 'babied' her daughter.

The fact, too, that the children were in danger of leading limited lives in other spheres made parents indulgent on many issues and led them to allow more television watching, to buy more gifts and sweets and generally to relax rules.

> At the moment she has more sweets than she should have but there's not a lot she can do anyway.
> (1981)

> Well we never really admitted it but I do in the back of my mind feel I have to make it up to her. I show her a lot more love than I ever showed the others. I love all the children but I show it more to Joan. It's not a different love.   (1981)

Others openly pitied the child and this also led to indulgent behaviour:

> B.   When we go over there [to mother's family] they always buy things – but out of pity for him, they feel sorry for him. They always give him more . . . we bend the rules, let him win, like. We feel sorry for him I suppose. With him we give him more because he's bad, I suppose . . . he had more love, obviously, because he's bad.   (1981)

As the children became older other factors came into it. One or two of the mothers of teenagers who were at boarding schools were inclined to be over indulgent when they came home: 'We may as well spoil him while he's with us.' Others voiced uncertainty about the best way of controlling their teenagers:

> The point is they [professionals at school medicals] can't tell you how to bring up your child. And the thing is she – now she is getting – she's getting naughtier than she was, or seems to be. Well, when I say naughty, she's getting rude and cheeky which isn't going down well in school so we've had a note from the school a couple of times now about it – you don't really know how to handle the situation, but then on the other hand, you get that with all teenagers, don't you – I find that with [sister] at the moment.
>
> (1981)

Those mothers who still relied on physical control obviously encountered problems as the teenagers – especially the boys – increased in size. A minority of mothers tended to avoid the scenes and tantrums which resulted from any attempt to check or control their teenagers by coaxing, avoiding the issue, or giving in. It should be stressed, however, that most mothers, even those who were lenient, could control their teenagers, and some teenagers were almost unnaturally biddable and obedient.

> I have left him in the house about half an hour. I've told him where I'm going and say 'Adrian, stay where you are, don't move, don't touch nothing.' He says 'All right Mam,' and he'll stay there, and he'll be in the same place where I've left him.
>
> (1981)

> It's not necessary to be strict, he's a very easy boy to live with. If he does something that displeases me, if I raise my voice, he's the one who gets upset. Mind you if there's something I particularly don't want him to do, I'd say 'No.' That's it and it is no – there's no further pushing, as long as I make it sound definite enough.
>
> (1981)

Punishment and rewards

Mothers were asked how they punished the child when he was naughty.

In 1972 smacking, although of a very minor nature, was widespread. 'Only a token to show she's been naughty', 'tap her hand' were two examples that implied a very small correction was intended. Only three mothers said they did not smack the child, although five more did not regard it as an effective or desirable form of correction. There was some evidence of the contradiction the Newsons (1963) found concerning the smacking of 1-year-olds: some mothers did not smack because the child would not understand, while others smacked because they thought the child would not understand anything else.

Twelve (32%) mothers seemed to rely mainly on smacking to correct the child; 18 (49%) mothers specifically mentioned some verbal correction. This was simply shouting, or saying the child was 'naughty', or using a certain tone of voice. This was especially common for lenient mothers. Some mothers said that other forms of punishment were not used because 'punishment doesn't register' or 'he wouldn't understand if I said "No sweets", like with his brother.' Thirteen (35%) other mothers, however, seemed to use alternative means of correction with effect. These methods of control were often deprivation of sweets or television, or, as one father put, 'blackmail, really'. Quite often the child was deprived of company (being put on the stairs, or put to bed, or being ignored). One boy was made to sit still on a chair until he stopped his deviant behaviour. Only a very few mothers admitted to using no methods of control at all. Asked what happened if the child did something *really* naughty, one mother replied: 'Well, that's it – she's really ruined', and roared with laughter.

By 1981, when the population were teenagers, the proportion of mothers using physical means to control behaviour had fallen. Whilst almost all mothers used

Table 6.5 *1st and 2nd choice of punishment 1981 (% in brackets)*

	First choice (1981)	Second choice (1981)
Physical	13 (25)	9
Verbal	18 (34)	2
Depriving of treat	10 (19)	2
Depriving of food	2 (4)	2
Sending to bed	6 (11)	2
Unnecessary	2 (4)	–
None	2 (4)	–
Total	53 (101)	

smacking to some extent in 1972 only 22 (42%) used it at all in 1981 and for only 13 (25%) was it the first method of control. Increasingly common was deprivation of treats – no youth club, money, outings, or staying with relatives and, particularly for the more able teenagers, these were extremely effective sanctions. Several mothers commented that the teenagers became very upset if parents verbally showed real displeasure. (See Table 6.5.)

Rewards featured less commonly in replies. Most mothers relied simply on verbal praise although one mother regretfully said:

> I tell her 'Good girl, very good girl, Megan.' I do praise her if she is being excellent but she never is excellent, hardly ever. I get in a temper 'Can you do anything right?' I wish I could praise her, I wish I had the chance to praise her, but she doesn't do anything right.   (1981)

Five mothers mentioned giving gifts or treats to their teenagers and eight gave special food. These eight included the two mothers who used no form of punishment. Three others gave money, three gave outings and two gave cuddles.

Fathers' attitudes to discipline

Table 6.6 shows how strict mothers felt fathers were towards their teenagers.

Table 6.6 *Fathers' strictness 1972 & 1981 (mothers' classifications) (% in brackets)*

	Original sample (1972)	(1981)	New sample (1981)	Total population (1981)
Strict	5 (16)	7 (27)	2 (13)	9 (21)
Average	8 (26)	5 (19)	–	5 (12)
Lenient	18 (58)	14 (54)	14 (88)	28 (67)
	31 (100)	26 (100)	16 (101)	42 (100)
No father living at home	6	8	3	11

Figures include 1 stepfather, 1972, and 1 stepfather and 1 brother-in-law, 1981.

In 1972 the majority of mothers considered that their husbands behaved leniently towards the handicapped child. Perhaps, if husbands had been able to speak for themselves, results would have been different since, when they were present, there was often disagreement between husband and wife. When asked about their strictness husbands were inclined to answer 'Oh, fairly strict, I should say', but they were instantly corrected by their wives – 'Fairly easy going I would say', or 'You bullies no one, he's not strict with anyone.' Certainly wives seemed to feel that most of the task of correction in the house was left to them. Some criticised their husbands for this – sometimes because it was not fair to the wives themselves, and sometimes because it was not serving the best interests of the child:

Well, with me, see, I do treat her the same as the others . . . now with him he do talk 'Come to Daddy, Daddy's baby.' Now I don't believe in that, see. She's $5\frac{1}{2}$, isn't she, let her think that she's the same as the others, she's not a baby . . . . He cuddles her more [than the others]. Give her a cuddle, aye, but not learn her on the babyish side 'cos I think the more you bring her out the more she's going to be when she grows up.   (1972)

The belief of most mothers in 1972 that they were the main disciplinarians in the family was as apparent in 1981 – 'I'm the ogre' said one mother and another about her husband, 'Mat is – Oh – beyond silly with him.' In fact only nine male carers were thought of as being strict with their teenagers and one of these was not the girl's natural father but her brother-in-law. This was not to say that strictness was not again seen as a valuable training exercise and two mothers, both divorced, remarked on the advantages that had resulted from their new partners' tougher approaches. Again, the link mothers made between firm discipline and gains in independence is clear. The following mother's marriage to the stepfather ended unhappily, and indeed towards the end of the marriage she felt the discipline had become too extreme, but she could still see that there had been advantages:

When I first met Don, Roger wouldn't walk anywhere, he wouldn't eat anything – I don't think he'd be alive today if it wasn't for Don because he got – well I'd gone down to 6 stones 12 pounds myself when my first marriage broke up . . . and honestly I was going into a nervous breakdown and he more or less took over – it was amazing how he did. And Roger, he got him to walk because he was determined and Roger would start crying . . . and would sit there cross-legged and wouldn't move and Don would say 'Come on, now, you've got to walk' and I was too soft you see, and I'd be in tears myself and I'd think 'Well, he's doing it for his own good' and he'd *make* him walk and Roger would say 'Carry, carry' you know, because funnily enough Roger could express himself at quite an early age. So in the end he got him to walk and he'd walk alongside the pushchair, but he was lazy *then*. And as far as food was concerned, all he'd eat was bananas, ice cream and Oh – a very limited amount of food he'd eat, he wouldn't touch dinners at all. So of course, when Don was there he'd buy a block of ice cream, show it to Roger and put his dinner in front of him – cabbage, sprouts, all sorts of things like that and he would make him eat it. And he'd be crying and I used to feel so sorry for him but he was such a skinny little thing. I think, honestly, eventually he would have caught some disease and died if Don hadn't been the way he was with him then. He was very very strict . . . and now he can't get enough to eat . . . . He'd have to finish everything before he got that ice cream. He was very tough but on the other hand Roger was so stubborn that he needed somebody like that but, unfortunately, it went to the extremes – in the end there was too much of it and children need a balance between love, affection and discipline.

(1981)

PROTECTION AND INDEPENDENCE

In 1972 a well-protected environment was rarely questioned because it was obviously appropriate when the children were young, but, by 1981, parents were under new pressures. Vying with the emphasis some parents put on normality and the new adult status of their teenagers was the need still to extend some protection towards them, and this to a degree that would not be appropriate (or even desirable) for the normal teenager. Parents had to reconcile the contradiction of insisting the teenager took more responsibility, like his peers, without offering the reward of extra freedom this usually brings, and which an aware Down's syndrome teenager could see others enjoying. How much the Down's teenager spots this contradiction is influenced by his own view of himself: how far he considers or accepts himself to be 'different'. This was not an aspect which was covered in any depth by the study but parents spoke in the following ways:

You've got to try to explain to them that they're different from the other children.   (1981)

He hasn't yet understood it's an illness – you know – to him it's – he just knows he's a mongol and that's it. I mean he watches the programmes of the children on television and we tell him 'There's a little boy like you', you know. Yes, it's never embarrassed him. [You're saying how normal he is so when you say 'you're a normal boy and a mongol – ?] We explain to him what mongols are – that they can't do as well as other children in certain things – like reading and writing. In things like tennis and what have you he knows he's at a par with them. He says mongols have been born differently, you know – you can't explain the medical side of it to him yet, you know. But he knows he has to be in a special place other than in the Comprehensive because he says himself 'They'll tease me,' you know.   (1981)

During the tests one girl said, 'I have a mongol handicap and I have a weak heart', but it was difficult to assess her understanding of this or whether she was simply parroting what she had been taught. Several parents said, or implied, that their children did not realise they were disabled but the boy in the following quotation who had been brought up very much in the normal rather than the handicapped world recognised disability but distinguished himself from the disabled.

He wouldn't go to the Jane Hodge home [holiday home] but I said to him 'Now, listen Frank, there are handicapped people there but they need your help' that's fair enough. He goes because he's giving them help.... I laughed at Frank, there was a normal fellow but he was short and our Frank said 'Mum, don't laugh, that's a part of life.' I said 'What, love?' He said 'I know he needs his sleeves shortened and his trousers, but I think he goes to the Jane Hodge home too and he needs my help.'   (1981)

In other cases, however, the carers emphasised their own teenager's lack of awareness:

He's in his own little world, he's happy. He doesn't miss things – he doesn't know what we know, so in his own little mind he's happy – he's happier than me.   (1981)

Two other sets of parents, however, put the opposite side of this very forcefully:

He's very much aware of his own handicap – oh, yes – he has been for years. He's completely conscious of his handicap and the difference there is between him and other children [How do you know?] Because he withdraws – and he's accepted that he's different to them and he keeps away. He stands on the outskirts of anything that's going on – you know – even when they ask him in, he stands back. He's an extremely sensitive boy – he hasn't lived with his handicap all these years without knowing what it's all about, has he? ... I've experience of a lot of children in the school, I know them quite well. They're aware, fully aware. Not in the school, there are no inhibitions there, they're all the same, but outside the school there's a difference.... How can there not be? They see other children walking around ... there's an old saying 'Where there's no sense, there's no feeling' and that's been carried through too far.   (1981)

M. I feel *for* her in many situations. The competitive atmosphere at home, she likes to do what [sister] can do ... she's become more reconciled to it recently, but when [sister] started cookery at school Catherine took an orange and polo mints to do her cookery – it's pathetic, the dinner lady did some concoction with it and she brought it home, but she *knows* it's not right – she's that little degree *more*, so she *knows* ... if she goes to Guides there are obviously lots of things she can't do – she goes in to a shell then and sits in a corner ... in any situation if she can't do or understand she does this shell thing. At an evening meeting of parents she sat in a huddle on the edge of her chair, hair over her face, sucking her finger ... she couldn't understand – the conversation was above her. Once she's out of it she's fine.

F. Another significant thing – this awareness of difference – is that she's *terrified* in the presence of other mongol children.

M. If she doesn't know them – there may be one or two in the school and she knows them but she has done since she was little – under 5 – she'd recognise somebody with a handicap a mile off and she's horrified ... at the mother and baby group [for handicapped children] I went to ... she spent the whole time on the floor with her arms round my legs and wouldn't go *near* any of the children.

S. And a competition on Blue Peter, she couldn't watch it, she turned away.

F. She said to me 'Not me, Daddy, not me ...'

M. That's one of the reasons we left the NAMHC ... the parties, etc. were pointless for her .... she wouldn't eat, she'd sit on my lap all the way through, she'd be petrified and when semi-toilet trained it was a disaster because it was the first thing she'd do.   (1981)

Part of how teenagers feel about themselves, and how normal they consider them-selves to be, is influenced also by how normal their lives are: how far they are protected and how far they are encouraged (and able) to take control of some aspects of their lives. Some areas in which the normal adolescent will be becoming increasingly inde-pendent will be considered here: freedom to go out and the teenager's wish for such freedom, pocket money, and choice of clothes. Details of where teenagers slept are also included although, obviously, this is not usually an issue at adolescence.

Freedom outside

Details of the freedom outside the house accorded to the teenagers were given in Chapter 2 (Table 2.2). There were 55% who were not allowed out alone at all, 11% had 'very limited freedom', 26% had 'limited freedom' and only 8% were able to come and go in a more relaxed fashion. There are obvious implications from these figures, both for the lifestyle of the teenagers and the amount of stimulation they receive socially and more generally.

Even children who were able to go out alone were vulnerable to any change in cir-cumstances. Five youngsters who had been given some freedom outside as children lost this as they grew up. Two no longer had siblings as automatic companions and so be-came more restricted, one teenager had shown he could not be relied upon and two had moved to new areas where they were not known and had no friends. It is of interest that the two latter teenagers clearly had not learned, as others do, 'to go out alone'; rather they were able to go out only in very specific circumstances. A change of circumstances implied new learning had to take place. For the most part, however, those who were allowed out in 1972 had extended their range by 1981.

The constraints on allowing more freedom included the obvious ones of the teenagers wandering off, and traffic. Very few parents were wholly confident of their teenagers on the roads and some quoted examples of their children simply walking into roads. One boy would dutifully look both ways, as he had been taught, but would fail to make any adaptation of his behaviour according to the conditions.

There was a further hazard for the teenagers. Although normal teenagers pleasantly learn to mingle in the social world by going outside their own homes, for the Down's syndrome teenagers such ventures could involve them in difficult encounters with other children who teased them or with shopkeepers who accused them of stealing. For the girls, too, mothers were becoming concerned that they could be 'taken advantage of'.

Since most teenagers were allowed such limited freedom outside, mothers were asked how far the teenagers themselves pressed for less restrictions. In fact, 72% of mothers did not feel their offspring were anxious to be allowed greater freedom. Those teenagers who had some experience of going out alone were more likely to wish to extend this, but those who had never gone out unattended were less likely to press for this novel experience and some parents were not sorry about this:

I wish his communication would improve but I never want him to be able to go out – like some teenagers you see – well they might be 25 or 30 – who get about and do sort of – they're borderline. Their families are far worse off than I am – I know where my son is but they don't know what their sons and daughters are getting up to and they get a lot of problems. With a boy living up the road there – he didn't do very much but he liked girls and he's quite – not very nice to look at – and whenever he made advances to girls they usually started screaming and shouting for help – he didn't do anything but he ended up in court on several occasions and his mother was fined hundreds of pounds. There's a girl up here who's been en-couraged by other teenagers to break into shops and to behave – well – very antisocially. So these people are worse off than I am. So I'm grateful that Donald will never be able to go out and about by himself – I think I would rather see him as he is, I'd like his communication to improve so that in after years he'll be able to say more – 'I'm not happy doing this' and 'I don't want to do that', but I never want him to go out, because he couldn't cope with this world.   (1981)

Some parents of the more capable teenagers, however, saw it as quite natural that their children should want to go out alone ('He needs freedom the same as other children and with me he gets it') and one stepmother found her teenage stepdaughter argued that she should be allowed out as others were.

> She definitely wants that bit more freedom but I'm not prepared to allow that yet. I don't think myself that she is that capable to cope – she forgets about the roads . . . she realises teenagers go dancing and to discos and it's hard to get her to understand why she can't go to the disco – obviously it's because there's not enough supervision – only the vicar, and I don't think he can control about 25 raving teenagers. If she got fed up and walked out and I thought she was there safe – you know. She can't go out on her own and she says, 'I'm going out, other girls do.' Some days she'll relate to the teenagers next door, other days not and she's back to being herself again and wants to stay at home and play.   (1981)

Only five or six teenagers, however, were able to use arguments in this way and most of the parents judged discontentment in their teenagers by their tendency to run off or attempt escapes from the house. Those who had stopped indulging in this behaviour were judged not to be feeling restricted and vice versa.

Some of the 28% who were felt to wish for more freedom would have been satisfied with more outings – supervised or not. In other words they were seeking more activity and action rather than pursuing more personal independence for themselves. A wish for outings is entirely natural for teenagers but normal teenagers can pursue these activities themselves. Understandably mothers of the Down's teenagers could be busy, or not inclined to be out and about every day ('especially not if it is raining' remarked one mother who was without transport and lived in a particularly inclement and isolated valley, which afforded few amusements) and the need for obligatory daily walks that are taken with babies and toddlers had extended far beyond the days when these activities normally cease. Such outings, when they were made, had consequently become, for the mothers, a more solitary exercise, lacking in the companionship of others in the same position.

Although there was a tendency for those who did not go out alone to be judged as contented by their mothers, and although the pressure for more freedom generally came from those who were allowed some freedom, this did not reach significance. More boys than girls looked for freedom (10 boys (36%) compared with 5 (20%) girls) but again these differences did not reach significance.

Pocket money

For normal teenagers under 16 the amount of pocket money given is a balance between what parents can afford, how much parents feel teenagers should be encouraged to have control over all personal expenditure (some giving larger amounts that must include clothes and all extras, and some giving smaller amounts not intended to cover these personal necessities) and how pressing and insistent are the teenagers' own demands. Few of these guidelines applied to the Down's syndrome teenagers: from many of the youngsters demands of any sort were rare, wishes for material objects were usually of moderate magnitude and the relatively small amounts involved meant that parents were usually, though not invariably, restrained from giving larger sums by considerations other than poverty.

Once the teenager reached 16 years arguably he was entitled to larger sums from his Non-Contributory Invalidity Benefit, but few felt their teenagers could cope with responsibilities of this sort. Parents were mostly influenced by feelings that the teenager ought to have some pocket money both to encourage independence and also to emphasise normality but, against this, some teenagers clearly did not understand the idea of money at all (for instance one tried to eat it), or if they did, did not understand amounts, or had few desires outside those that were met routinely at home. As many as 22 (42%) teenagers had no regular money of their own at all and, indeed, the scores on the Gunzburg PAC for these teenagers were lower on average than for those who did have pocket money (46.3 compared with 72.6). However, there were teenagers with low scores (in the 20s) who did have money and yet others with scores in the 80s who did not.

The amounts involved for those who did have pocket money were small: 24 of the 31 who had money had a pound or less, and 14 had 50p or less. The maximum was £6. Sixteen boys and 15 girls had pocket money although the boys tended to get more than the girls (£1.30 compared with 95p) in spite of the fact that on average girls were more competent. Even these amounts give a deceptive impression of the independence of spending power since the sums were often given in daily instalments as 'money for school' or 'money for Gateway' and so such teenagers had little unsupervised spending. Progress, could be made here, however, and one boy, whose money was entrusted to the bus driver, had progressed from throwing it away to beginning to see that it was useful. In fact this was a stage that many of the teenagers had reached: seeing that money had a value but without understanding what that value was, or being in a position to consider expenditure, or to budget. Only four or five could be said really to appreciate money and the mother of one of the brightest boys said, 'Money means nothing to Colin.' Some of this lack of interest can possibly be accounted for by the teenagers' complete lack of avarice. Several mothers said that they were happy to meet any request of their teenagers since their demands were so very few and so modest. Clearly this is a state of innocence reminiscent of young children who do not yet understand that their environment can be changed, or that money can help to do this. Even those who had more substantial amounts were not thought fully to understand money. The 'richest' boy was given money so that he could 'pay his own way' as others do.

> Yes, we give him six pounds – well that's the whole week and for the disco. We take him out twice a week and let him buy his own pop and crisps. And he buys sweets . . . . Well he does down pop after pop, it's terrible, and crisps – packet after packet. You can't catch him, mind. He puts it up there and says, 'That's mine now' . . . . And like he'll say, 'Do you want a lager, Mam?' and he'll buy a lager for us all. And then perhaps he'll buy a little car or a record. [Does he understand about money?] Oh, I think so. He can't count what he's getting like. [Can he understand if something's two pounds and he has one pound that he can't get it?] Oh, no, no . . . [If he runs out do you give him more?] Well, if he needs it, but it's very rare he does, he doesn't go anywhere.   (1981)

Only one girl, who mixed with normal teenagers, seemed to be more like her normal contemporaries and was described as 'money mad'.

> M.   She's terrible for money, she has it every day . . . she's buying for others, she's sharing it. She has about £1 a day – well about £5 a week on average . . . she only spends it on the kids, she's buying them all sweets. I give her 25p to 30p in the evening, and my father – she goes round without us knowing and *he* gives her money. So it do work out about 90p a night and in the morning.

> GM.   And in the off-licence she's buying for all her friends. And 10p to 20p to go to school, to buy Kit Kat or something. She doesn't eat breakfast, does she? Very rare.   (1981)

Clothes

By the mid-teens most normal teenagers have acquired a great deal of control over what they buy to wear and what they choose to wear each day. For the Down's syndrome teenagers the everyday choice was left to only 24 (45%) of them; of these, four were only just beginning to have independence in this sphere and many were not completely autonomous in that their choice was checked by mothers for suitability. Most of the teenagers who did not choose their own clothes were said not to be interested. Some of this indifference could be accounted for by the level of retardation of a number of the youngsters in that the average Gunzburg score of those who did not choose their own clothes was lower than for those who did (47.2 compared with 79.1), but there were some teenagers whose scores were above average but yet who displayed little interest. More girls (15 (60%)) than boys (9 (32%)) were interested in what they wore every day but the difference did not reach significance.

A similar number of teenagers were also involved in decisions about buying their clothes. Fourteen girls (56%) and ten boys (36%) showed interest in the choices made at shops but, again, at least 20 teenagers were 'not interested'. Once more, there were differences in the average Gunzburg scores of those who chose clothes to buy and those who did not (79.0 compared with 47.3). Only 17 teenagers both chose their clothes daily and decided what to buy in the shops. All who were involved in buying clothes did this with an element of supervision and the final purchases were a compromise between parents and teenagers.

> He'll say he likes this colour but *I* choose them . . . last week I had to take him to buy trousers and he was saying 'This colour' but I thought it was a bit light so I said, 'No, you must have a different colour' and he was quite happy.   (1981)

Two or three teenagers were beginning to make progress into greater independence. One school encouraged parents to send shopping lists and money so that teenagers could shop in school hours. One boy, although he was still accompanied by his mother, paid for the clothes himself with money or with a cheque given by his father. One teenage girl was extending her independence to much wider matters.

> When I did her bedroom out recently – the worst thing I did, it cost a fortune – I told her she could choose her own curtains and own cover and a nice shade and she did her room the way she wanted. She cost me a pair of velvet curtains for her bedroom. I said to her: 'Being as you're on holiday, we can go and choose your own choice, whichever you like now you can have.' I thought this is a big thing, a big step to choosing her own things, and we went into the shop and the first curtains she saw were rose velvet curtains and she fancied those and I said, 'Let's have a look round the shop, there are loads of curtains,' but she still came back to those velvet curtains and I thought I had *said* and I thought well, it was something for her to have decided herself – up till recently she hadn't been bothered about choosing her own things – I would say 'Do you like this?' and she'd say 'Yes.' Now I think she's coming more aware of what she likes and what she wants, so I let her. And then a duvet cover and a shade. She chose a nicer one than I had for us, the colours all matched. And funnily enough I noticed that last Christmas [when] I bought her a kilt. I said 'Go around in Marks and Spencer's and see if you can find yourself a blouse to go with it' and she picked a blouse that went really nice. [Did you go with her?] I said 'Take the kilt around.' She got a blue blouse that went nicely with it and I saw perhaps she had a good eye for what went with what, you know. [Did she go with the money?] She brought it to show me. You want to see – especially at today's prices.   (1981)

Apart from the lack of interest shown by the teenagers other factors prevented parents giving more responsibility to their children. Several mothers had problems finding clothes to fit teenagers who were short and broad. Not only were such clothes unavailable and expensive but they were also frequently old fashioned and unsuitable. Costs were added, too, if alterations were necessary and incontinence made for further difficulties. For some mothers these problems, together with uncooperative teenagers, made shopping a nightmare. The following mother preferred to use catalogues so that trying on clothes could wait for her daughter to be 'in the mood': 'She's worked herself up on the bus, and I've worked myself up keeping her quiet and we're not fit to do shopping – we're in no fit state [when we get to town].'

Sleeping arrangements

The bedtimes of the children and teenagers are shown in Table 6.7.

Table 6.7 *Bedtimes of the children and teenagers in 1972 and 1981 (% in brackets)*

	Original sample (1972)	(1981)	New sample (1981)	Total population (1981)
Before 7.00	9 (24)	2 (6)	–	2 (4)
7.00–7.59	16 (43)	1 (3)	–	1 (2)
8.00–8.59	⎫	2 (6)	2 (11)	4 (8)
9.00–9.59	⎪ 6 (16)	14 (41)	9 (47)	23 (43)
10.00–10.59	⎬	6 (18)	4 (21)	10 (19)
After 11.00	⎭	–	1 (5)	1 (2)
No fixed time	6 (16)	9 (21)	3 (16)	12 (23)
Total	37 (99)	34 (101)	19 (100)	53 (101)

In 1972 the bulk of the children went to bed before 8.00 p.m.; by 1981 most teenagers went before 10.00 p.m. Although the proportion who had no fixed bedtime had increased, it had not done so substantially. In 1981, at the extremes, one girl went to bed at about 5.00 p.m., and one boy at 6 p.m., while another usually went to bed with his mother in the early hours of the morning. All three were severely retarded and this could perhaps indicate that, for such teenagers, all semblance of a normal routine had been abandoned. There was a tendency for girls to go to bed slightly earlier than boys, but the difference was not significant.

Table 6.8 shows the sleeping arrangements made both in 1972 and 1981.

Table 6.8 *Sleeping arrangements 1972 and 1981 (% in brackets) n = 52*

	Original sample (1972)	(1981)	New sample (1981)	Total population (1981)
With parents/carer	16 (43)	10 (30)	3 (16)	13 (25)
With others	11 (30)	9 (27)	5 (26)	14 (27)
Alone	10 (27)[a]	14 (42)[b]	11 (58)	25 (48)[a]
	37 (100)	33 (99)	19 (100)	52 (100)

[a] Door locked in 3 cases
[b] Door locked in 2 cases

By the time they were teenagers most of the major problems of wandering at night and overactivity had ceased. Only seven teenagers presented severe problems, although others disturbed their parents, briefly, most nights when they went to the lavatory. It has been said of 12 teenagers that they sometimes wet the bed at night although, for most, sheets were not changed until morning. Others liked company at nights and at least four teenagers tended to climb into someone's bed at night. One sister described night habits as follows:

> Last night he's been sleeping with me and the night before he slept with [brother] . . . he can't go to bed and sleep through because he's up and down all night changing beds, you know. And there's two beds in the front bedroom and he'll spend an hour in his own bed and then creep into Daddy's then, see. Then into the same bed as me with a long pillow between us because he's a funny sleeper. Half the time he'll sit up and sleep with no blankets on him . . . we'll spend all the night putting blankets over him.   (1981)

In spite of there being fewer problems in 1981 a quarter of parents still felt it easier to have the teenager in their own rooms at night, or had given up attempts to dislodge him. Three teenagers had only recently made the transition, one with advice and help from school. Two other parents were only able to get relaxed nights themselves by locking the teenager's door and one had put reinforced glass in the windows.

It is important to stress that no parent felt able to leave the teenagers alone in the evenings or overnight.

SUMMARY

Not surprisingly, mothers varied among themselves in how they *did* discipline their children and also how they felt they *should* discipline them. By the teenage years there was a more general (though not universal) agreement that an insistence on acceptable forms of behaviour was both possible and desirable.

Rules also varied between families. There were some who were concerned about the potential inconsistencies in providing adequate protection and at the same time encouraging independence, but very many parents did not question the degree of protection they gave their teenagers. They considered the physical safety of the teenagers to be the paramount consideration. They were also able to avoid their teenagers making mistakes (e.g. as regards dressing and in financial situations) and they considered it part of their caring role to do this. Many parents saw their role as one of protecting the youngster by avoiding risks rather than courting them. It should be emphasised that there was no clear relationship between the abilities of the teenagers and what they were allowed to do.

No judgement is made here on who was right and who wrong in these decisions but it is worth pointing out that this approach is likely to be at variance with the new moves towards normalisation advocated by professionals. The implication is that some parents will not be ready to accept such moves and will need to be convinced that they are in their child's best interests.

7 The Social World of the Down's Syndrome Child and Adolescent

This chapter describes the friendships the Down's child and adolescent had with others and his encounters with the opposite sex. It also describes his leisure activities. These issues have a crucial impact on the quality of the youngsters' lives. The patterns adopted in these areas were, again, heavily influenced by their parents' perceptions about the needs of Down's syndrome children and teenagers.

FRIENDSHIPS

Friends are usually important to all young people as an end in itself, but they also serve the purpose of introducing each other to the normal way of life of their peers. As one mother said of her very bright, but rather isolated daughter: 'There's no one her own age to show her how that age behaves.'

This is not something for which parents, who are inevitably of another generation, can compensate. Siblings can help to some extent but only 23(43%) of the Down's syndrome teenagers had a teenage sibling living at home and, for 10 of them, the sibling was of another sex. Another problem for the teenagers is that it is possible that social skills actually improve with practice but may fail to develop or atrophy without use, so creating a deteriorating, self-perpetuating situation.

Friends at school

School is one of the commonest places for making friendships. The Down's teenagers almost all attended special schools that were not local and this not only effectively isolated them from the children round about but also, because of the distances involved, reduced the chance of continuing school friendships at home, out of school hours. Indeed, it was usually only those with parents who made special efforts in this direction who did any such visiting after school. Only five teenagers saw others from their own schools at home on any regular basis. For just two of these teenagers (both at ESN(M) schools) was the contact informal in that one boy would call casually on one of the Down's boys. The other – a girl – was visited by a brighter pupil, but she was as much a protector as a friend and would come to look after her while her mother was busy. Another three teenagers had more limited contact with school friends and had meetings on special occasions.

Difficulties in pursuing such friendships were predictable. There were rarely local children at the same school and those that there were were of a different age, sex, ability or personality so that the friendships did not flourish. Other children lived at such a distance that transport had to be arranged. Not only this but there were no informal meetings among mothers (such as outside the school gates) where social arrangements could be made casually. Mothers hesitated to get involved in social encounters that could be embarrassing, particularly since it was felt it could not always be assumed that another mother would be willing for her child to mix outside school. Above all, the teenagers usually lacked the imagination to press for out-of-school meetings so that, if they were to take place at all, parents frequently had to take the initiative themselves. When an exception to this occurred, the result was not successful:

> He had a friend last week – she sent her 'phone number home and I had to phone. The mother was not too pleased actually. I said 'Is Melissa there?' She said 'Who wants her?' and I said 'Well, my son goes to your daughter's school and she's given him the number for him to 'phone her.' She said 'Oh, she's always doing stupid things like that.' She let him speak to her – she was a bit rude. He said 'Melissa, come down my house Wednesday and I'll take you to the disco.' That was it. 'Tarra.' He was so thrilled over that but the other mother didn't seem to like it.   (1981)

Other friendships

Table 7 .1 shows the friendships of the children in 1972 and 1981. The Down's children had encountered the problems of friendship with their normal peers from their earliest days and in 1972 parents often mentioned the problem of the relationships between children.

> Even by the gate you hear them say, 'Look at that little Chinese girl' and things like that, you know, because the children don't think of it. They are far more cruel than grown-ups. And they poke sticks in. She hasn't got the sense to know there's danger there, you see. She's been protected by me for so long . . . . But we heard a lot of mongol children have been out to play and nothing seems to happen. But I couldn't, you know, I'd be afraid.   (1972)

Table 7.1 *Friendships 1972 and 1981 (% in brackets)*

	Original sample (1972)		(1981)	New sample (1981)	Total (1981)
Friends	5 (14) ⎱	13 (36)	11 (32)	5 (26)	16 (30)
Friends through siblings	8 (22) ⎰				
No friends	24 (65)		23 (68)	14 (74)	37 (70)
Total	37 (101)		34 (100)	19 (100)	53 (100)

Sometimes, however, the relationships were good and parents used this to encourage the child further. In fact, parents felt those who saw little of normal children were often held back.

> Now she's got these little friends and I say to her – say she doesn't want to write and doesn't want to read – I say 'Well, you know Dianne can read and you know Ceri can read and you want to be a scholar like them.' Oh yes – you see she wants to be as good as they are – you use this sort of thing. The things she sees them doing, she wants to do.   (1972)

When children could hold their own with the others, mothers were clearly delighted: 'He was in school [normal school] and this little girl said 'You're a mongol' and Hafryn turned round and said 'You're adopted', and it was her that went to cry, not him. You'll never step on him.'

It must be said, however, that even at this early stage relationships between the children were not always on equal terms. Often the normal child was older or younger and parents very rarely felt able to leave the child to fight his own battles. Only three mothers said they would leave the child if he was in difficulties with other children, while over half said they would leave siblings in a similar situation. A few were inclined to watch and leave well alone if the child showed that he could cope.

As Table 7.1 shows, there were children who had friends mainly because they had siblings of a similar age and they all played together. Sometimes the Down's syndrome child was included in the group but participation was often confined to watching. Not surprisingly those children who were allowed to play outside were significantly more likely to have friends. Of those who were allowed out eight (80%) had friends, compared with only five (18%) of those who were not.

In 1981 there were still problems. Only two teenagers enjoyed friendships at home comparable with those of the normal teenage population. One boy (very capable, although in the ESN(S) school) was in the local youth club and this involved him in many normal friendships and activities – not all of which were wholly desirable:

Last year the police came to see him. Two other boys would go over there and paint the doors on the building site and because he was with the boys and they done it and [policemen] came over and spoke to him and told him not to do it. He's never been over the building site since. The policemen had to go to everyone. He's the same as them – if they do it, he'll do it. [Did he know it was wrong?] He knew he shouldn't do it, but he did it. (1981)

One other teenager, in spite of being in residential school during weekdays, had a close friendship with a neighbour. This was the girl who had been friendly with Dianne and Ceri in 1972. The family had moved house since then.

They've been friends since we moved – they're still friends but they don't see so much of each other now Clara is away, but that little girl has never treated Clara any differently to any other child she plays with, she's never given in to her then. If Clara wins a race from Mair she has won, Mair has got no charity towards her . . . and this is the best friend she could have had. When they play tennis they play to win – I've seen them out here till 10.30 at night and one won't give in to the other, you see. Mair is as determined as she is. (1981)

This was not typical however and most parents were conscious of their own teenager's disadvantaged position.

In all 16 (30%) of the teenagers had some sort of contact with others who were neither relatives nor attending the same school but, with occasional exceptions, the friendships were either with other disabled children or with children who were younger than themselves. One girl would play with 6- or 7-year-old girls in the park with her mother looking on, a 9-year-old girl used to ask to take one of the Down's boys on her pony and others were children of family friends.

Not only were the friendships rarely with peers, but sometimes they did not involve active interaction, or the relationship could lack any semblance of equality. In these instances some parents continued to feel the teenager was isolated, although it sometimes seemed that the teenagers themselves were not seeking friendships.

I'd like him to have more friends, but Charles doesn't want them, you see. Two little girls who've been constantly coming to ask to play and I say 'Yes' but often, after 10 to 15 minutes, that's enough. He likes Jane who's 13 but sometimes he won't have them in at all. She's been back and forward occasionally over the years, you know. They go in and talk to him and play snooker, you know. They go in there but they don't actually play with him, he's still on his own, but he doesn't mind them coming in. (1981)

She watches them, she likes to watch a lot. They play hide and seek, now Sheila doesn't like that game, she's quite happy just watching them play among themselves. Joan and Marion come in to play the records. We send them all upstairs – she's got a record player upstairs – oh, they come in often. [Does she go to their houses?] Not very often – no. What it is I think, Sheila doesn't go to call on them you know . . . . She's never been allowed to go down the steps, see, and she wouldn't go unless she asks, so she doesn't bother. [Could she go?] Oh, yes. We sent her one day – we watched her in the window and we sent her with a piece of cake from her birthday – she likes to take it herself. [So she can go?] Oh yes, she's rather lazy that way. No, if they didn't come it wouldn't worry her. She's quite happy to be on her own. (1981)

[The most difficult thing] is other children accepting. Judy would love to be out playing, she's not aggressive so she wouldn't quarrel with them but they move away, I think, and then I look out and she is there on her own – perhaps they've run off over the field and she won't follow. (1981)

Sadly, some teenagers who used to have good friendships with others, were being more restricted as they grew older:

We let her go out and about a bit because we were advised to treat her the same as the other children and to let her get about and mix as much as she could. We've got her to do all these things and it seems because she can do so much now you are paid back in another way – but then, on the other hand, I wouldn't like her to do less . . . . We're trying to keep her in now . . . we've allowed her to go out and mix but the only children she can really play with now, bar Mary, are younger children than herself which I don't think is a very good idea, because they're only about 5 or 6 and they sort of treat Jill as one of themselves. But then there was a little problem. They came and told me Jill was being rude and things like that. So now I try and keep her in and I say 'Don't go and play with the little children any more' because they're too young and I don't want any parents coming here and complaining to me and saying to me to keep her in. They said that she was showing her bosom but I don't know whether she was – I mean she got into trouble for it but she said she wasn't doing anything. I just don't know . . . the terrible thing is they could ask her to do something and she would do it without giving it a thought. Children do take advantage of her, I think. The problem with her really is her mind, isn't it? Years ago – I don't know about it – but I was told that she was told to lick the floor and she done it, you see. You get kids doing things like that . . . . Well, I'm hoping that she wouldn't do it today but the point is that we try to keep as much of an eye on her as we can . . . now that she's getting older well, we feel that if anything happens, I mean we're going to get the blame for it, you know.   (1981)

These problems did not, however, arise for the majority of teenagers (70%), since they were very isolated from children who were not at their schools or in their families.

Jip the dog is the only playmate he's ever had.   (1981)

He's always looking for someone to play with. When we go on holiday he's not still long – one or other of us has to be playing with him all the time.   (1981)

When you have a child like this, people don't realise, you can't ever let them go out to play, and no one comes to play with them, so they're really very lonely children.   (1981)

Difficulties with friendships

The barriers to making contacts (not to speak of friendships) with other teenagers were all too predictable. Again and again schools were said to take children away from their local areas and so were held to be responsible for limiting contact with others. Not only did this hamper the continuation of friendships with children at the same school but it affected the making of friends at home, too. Even those who did know local children were disadvantaged in that they lost the intensity of contact that can be built up between those who both live and study together. All friendships for these children were inevitably diluted and so were broken more easily. The detrimental effect on relationships of segregated schooling is a particularly important consideration for children who are, in any case, less well equipped than others to overcome barriers in this sphere (both socially and because of their limited freedom). Attendance at residential school is likely to exacerbate the problem further, but these schools have the advantage that opportunities for informal contact exist there, albeit that such contacts are restricted to other disabled children.

Another major difficulty, possibly not unrelated to the last, arose from the attitudes of other children who were hostile or unsympathetic to the teenagers. Almost a quarter of parents mentioned these problems spontaneously. The following quotations cite examples that took place with parents there: children were much more vulnerable to actual teasing or bullying if alone:

M. The biggest problem is going out. The children can be so – horrible, you know . . . . You can see them looking and chattering – that's horrible, that's nasty. But otherwise there's nothing to worry about at all, is there?'
F. The very young ones don't understand so it doesn't make any difference to them.
M. It's when they get to know, to understand that she's different, you know . . . at about 10. It's the most upsetting thing, otherwise we're as happy as Larry with her, but I suppose that reminds you, when you see them.

F. Particularly if you take her on the beach. That's one of the hardest things to do.

M. You'll find they come up and look, and then it's upsetting. Of course, Diana doesn't understand – she just says 'Who's that? What's his name?'   (1981)

Well put it this way, I'd rather people came here to me than ask me to their houses. I don't like taking him to people's houses especially if there are young children there. They just seem to sit and they stare and then they start. They want Pete to play, but it's teasing they are, and it upsets me a little bit to think he doesn't understand and he'll go out and they'll tell him to do this, and do that, and he'd do it all for them – they're sort of putting on him, it does upset me a little bit. So I think 'Right, I'm not going there.' (1981)

One boy had encountered difficulties when he first went to the local disco, but he had persisted in his attendance and gradually the problems passed. Some parents emphasised that the local children had all grown up together and so there were no such problems. Two teenagers, who had enjoyed such contacts, had lost all their friends when they moved house. Isolation increased as siblings left home or pursued their own activities and so no longer acted as a bridge between the Down's children and other children. Nor were siblings offering companionship themselves to the same degree as their own activities became more adult. Childhood friends, too, were growing away.

Of Stephanie's age she still has friends in the neighbourhood but they're the same age exactly as Stephanie and gradually it's decreasing. They used to play together *very* regularly in this garden, in that garden, everywhere . . . most of her friends now are school friends.   (1981)

The friendships were ever fragile and difficult to replace when lost. One mother of a very bright girl, who had moved a number of times, described the problems in her new area:

She relates to adults far better than she does children, she's fine with adults and I don't know how I can get round it. I'm hoping this street party next week – I'm hoping she'll get to know some children. There's a little girl next door – 10 – younger, I know, but perhaps she'll get to know her, I don't like to impose Sophie on neighbourhood children in case they don't want it.   (1981)

Teenagers themselves caused some of the problems in that they did not always welcome friendships and would refuse to join games even when invited, or were shy or indifferent. One or two rejected younger children who were the only ones willing to play with them. A minority of parents, sensing antagonism, would keep the teenager in or avoid unnecessary exposure of unacceptable behaviour (e.g. poor table manners). This could restrict contacts further and no doubt perpetuated the problem of strangeness. Some behaviour, however, was hardly likely to be acceptable to anyone:

The only thing is some of the children get scared of him now and again. I take him up the shop and he pinched somebody's sweets off them . . . he's got an awful habit of smacking people – he doesn't mean to hurt them, he thinks he's funning around – he laughs as he's doing it . . . if children tease him we just let him go, he'll do the rest. Have you seen the Incredible Hulk on television? They used to tease him. There were a couple of kids – he got out and ran after them – they soon run. But all the kids round here are all right with him – but strangers . . .   (1981)

Encouraging friendships

Overcoming all the difficulties was not easy. Some parents compensated by incorporating their teenagers into their own activities, others concentrated on friendships with other mentally handicapped people, and some were content to leave it as it was.

Clearly those Down's syndrome teenagers who had reasonable skills in self-care and who had been encouraged to go out alone were more acceptable and easily integrated. Similarly, those who had siblings of a similar age had been introduced to the peer group in a natural fashion as children, albeit that the advantages did not last until the teens.

Mothers varied in the degree to which they would take strong measures to develop friendships. There were two mothers who recognised that extra attraction was needed and stoically accepted a degree of imposition in order to foster normal friendships.

There's a boy from F. who's been over – he'd come every night for about three weeks and then he stays away for about six months, you see, and comes back again . . . . I think he just comes to have a – well – Malcolm gets nice things around here you know – meals – and things like that and he gets the same when he's here . . . . He's 16, a very stunted little boy – he looks as though there's something wrong with him. I think he's a little boy who's not not quite normal up there. They get on great . . . . I always welcome him in because Malcolm likes having him here, but you can't lay any conditions – 'You can't come if you stay away' – so they take advantage, don't they? I don't suppose they want to play with him all that much.

(1981)

In one interview a question to a mother about the expense involved in keeping her daughter produced the following revealing postscript:

GM. And you've got to give the children a little something – for looking after her.
M.   Yes, you know, like when the girls are playing with her, when they goes out I gives Angela money and says 'Right, there you are girls' 'cos they stays with her, you know.
GM. Just to keep an eye on her, mind – well, say they're having chips, 20p for her and for her two friends.
M.   That's when my mother was – well, *she* does that. Well, you know what children are like – if they've got a friend that's – more or less we're buying her friendship, you can look at it that way, can't you?

(1981)

Others were not prepared to use this strategy and indeed discouraged these sorts of contact:

I used to have children in when she was younger but I found they used to come and didn't play with Pat but with her toys and, not only that, I found Pat wasn't very interested in them. She'd have about ten minutes and then she'd leave them to look at TV. We stopped them coming. [Was that difficult to do?] Yes. [Did she never go to their houses?] No. [Were the others keen to come?] Yes, they'd queue up at the side door – we had all the toys. In the summer we'd go out the back and have all her toys and whatever she wanted. They'd knock at the front door, 'Is Pat coming out?' Well, Pat never went out. 'Can I come in to play with her?' and we said 'No.' And then they'd be more interested in what I was cooking out there.

(1981)

Although it was impossible to gather objective information, it seems likely that the type of neighbourhood a child lived in could foster or hinder the development of friendships. Middle-class families with well-protected and fenced gardens could become isolated islands. One mother with a very able Down's teenager had recently moved into such an area. She was reluctant to invite rejection from a girl next door by making positive overtures. In contrast a mother living in a different type of neighbourhood described the sort of interaction between mothers which could help children to mix. She lived in an area with rows of terraced houses that all fronted directly on to the pavement. In 1981 her daughter mixed well with the local teenagers:

In the summer evenings I used to sit out there till about nine in the night and that is what I done for months and months and for a good few years . . . she just wanted to be with the children and I used to take a chair out there . . . friends used to sit out there together, the other mothers with their children. I would sit out there first, one would come, then another would come and it ended up about five or six parents . . . we just used to sit there – take a deck-chair out the front and we would sit there. Even in the children's holiday we would sit there. [Do you still, now you don't have to watch her?] We still do it now in the summer evenings – it's for my own good now. If I want to just go out there and sit – well, just to have a natter, then, put it that way.

(1981)

Initiating and fostering relationships is not an area that lends itself easily to intervention by services, although one parent, living in an area where community services were being improved, had been told of the possibility of a young woman volunteer who could befriend her daughter and spend a few hours with her on a regular basis.

ADOLESCENCE AND SEXUAL DEVELOPMENT

Several workers report that, although there is some variation, sexual development in

Down's syndrome individuals is underdeveloped and that sexual urges are likely to be minimal or generalised to showing affection to everyone (Gibson, 1979; Smith and Berg, 1976). Brinkworth (1983), however, suggests that those with more near-normal achievements may have more average sexual desires and may also be more fertile. It is unfortunate that his paper concentrates on the sexual problems of girls rather than boys, because in fact this study in South Wales found more problems associated with masculine sexuality. It seems likely, as with so many aspects of Down's syndrome, that a wide range of responses is found and that, just as generalisations about social abilities of Down's people are unwise, so too it may be misleading to attach a stereotype to the sexual behaviour of Down's individuals. Fertility, however, is generally assumed to be low for both sexes and certainly there are few recorded cases of women with Down's syndrome becoming mothers – although this could result from extreme protection and lack of opportunity rather than from low fertility. Moreover, most work in this area has investigated the situation of institutionalised subjects and so may not have much relevance for people brought up at home. There are no recorded cases of a Down's syndrome man having fathered a child, although obviously the link between paternity and birth cannot always be confidently made. It is possible that, with improved health and longer life spans, the fertility of Down's individuals could increase.

Adolescence can present problems for normal families, although Hill (1981) casts doubt on the notion of exceptional problems being inevitable during adolescence. Nine (17%) of the parents of Down's syndrome teenagers said they had encountered major problems and 14 (26%) minor problems during adolescence. While more boys than girls presented problems, (15 (54%) boys compared with 8 (32%) girls), the difference was not significant.

Problems mentioned were changes in mood, including increased stubbornness and tantrums, and one mother attributed her son's unwillingness to go out to his age. Other problems for the boys were more extreme: tearing clothes, pulling others' hair and outbreaks of violence. Adolescence was thought to be one possible explanation for the behaviour of the boy who had started to hit himself although other explanations – changes of school and his inability to communicate – were also put forward. For the most part, however, those who said there were adolescent problems were referring to some aspect of sexual behaviour.

Families in this population of teenagers were asked about sexual problems they had encountered with their children. Answers depended on how frank parents were prepared to be (one important evasion is known to the interviewer through another source and so cannot be quoted) and also depended on their perception or interpretation of behaviour. As the following extract illustrates, it is not always easy to agree how far behaviour is simply natural friendliness and how far it has a sexual overtone.

> F. He's girl mad . . . he is attracted to the opposite sex.
> M. We took him round the country a fortnight ago. He had five young girl friends and he couldn't wait to get back to see them all the next time. He is friendly.
> F. Especially with women.   (1981)

Attitudes and expectations of the parents

Down's syndrome teenagers were very dependent for most of their activities on how parents perceived their needs. Relationships with the opposite sex were no exception although this would, for most people, be a particularly private aspect of life.

How parents viewed the sexuality of their offspring depended upon their expectations of what was normal for an adolescent with Down's syndrome. This in turn affected their attempts to influence or control sexual behaviour and, as a continuation of this, the sex education they thought appropriate for Down's teenagers.

Boys were more commonly expected to experience sexual urges than girls and similar phrases to those quoted below were used by about a third of the boys' parents.

He's got normal feelings.   (1981)

He has the natural instincts of a boy that age.   (1981)

Come on he's 16.   (1981)

I mean, I'm a married woman and I know the feelings he's having.   (1981)

In contrast other mothers said such things as: 'He never bothers – he thinks it's all a laugh, just talking. I don't think in his mind he's that old, that way . . . . If he sees a girl passing he goes "There's a lovely pair of knockers" – that's nothing.' A few mothers had expected their children to have sexual feelings and one mother had been told 'Sex is not part of their lives.'

In contrast, fewer carers of girls expressed similar expectations of normal physical feelings, although some were prepared for this.

GM. I expect we'll have to watch her all the time, where she'll be and where she'll go. I think she's got
     the same feelings and everything as any girl of her age.   (1981)

I suppose she's got the same feelings as anyone else.   (1981)

I've heard her saying about boyfriends. Every boy she sees about her brother's age she says 'My boyfriend' and she remembers the name and they're all her boyfriends but there's no real problem, we smile
it off, but I often wonder what she's thinking. If my daughter's boyfriend is here she likes to get between
them and put her arm round him – she wants attention . . . . I wonder how she feels herself, she's jealous,
and she wants *her* boyfriend.   (1981)

The above quotation emphasises the realisation that Down's teenagers may be wishing for normal physical sexual expression and they are denied not only this aspect but also the social dimension of sexual relationships. This aspect possibly received more emphasis as a loss for the girls. Social mixing was linked in many parents' minds with the dangers of physical encounters. Both boys and girls were teased about 'boyfriends' and 'girlfriends' and several teenagers had expressed their intentions of marrying.

He says 'I'm getting married one day' and I said 'I hope so, love' but I said 'You've got plenty of time'
and he said 'You can't keep me for ever, you know that, don't you?' and I said 'Yes, love, I know that.'
                                                                                         (1981)

Two carers of the girls did not entirely rule marriage out. Indeed, marriages of Down's syndrome adults are not unknown (Cunningham, 1982). On the issue of motherhood, however, it has been suggested that the care Down's syndrome mothers give to their children resembles the relationship between child and doll rather than that between mother and child (Lejeune, 1983).

Well, I know Judy perhaps *could* get married, she talks about getting married, but that would be a big
problem wouldn't it? [You wouldn't want to encourage her?] No, I wouldn't encourage her to have
children [Would you stop her?] I don't know what to say. Really I wouldn't like to stop her because she
has had everything else a normal child has had in her life, but you've always got it at the back of your
mind, would they be able to cope? . . . It would have to be somebody with a little bit more – because she
loves children, and this new baby that we have got, I mean she knows where it has come from and she
gives it so much love you think – well is it cruel to stop [her]?   (1981)

S. I'd like her to be married to a man who could look after her – I would have no worries then. [Do you
    think that's likely?] Not likely – you never know, though, she might get married – you never know.
                                                                                         (1981)

Most parents, however, merely paid lip-service to the idea of intersex friendships and usually did not feel it necessary to foster this aspect of their teenager's experience as they fostered other facets of teenager life. Where friendships did occur in school or at Gateway Clubs, parents were usually tolerant. 'Trouble in school', however, which usually meant no more than kissing and horseplay, was felt to be rightly discouraged. Adequate supervision at the Adult Training Centre (ATC) was a major concern for the girls' parents. Only one boy was suspected of having more tangible sexual experience.

M. I say he's not to go with the girls [at discos] – he's watched over there.

F. Nothing untoward has happened that we know of – he did come home with marks on his neck and, I'm not being funny, but they looked like bites. He was getting them from school and when I said 'Where did you get that, have you been fighting?' 'No,' he said, 'My collar's too tight' and he always wears an open collar so it's not his collar . . . and he laughs and says 'My collar's too tight.' [Do you think there is anything?]

M. I don't know.

F. I honestly don't know. (1981)

Of course, even where parents did not discourage, or even welcomed friendships with the opposite sex the parents of the other teenagers could be less cooperative. A few mothers actively encouraged such friendships, taking care though that physical barriers were maintained. One mother, for instance, warned her daughter not to let her boyfriend touch her breasts. The following quotation is from one of the few mothers who did welcome contact between the sexes:

Well, the only girls he meets are those in school. Rhiannon is his girl. They walk around holding hands, as far as I know, but that's the only girl he's got a relationship with. It's a very innocent thing . . . we've had her here occasionally in the holidays, my husband fetches her over. They go for a walk in the park, with me walking five yards behind. He won't go without me. I think it is the most beautiful thing to see them walking ahead hold hands . . . . Well, you see, they are very vulnerable these children to other – to the public, you know, they'd laugh at them and that sort of thing and I'm always there on guard because I'm fighting fit. I'm like a dragon – nobody would dare look twice at them, but they walk ahead of me, you know – they think they're courting. I think I find that sad. It hurts quite a bit – well, it's that time you feel he ought to be going out with girls. (1981)

The boys

At least half of the boys had begun to show some interest in girls. This interest was often on the level of small boys' smutty talk or confined to noticing and commenting on women's 'sexy legs' and so on, but there was a growing interest towards girls in school or at Gateway, towards women in the family or – more distressingly for parents – towards females outside the family. One boy spent his time, harmlessly enough, cutting out pictures of women from magazines – 'Never men', said his mother darkly but tolerantly.

He pretends he's got a woman in bed with him, you know – I hear him talking to her and he's got nobody – I've heard him often enough talking to her. 'Are you all right now?' I hear him say and 'I love you', you see. Oh, its comical – I have to go downstairs because I'd only laugh. Oh, yes, he's a grown-up boy now, you know. He's got the telly sometimes by his side in bed and I go in sometimes and open the door and I can see him kissing the telly. 'Oh, you've got your girlfriend, have you?' and he goes shy then. The social worker came here one day and said Raymond was meddling about with the girls and boys – well, that was very embarrassing for me. I said 'Well, I'm sorry I don't get trouble with Raymond at home here, he's in school and should be taught if he's doing something wrong. I won't say nothing if any of the school masters give him a slap.' . . . I'm turning my back on him in the morning and putting water for him in the washbowl . . . and he catches hold of me from behind – the back you see – and he puts his arms around up here then, you see. 'What are you trying to do?' And he just laughs. 'Now, don't do that to Mammy – or nobody else'. [Isn't he simply being affectionate?] Yes, it is just affectionate, but I don't want him to do that because he'll be condemned in school for doing so – but as my daughter said, that's the only love or anything that will satisfy him that Raymond will have – but I don't want him to start off like that you see, although I know he's deprived . . . . Raymond is very sensitive to tell you the truth. He took a fancy to a girl at Gateway and he couldn't have her and he was running home here very moody and crying and he would be very upset . . . . I don't know if that had put him off going to Gateway – that he couldn't have the girl he fancied – so I would tell him 'Look Raymond *bach*, there's plenty of girls to be had, next time you'll be in the Gateway and perhaps there'll be a lovely girl there and perhaps she'll only want you to dance with her. That girl fancied someone else, you see, you've got to leave her go with who she wants to – you can't claim her, you see.' He was still crying. 'Next time, next time' he'd say – he forgot it then, you see. Oh, he won't keep on all the time, but that time he was upset. (1981)

Other parents simply said their boys 'liked girls' or were 'very interested' or wanted to kiss girls (or 'anyone and everyone'). Only two mothers expressed strong worries about their boys' interest in local children. Both of these mothers were also very concerned about relationships within the family.

I very rarely leave [teenager sister] with him. We had some problems years ago and I don't think I've really forgotten that. He was a bit awkward – well he was – Roger is inclined to think – I don't know if it's a baby way, or part of growing up, but we had problems. He's inclined to walk about with nothing on you know and – er – [sister] had a couple of awkward moments . . . he tried – you know – something on – it was only a question of something very, very little but it frightened us into thinking it could become more serious if he got away with it . . . . The problem now is that we've got a three-bedroomed house and [young brother] has to sleep in the same room as Roger . . . it's more silliness than anything . . . but he's inclined to mess about . . . . Let's put it this way – you're never very sure of *what* might happen – it's something I'd hate to happen and I cannot say positively to you now that it wouldn't happen . . . . I've always got it in my mind, I'd never leave her for any length of time. [Sister's] a very strong child and she could cope with him to a certain extent but I know I'd hate it to have to happen . . . . It seems to me as far as Roger's concerned we're happy with him, he's a great kid, but this is a problem beyond his control, you've got to try to understand it, but when you've got younger children it is a big problem.   (1981)

With my grandchildren, I'm afraid to let him go upstairs with them. Well, my son came the other day and told me Alistair likes to take his pants off and he likes them to take their pants off so I don't know what sort of trouble I'm going to have to – I'm a bit nervous. I mean he might have only been saying 'Mine's bigger than yours' or something like that – they do do that, you know. I mean I can't get to the bottom of it really because Alistair can't tell me and the little ones are too embarrassed, because they're only 7. And we took him to the park on Thursday afternoon – only to the park, my daughter's son – he's 11 – and the baby and myself – well for a long time he sat on the bench with this girl and he was putting his arms around her, you know and – er – I don't think she minded, and she was only a young girl but in the end I could hear her saying 'Oh, leave me alone' so I called him over and he came – reluctantly – and then played ball and I played ball with him, but I mean *I've* got to play ball and I've got to be careful with my foot, I've got to do all the playing with Alistair – nobody else have done it, not since Alistair was born . . . . I said to my daughter, she's got a little girl and she idolises Alistair and she's 4 and they always want to go upstairs and I said 'For goodness sake don't let her go upstairs for my peace of mind.' . . . I mean I wouldn't like him to corrupt her.   (1981)

Five or six mothers mentioned that their sons showed some sexual interest either in themselves or their daughters, although this amounted to little more than 'noticing' or being too demonstrative in embraces.

Fortunately apart from one or two occasions when he gets a bit personal with his sister or with me perhaps, he relieves his feelings by tearing his clothes . . . . Well he touches [sister] sometimes and he says – er – 'Tits' – she's embarrassed, you know. I don't know where they get these things from, but he does. I remember once my sister was here and he was tearing his clothes and my sister's a health visitor and she said 'It's his age' and suddenly he went up to [his sister] and he just put his hand up her skirt and I said 'For God's sake Donald, go and tear your trousers.' We laugh about it, but I meant it. There are so many worse ways he could express his feelings.   (1981)

Other sexual problems for the boys centred around masturbation. Whereas the growing interest in girls was across all ages the 13 boys who were known to masturbate were on average slightly older than those who were not known to do it (16 years 7 months compared with 15 years 11 months). For only three boys was it a major problem, since, for all but one, it was, or had become so with persuasion, a private activity. The following mother had encountered problems in enforcing privacy.

At the moment the major problem is masturbation. We've had trouble at school, in the house. I have got him into the bedroom – well he has gone into the bedroom, but if he hasn't gone into the bedroom and he's on the floor he gets nasty – he gets very violent if you interfere with him. The doctor said, 'You must leave him alone, he's human.' I said 'Well, it's all right if I'm here on my own, but if people call it's very embarrassing – and you know they play with themselves when they're out.' And he says they can't satisfy themselves so they get nasty inside . . . . I think this is what makes them so angry. He said this is the problem – he can't satisfy himself so – er – he's wild for a time after then, you know. It's – oh – all the time.

He's all right if I can get something in his hand, you know – a puppet or a toy – and talk to him . . . . Well you should hear the conversation here some days, people would think I was nuts: 'Stop playing with yourself', 'Hands out of your trousers', 'Leave yourself alone' – Oh, it's terrible . . . . I mean he's a normal 17 – he'd be out with the girls and he could be interfering with girls but he hasn't connected that, which I'm grateful for . . . . Well, they gave me some tablets for it but I had to take him off them . . . . Oh, he was depressed – it wasn't agreeing with his other tablets. He used to cry, break his heart and he's never been a crying child and I took him up to the hospital and said 'There's something wrong – he's not very happy, he's crying and sits in a corner and crouches like this' and he said 'Well, you must persevere', but when I came home I said to my husband 'I'm taking him off them and that's it' I said 'I'm going to put up with the problem' . . . . Well, I ignore it . . . if he's on the floor and started I just have to leave him because you daren't touch him and he's nasty and he'll kick out. Well, if I see his eyes start to roll and he'll go down to the floor and his father will say 'Bedroom.' (1981)

Another mother had found sex presented no problems:

No – he's quite normal. I don't think they've introduced sex and things into the Centre as yet. I mean he comes home and says 'Nice girls', he likes so and so and – but that's as far as it goes. We don't encourage it, you know, but we don't discourage it either – we just – we tell him. 'You'd better start saving if you're getting married', you know, things like that but, obviously, he watches TV and I don't think he's that stupid. (1981)

The girls

The sexual problems of boys frequently presented more problems for parents than did those of girls. Presumably this was partly due to the fact that the final sanction for the boys was seen as criminal charges, while for the girls it was the more private pregnancy. The former would provoke public blame and condemnation but the latter was more likely to attract pity. As well as this, a girl making advances to a boy or a man is seen as less threatening than the opposite situation. Whereas problems for the boys had centred around protecting others from their advances, the first consideration for girls seems to be to reduce sexually provocative behaviour to a minimum and instil in them a sense of 'proper and improper', as one parent put it.

Well, she's a bit on the – she likes showing her bosom and that sort of thing and wiggling her bottom, which we've allowed in a way because, when she was younger, it didn't seem to be so bad but she doesn't know where to stop now and she's 16 going on 17 and she's friendly to everyone. She'll go up to a man and tell him she likes him. She was sitting by a man on the bus the other day and he's not two penny worth, sad to say, and I mean she was telling him she liked him and things like that. On the bus – she just wants to go and sit on her own somewhere away from you, she's inclined to do that. When she was little it wasn't too bad. Oh, she'll talk to anybody, if she's down on the beach she'll move away from you, you've got to watch where she's going and who she's talking to and try to stop her from doing it. I find it's very difficult. (1981)

In contrast others said their daughters were not forthcoming with strangers and, in all, less was made of the girls' own instinctive sexuality. Rather the fear for girls was that they would be taken advantage of by both the mentally handicapped and normal population. Oddly, in view of the protection given to the girls, pregnancy was a major worry and parents were more protective still when periods started. Obviously it was not always easy to make the distinction between attack and invitation:

S. She do like men, likes to sit on their laps, touch 'em and kiss them. This is why I don't want to let her out very often. She wouldn't have to be coaxed into anything. She likes attention and you can get some fellows – well you read about it often enough, don't you? (1981)

At the moment, you see, we do shelter her, I think she would be easy going – I think she'd be game for anything like that. (1981)

Similarly, less reference was made to actual advances that girls made to men and boys, although some girls obviously liked men and were overenthusiastic in family embraces. Girls often showed their consciousness of sex in speech rather than action. For instance, they would comment on scenes shown on television: 'I know what they're doing, they're being rude.' Masturbation was not always brought up with girls, since, as Brinkworth (1983) points out, it can be a more discreet activity in girls and may pass unnoticed. Two mothers showed concern about masturbation because their retarded daughters embarrassed other family members.

Sex education

Parents attempted to deal with all these problems in a variety of ways. Some avoided television programmes with a strong sexual content and verbal correction was commonly used to both sexes. Boys were told to kiss quickly and not to kiss men at all, but to shake hands instead. One mother had been caught out on this:

> He is beginning to start . . . if he sees any girls out, you know, he starts kissing them. It is a problem . . . some don't like it, some of the women, and he's that strong he won't leave them go. I say, 'That's naughty, don't do that.' He did start kissing men and I stopped that. I said 'You should shake hands with men, kiss girls.' So now he does. It's our fault really.   (1981)

Only one carer had considered putting a Down's teenager on the pill, but she had rejected the idea because there would be no warning of side effects. One boy's mother wished drugs were available that suppressed these instincts and another thought the boys should be 'circumcised' [*sic*].

Sex education as a means of dealing with problems was usually limited to warnings rather than explanations. In fact, 19 (36%) parents felt that sex education was neither necessary nor, indeed, possible. Only five mothers – all with daughters – had attempted any real explanation of physical changes and none of the boys had been given any information. For the girls, of course, the topic could not totally be ignored and it was particularly sad that some girls could not adequately be prepared for menstruation before the event. One mother described her daughter's shock at her first period.

> I found her sitting in the dark just before she went back to school. We both missed her and I said 'Where's Jessica?' – we both thought the other had her and she was sitting there – seven o'clock in the morning, in the dark, really scared. I took her upstairs and talked, I had everything ready and she was fine. I think the fact that there was a mess on the sheets upset her and she thought she'd made a mess and been naughty. To her it didn't mean anything – just a mess and I had no way of warning her beforehand.   (1981)

Another mother spoke of her daughter's 'hysteria' but others had accepted it calmly. Apart from the five girls mentioned, explanation was confined to practicalities rather than linking menstruation with sex and pregnancy, which mothers hoped were contingencies that would not arise anyway. Seven mothers of the more retarded children offered no explanation at all. Eight emphasised that this was something that happened to all women as they grew up and instanced friends, sisters or themselves as examples. Three girls had obviously had some explanation at school and those who lived in residential schools had the advantage of seeing how other girls coped. Explanations of why this should happen were superficial. One sister described it as 'waste blood' and a mother outlined her own explanation as follows:

> I didn't explain it. She thinks she's – well – she says 'a bad bum' and she thinks she's cut herself. I say 'No, Mammy and Sister, all little girls – all the same. All little girls have to wear pads' but other than that, nothing, no further. She listens, 'cos she said, 'And [sister]?', 'No, she's too small, but a big girl like you, you're big now, like Sister' – she calls S. 'Sister'. And she's accepted that. You can't go further, that's all.   (1981)

Some mothers did try to instil a need for discretion into their daughters or, as one mother put it: 'This is girls' talk, because *everybody* knew when she wore a bra.' Only a few mothers brought up the fact that the growing maturity of their daughters without a similar development of other normal feminine activities was something painful for themselves, emphasising, as it did, the lack of growing companionship and shared interests that can come at such times. As one mother said, 'I get a lump in my throat sometimes when I think about that.'

As to further explanations to both sexes only 6 (11%) mothers felt that their children had any notion of intercourse, 27 (51%) of pregancy and 21 (40%) of birth. Most had gained their knowledge of pregnancy through a relative being pregnant and television seemed to be largely responsible for knowledge about birth. ('Go out, Mammy, it's too rude for you to watch', said one boy to his mother.) Nineteen teenagers (36%) were thought to be innocent of all such information and indeed one boy had only recently discovered the difference between men and women. This was probably unusually late and one 5-year-old boy in 1972 had caused some surprise in school with a very explicit drawing of a man and a woman. Explanations of intercourse were rarely attempted by parents and indeed had sometimes been avoided even for the normal siblings:

> There's the other part I haven't got to yet, you know, I will have to do it, I will have to tell her . . . when she looked at the television she said, 'Look, Mam, he was on top of her' or something like that and I say 'Well, there's a terrible thing' – well, it wasn't the time so I didn't bother to say then . . . because I never have been able to explain, even to my daughter. I just told my daughter before she went to grammar school 'There'll be bigger girls there that'll give you wrong ideas about things . . . . You are like your father because you are part of your father', so that was all I could tell her.   (1981)

One mother simply said: 'Boys make babies and girls have babies', but was at a loss how to elaborate on this since she said, 'It's like talking to a 5-year-old'.

Warnings about the opposite sex, however, were often felt to be necessary, in spite of the fact that the teenagers were rarely left without supervision. Warnings to boys were confined to 'not touching' girls although more than one mother was afraid that warnings would serve to encourage rather than the reverse.

> Well, I think the school should give some guidance as they know better than us how to put it, preferably from the doctor. Whether it would sink in or not I don't know, but at least he'd have been told. I mightn't put it the right way, you know – I might make him more interested, you know what I mean, and I wouldn't like to do that.   (1981)

Warnings to girls were considered very important and varied in the level of interaction allowed from the extreme 'don't go near boys, they'll harm you', to 'don't bother with boys, they can be very cheeky', to the lesser 'don't go on their knees or get too close'. One mother's warnings were very explicit:

> Well, yes, I suppose I've tried. I've said she mustn't let boys play with her down below and things like that, but you see she's allowed to watch TV and there's such a lot coming on TV that it's ridiculous . . . .

In fact some mothers took it in their stride and simply continued early lessons:

> I did [warn her] years ago when she was at school you know – boys and girls – you know how they are and that, and she was on about something one day and I said 'Not even girls' I said 'Don't let anybody touch you – or touch your knickers.' 'Oh, I won't, Mam' – when they were small, fairly small this was. I think she knows – well – nobody's supposed to – with Clara. I haven't fully explained, I don't really know what to say to her really, it's awkward, but everything [else] has just fallen into place and this will too.   (1981)

One mother of a very bright and presentable girl was reluctant to make her afraid and distrustful. Those with more retarded children did not know how to set about protecting their daughters other than by giving extremely close supervision. The need for modesty was stressed, but a minority were afraid that, even if their daughters did not actually invite advances, they would not necessarily discourage them.

Possibly because of the difficulties of making an explanation understood, over one-third of parents felt it was not possible or really necessary in view of the protected lives their teenagers led. Only six (11%) parents felt that explanations should come from home, although seven (13%) saw it as a joint responsibility with the school. Most (18 (34%)) felt that the school was the best place for this sort of instruction and three parents were unsure who was best to deal with these issues. School was favoured because the staff were considered to have expertise that would enable them to ensure the children comprehended the message, or because the children took more notice of instruction from school and five mothers felt there would be less embarrassment in a group of other teenagers of the same age. Two mothers felt their teenagers' particular schools were perhaps unsuitable because attitudes were judged to be too repressive in one and, in the other, too 'airy fairy'. 'They say they do dancing, and games and exercises and there's no problem.'

Other parents had gone to their doctors for advice on sexual matters, although one GP had simply advised, 'Tell her if she goes with anyone she'll have a baby', which could be regarded by some of the girls as encouragement rather than a sanction.

In fact, although parents worried about attacks on their boys and girls from outsiders, only one girl had had an unpleasant sexual experience and this, as with many such incidents, had been from someone in the family, against whom there could be little advance protection.

OTHER ACTIVITIES

There were considerable differences in how far parents managed to provide an interesting and varied life for their teenagers. A major contrast with normal teenagers was that activities had to be initiated by families or needed their involvement or support. Where families were reluctant or unable to provide many facilities, the teenagers were unlikely to be able to compensate for this themselves. Cheseldine and Jeffree (1981) describe many of the activities of mentally handicapped teenagers as family orientated or 'solitary' and 'passive' and suggest such teenagers may be as disadvantaged in the sphere of leisure as they are in access to work. This study in South Wales certainly gives confirmation to this view and implies that teenagers may be vulnerable to secondary handicap because of it. The amount of stimulation teenagers received at home was largely dependent on their parents, who firmly possessed the initiative, and their perception of the needs of a Down's teenager. Not that these perceptions always resulted in action: 'Now Maralyn is 15, she should be starting going to discos, but where I go she goes, sort of thing . . . she just wants to sit and eat. If I want to take Maralyn I have to give her a pile of sweets.'

Although there was considerable overlap in activities, parents attempted to make a reasonable life for their teenagers in a variety of ways. A few continued to promote patterns of behaviour and activity that had developed during childhood. This was understandably more common when there were young siblings still at home. A common choice for others was to absorb teenagers into their own way of life – visits to relatives, churches, pubs, clubs, dances and coffee mornings increasingly included the teenager. This worked well, except that such outings usually involved companions who were at least a generation older than the teenager. For some teenagers most of their contacts at this stage in their life were with people either younger or rather older than themselves. Also some parents participated in few activities themselves because of ill health, poverty or lack of inclination. Another solution, which most adopted in varying degrees, was to concentrate on activities for handicapped people.

Turning to actual activities, it should be said, some teenagers were leading very full and interesting lives and it was a minority who did little except sit at home. Indeed, some parents remarked that the teenagers led a more varied life than their sibling with

Table 7.2 *Club membership*

	n	%		
For handicapped teenagers				
Gateway	8	(15)	⎫	
Youth clubs	5	(9)	⎬	19 (36)
Guides or Scouts	3	(6)	⎬	
Faith and Light group	3	(6)	⎭	
For all teenagers				
Youth clubs	2	(4)	⎫	
Guides or Scouts	3	(6)	⎬	7 (14)
Young farmers	1	(2)	⎬	
Regular disco	1	(2)	⎭	
No regular attendance at clubs	27	(51)		
Total	53	(101)		

youth clubs, swimming clubs, special holidays, parties and trips at school all part of their usual activities. Twenty-one families (53%) had weekly outings together and only 6 (11%) had none at all. Sixty per cent of the teenagers went shopping regularly and only 6 (11%) never went. Only 23% had never had a holiday. Swimming was a popular pursuit and some teenagers were very competent. Only 19% never swam at home or at school. Significantly more boys than girls were taken swimming at home. Half of the teenagers attended some sort of club, although only seven of them attended clubs with their normal peers (see Table 7.2).

Parents were prevented from providing even what they saw themselves as an optimum background for their teenagers for a wide variety of reasons, however. Some of the obstacles to a richer lifestyle were interdependent, but it was possible to divide them into those that arose largely from the teenager, those that arose from the parent, and those that arose from what can loosely be called the environment. When the whole list of problems and restrictions is given it is surprising that the teenagers led lives as active and full as they did. Sadly, for some families, the reasons were linked and their teenagers suffered from such a variety of disadvantages that more than one parent would sympathise with the mother who stated, 'Well, I think he don't have no life.'

Problems connected with the teenager

From the earliest days poor health had caused problems. Apart from the general restrictions imposed on activities resulting from being kept away from school or indoors for short periods because of poor health, a few children suffered more severe deprivations. One boy had been educated at home for three years because his mother judged that his heart condition warranted this. Others were excluded from swimming, or camping, or pony riding at school. Another boy never used public transport because of a (possibly chance) remark of his doctor when he developed epilepsy. Another boy had his hands almost permanently tied because he attempted to injure himself whenever he was released. The association of mothers' assessments of health and the Gunzburg score of their teenagers was noted in Chapter 1.

There is the general and important problem of mobility. Those who had experienced a fuller life when they could use pushchairs suffered restrictions as they outgrew them, and even the two who had graduated to wheelchairs were still restricted because mothers found them heavy to push. It has been said that the restrictions to mobility were not only physical. Some teenagers had become more sedentary and generally less keen to go out and a few disliked buses or crowds. Also, the behaviour of some teenagers, obviously noticeable as the child grew, deterred some parents. In general too, the work involved in preparing a trip with an unwilling, troublesome, possibly incontinent teenager who had to be washed and dressed before leaving detracted from the enjoyment and made some parents avoid outings when they could.

Children and teenagers who actually had had accidents were subsequently treated with more caution. One boy had never been taken to the beach again after he had almost drowned, another would herself not return to the beach after she had been covered in 'leeches'. Similarly, clumsiness in the home would discourage further attempts at domestic activities. Understandably parents were less inclined to keep trying in a situation that had once proved unsuccessful.

Most importantly, unresponsive teenagers gave little incentive to parents to initiate or continue with their efforts to provide a stimulating background for their children. It is this sort of influence that can strike at the roots of normal parent–child interaction resulting in subtle distortions. (See Mitchell (1976) for a review of the types of speech mothers use to mentally handicapped children compared with those used to normal children.) There was further discouragement for those parents whose children did not play with, or even destroyed, toys that were provided. Those who did not express needs or wishes were sometimes assumed to have none, although arguably their needs were greater than those of the average Down's teenager. The apparent freedom given to the teenager whose grandmother said 'Sheila can go if she wants to' is misleading since it was highly unlikely in this instance that any such wish would be expressed. Parents needed to be assertive themselves if their children were to lead full lives, and indeed parents of even the more able teenagers implied that their children, if allowed, would become more passive and inactive. The mother of one extremely bright and personable boy who, in times of full employment, would easily have been a candidate for open employment, when considering the Adult Training Centre made the following comment:

> I've never been to [ATC] so I shouldn't really say anything about it, but I've seen some of the people who go there – would Colin go backwards . . . . I know they make wrought iron gates, they do lots of things there. I've heard but I haven't actually been to see it – he must be occupied, he'll go like a vegetable if he isn't occupied. (1981)

These influences could lead to a vicious circle being set up with unresponsive teenagers receiving less attention and becoming more passive still as a result.

Problems connected with the parents

Since parents of these teenagers were older than average when they had their babies it was predictable that by the time their children had reached their teens some of them were becoming conscious of the limitations imposed by age. Sometimes they themselves felt less inclined to go out and about and yet, if the teenagers were to lead lives outside the home, this was needed. Hours spent playing with and encouraging their offspring were becoming irksome for a few mothers. The reasons were in part physical in that health problems could result in less strength and patience, but mentally too some parents were beginning to feel that, at their stage in life, they should be allowed to relax and follow their own interests.

> Yes, she's stubborn and doesn't want to bother, you know, and gone lazy. Sitting down here for years she's gone lazy. No one to take her in hand, no one got time to bother with her. I've got around to telling her 'You wash yourself now, you can go to the toilet yourself' but by the time I get to where she's washing, she's soaking. And I haven't time to train and teach her. Rather than persevere and have the patience, I'd rather not bother. I'd have more work changing her and wiping her down, it's the patience and time they want which you haven't got to give 'em. (1981)

For some teenagers it was not a diminution but a total withdrawal of contact with one parent if a mother or father had left the family home or had died. In addition, one or two fathers had jobs that took up most of their time or had unusual hours. In contrast to this, however, one positive feature of ageing was that some fathers were retiring and so becoming more rather than less involved with their teenagers.

The majority of parents continued to show as great a wish as ever to encourage their teenagers but some clearly possessed little talent in this direction. Problems were increased too when the well-tried and established patterns appropriate for both normal and handicapped younger children became redundant and inappropriate for teenagers and there were no obvious and familiar patterns with which to replace them. A minority of parents showed little understanding of the needs of any children. One father (subsequently divorced) would not allow any noisy play indoors. Two parents, totally unaware that they were being restrictive, expected their very disabled son to sit still in one place. Their policy was to some extent the result of the boy breaking things in the house.

> Well he knows he can't roam about in the house. He comes in, he knows his seat. He's touching things now and again but all you've got to do is just shout at him. Like the other day he tried to switch on the television – we said 'Stop' and he stopped.   (1981)

Other restrictions resulted more directly from their feelings about Down's syndrome and disability. Some parents felt embarrassed even when there were no overt adverse reactions from those outside. A major difficulty was a parent's natural wish to protect the child, which could progress to over-protection, or lead to parents being over-helpful with everyday tasks.

Problems connected with the environment

Some of the problems that arose for teenagers resulted from the physical or social environment in which they lived. Certain of the problems were obviously amenable to change.

Over and above all else, personal and/or community poverty exacerbated the problems of handicap. For those with greater than average needs greater incomes were necessary but not always available. Almost all families received the attendance allowance. In poor families this usually went simply to relieve poverty rather than to expand horizons. However, in areas of high unemployment and impoverished facilities, in simple economic terms some of the families with Down's children must have been better off than their neighbours. In such areas, though, expectations about acceptable lifestyles for everyone were severely restricted to levels that would not be contemplated by those living in the more affluent parts of the country.

Limited resources particularly affected mobility. The very poor clearly could not afford cars and only four teenagers qualified for mobility allowance. Public transport was expensive anyway and the problem was made greater because double fares were needed for all journeys. This expense arose whether the outing was intended for the parent or the teenager, if there was no one with whom the youngster could be left. A cost of £2.90 to visit her sister six miles away was quoted by one mother. Only one mother told of a service (prisoners minding children while mothers shopped) to which she had no access because she could not afford the trip in to town. Others mentioned the expense of attending hospital clinics. One boy did not use buses because it was difficult to get on and off them and one or two teenagers only travelled by taxi.

Longer journeys were also restricted and, not surprisingly, holidays were not a regular feature in poorer families. Of the 12 families who had never had a holiday, 5 were in social classes IV or V and 8 were from one-parent families. Social classes I or II accounted for 8 of the 13 who had been abroad.

There were also more general difficulties. One mother, living in a particularly disadvantaged area, said that people had stopped giving parties because of the expense. Others spoke of the expense of buying special toys for their children. It was suspected that one mother refused to allow her son to attend school partly because the weekly boarding place offered meant she lost the full attendance allowance. A day place was not offered. Another changed her child's attendance from weekly boarding to a daily basis probably for the same reason.

Some environmental problems were less open to improvement or change. Hilly or uneven terrain could make mobility more of a problem for the less agile teenagers and presented special problems for the two with wheelchairs. Those who lived in the more isolated valleys had few local facilities and reaching those available outside involved lengthy and expensive journeys. For delicate children the weather itself could make out-door trips difficult as well as ill-advised.

> Well, getting him to stay in is my biggest problem. You know – he wants to go out – well, take the weather we've had, now there's nowhere you can take him even. There's no shelter you can go and sit in with him when it's pouring with rain.   (1981)

A few had experienced extreme housing difficulties. One mother had lived in a single room with her three children for six months when she left her husband. Other homes were small and cramped and did not lend themselves to any boisterous activities that needed space. Moving house could cut teenagers off from their old contacts and result in greater isolation.

Yet more difficulties arose from the attitudes of other people who stared at or ridiculed the teenagers when they ventured forth. This was a problem even when parents accompanied their children so it did not encourage outings and understandably made parents reluctant to allow teenagers out alone where they could be exposed to such abuse.

Poor services added to restrictions. The discrepancy between the numbers experiencing mobility problems and the number receiving mobility allowance has already been mentioned. Several parents who were over-protective and consequently limited the lives of their teenagers could possibly have modified their behaviour if professionals had pointed out how to do this. Poor public services (e.g. badly maintained playgrounds, poor bus services, no local swimming facilities) had as detrimental an effect upon the Down's syndrome teenagers as upon anyone else: possibly more since alternatives were less readily available.

Although more attention has been given to the problems of providing a stimulating background it should once more be emphasised that there were parents who overcame all difficulties, or encountered few, and who did provide a rich and stimulating environment for their children. One mother described her own approach as follows: 'We've given him every opportunity to do everything, to see where he'd shine the most and he's shining at sport. Anything he wants to do he's allowed to do it, you know, if it would be beneficial for him.'

The problem of providing ways of life more appropriate to the teenagers as they left childhood was discussed earlier. The crucial distinction between the Down's syndrome teenagers and their normal peers was that the role the Down's syndrome teenager adopted was largely given and shaped by his parents and lacked the element of personal choice usual in the non-handicapped population.

SUMMARY

Despite the fact that there were variations in the friendships and activities of Down's teenagers the majority of the population were leading comparatively restricted lives socially. Although teenagers could learn self-care skills, could learn to read and write and so on by themselves and without reference to strangers when they moved into the social sphere, the teenagers were dependent on people outside the family and the responses they made. Undoubtedly parents did not always encourage interaction with the normal world as forcefully as they could, but there again there were certainly occasions when the Down's teenagers encountered hostility, ridicule or discrimination from members of the community that justified the caution of parents, or made it understandable.

Part 3
Variations in services for families

8 Early Help for Parents

The previous chapters have outlined the impact Down's syndrome has on parents' lives and the problems parents encounter in the day-to-day management of their children. Services are intended to help parents with their task and generally, as far as possible, assist in 'putting things right' by minimising any negative effects of disability. To these ends some services are directed primarily to the child in order to improve his health, skills and education whereas others are concerned to give parents relief from care, or to help them to realise the full potential of their children. These distinctions have become blurred in the delivery of services and different services can provide the same type of help. For instance, advice can come from any quarter, and early teaching is no longer the prerogative of educationalists but nowadays can also involve health professionals. The effects of services, too, are inevitably interdependent. A boarding-school placement, for example, can provide a balanced environment of care and stimulation for the child and also gives parents relief from full-time care. This can be beneficial not only for the parents themselves but may also benefit the child in that parent–child relationships improve, and the child may be given greater encouragement at home because of the fact that parents have time to recuperate from the strain of full-time care. Similarly a heart operation whose primary aim is physical, to keep the child alive and healthy, may have secondary mental gains for him as he becomes more able to explore his environment. His parents too, relieved of the expense, burden and worry of hospital visits and illness, can make a more constructive use of their time with their child.

Services for all mentally handicapped children have improved both in quantity and quality in the last decade, with attendant improvements for families, as the following chapters show. Down's syndrome is an interesting condition to monitor in relation to delivery of services, as it falls on the borderline of what is considered to be severe and what moderate handicap and people vary in how they view the condition (Shepperdson, 1983b, 1985b). In addition, Down's syndrome people are often categorised, not by their actual and individual abilities, but according to a stereotyped and general approach. These factors have affected the delivery of some services, usually to the detriment of the Down's syndrome population. So, there have been problems in the introduction of the attendance allowance, the Family Fund and, to some extent, the mobility allowance for the Down's syndrome population who were often considered 'too good' to qualify. Paradoxically, in their allocation to schools Down's syndrome children were, in the past, frequently regarded as 'too bad' to be allowed into the education system at all, or into mainstream schools after 1971. Some of the advances in recent years are due to the fact that, increasingly, people with Down's syndrome are being judged on their own individual characteristics. This has led to a fairer, and more acceptable, access to services.

EARLY MEDICAL HELP

The State, particularly in the field of medical services, is greatly concerned with all pregnancies and child care. Where there are unusual circumstances (an older mother, or the outcome of a pregnancy is a handicapped child) it could be expected that official services would be more involved than ever, but this was not usually the case for the parents of this cohort.

One major problem in this study of the early services is that information is all obtained retrospectively. In any case, mothers are not always accurate informants. They do not always remember what they have been told, or see the significance of what is being said. For instance, Leonard *et al.* (1972) monitored carefully what was said in genetic counselling to parents who had children with genetic disorders. They followed up the parents six months later to ascertain what was remembered. Mothers denied categorically having been told things that, in fact, had been clearly stated. Some denied having had any genetic counselling at all. For many parents in this population, an additional problem was that information was being given at a time of great emotional stress and some parents found they could not remember what was said. Talking about genetic advice one mother said, 'Well, he did talk to us about blood tests and – it all happened the same day he told us about Roger and really, I was so blank, I didn't take in all he said.'

Again, parents, especially those who had not been given a clear early diagnosis, were inclined to hoard any scraps of information that could imply the child did not have Down's syndrome after all: 'But I still don't *know*, you know. I met another person who had a mongol child and she came to the house and said "Don't think for a minute that child is a mongol" ...'. Others could think they had not been told, even while repeating words that showed they had in fact been given a clear diagnosis.

Parents cannot be blamed for wanting to select from the information they are given the comments they would most like to be true and all these qualifications should be borne in mind when considering the following sections. Equally, however, criticisms of treatment and services made by parents should not automatically be dismissed as untrue or exaggerated. Information was gathered from the original sample in 1972 and from the new sample in 1981. The information is kept separate in the tables because of this difference.

How mothers were told about their child's handicap

How a parent is told about her child's handicap has been a common subject of complaint. It is still a particular problem where there is uncertainty over diagnosis (Quine and Pahl, 1986). Evidence shows that parents wish to be told as soon as there are anxieties about their baby and that follow-up contacts are necessary after the initial disclosure. (See Hewett, 1975, for a review.) In the early 1970s hospitals began to lay down more specific guidelines (e.g. Bendix, 1975) and there is now clear evidence of improvement for Down's syndrome births, at least (Murdoch, 1984; Appendix 2.) (See also Cunningham *et al.*, 1984, on how further improvements could be made.) Birth events for the South Wales Down's syndrome population followed a fairly typical pattern for children born in the early 1960s. Since these events form an important part of parents' experiences with services, and indeed set an example of what was to follow, a brief account is included here.

A variety of both health units and of staff in these units were involved in the Down's child's birth and the post-natal period. The child was sometimes born at home or, more usually, especially since mothers were often older than average, in hospital. From there the child was sometimes transferred to another hospital or sent home, to be followed up by the general practitioner or at clinics. Clinics were sometimes attached to the general practice, or run by the local health authority, or attached to the specialist hospital. Even within these various units the staff whom the parents met were not always the same, and in a series of visits a parent could meet several different doctors. Possibly because of this assortment of units and the numbers of staff who could become involved, parents were told about their children in a variety of ways.

Table 8.1 shows that most mothers were told about their child in the first few months of his life. It is clear, however, that many professionals cannot have shared information with parents as soon as possible.

Table 8.1 *When mothers were told their children had Down's syndrome (% in brackets)*

	Original sample	New sample[a]	Total
Under 10 days	12 (32)	5 (31)	17 (32)
11 days to under 3 months	13 (35)	5 (31)	18 (34)
3 to 12 months	8 (22)	5 (31)	13 (25)
Over 12 months	4 (11)	1 (6)	5 (9)
Total	37 (100)	16 (99)	53 (100)

[a] Information for three mothers not available.

Table 8.2 summarises how mothers were told about their children.

Table 8.2 *How mothers discovered their children had Down's syndrome (% in brackets)*

Circumstances	Original sample	New sample[a]	Total
Maternity hospital/specialist/general practitioner involved in the birth	10 (27)	7 (44)	17 (32)
Specialist/general practitioner called parents to see him	5 (14)	2 (13)	7 (13)
During treatment	5 (14)	3 (19)	8 (15)
Routine visit to doctor	2 (5)	1 (6)	3 (6)
Parents guessed and asked	6 (16)	2 (13)	8 (15)
Saw own records	3 (8)	–	3 (6)
Not told accurately	6 (16)	1 (6)	7 (13)
Total	37 (100)	16 (101)	53 (100)

[a] Information not available for three mothers.

In 17 cases the mother was approached and told by staff in the maternity hospital (often by a visiting specialist), by the general practitioner involved in the birth, or by a specialist, that something was wrong. Usually this happened within a few days of the birth, although in five cases there were journeys to and from a children's hospital before a diagnosis was given.

In seven more cases the general practitioner or specialist asked one or both of the parents to call to see him, or, in one case, the GP called on the mother within 48 hours of her discharge from hospital. Generally this occurred a little later (from 10 days to 6 months).

There were eight cases in which children needed treatment of some sort and in each of these mothers were told during this period. In six cases this was done by the specialist and in two cases by the general practitioner.

Three parents learned through routine visits to the doctor. It is not clear when these parents would have found out if the routine visit had not been made.

In eight cases parents guessed something was wrong before anything was said and insisted on explanations. There were more mothers who suspected something was wrong, but not all asked about it. Their guesses were not always the result of the child's appearance or behaviour. A slight word or glance from hospital staff was sometimes enough to alert mothers, and this could happen even in the delivery room. Obviously these mothers could not rest until they learned the truth. When fears were not dealt with speedily or were successfully allayed, mothers were generally critical. When a mother suspects very early, even the most efficient hospitals with a well-thought-out policy are put at a disadvantage.

Three mothers found out by looking at their own records in hospitals and clinics.

Seven mothers could be said not to have been told the child was a Down's syndrome child although, in some cases, they were told 'something' was wrong. In one case the father was told after two days but was advised not to tell his wife – 'she would find out for herself'. In fact, she was told after one year by a specialist who said that the child would be 'slow'. Two parents were told the child would be 'slow', but not what was wrong, and the implication seemed to be that eventually he would be like other children. Another baby was sent for blood tests at 6 months but the parents knew nothing of the results and, no doubt because the child was reasonably competent, enquired no further.

Details of how and what some of the uninformed parents were told are given here since it seems curious both that information of this nature should be withheld and that parents could live with their child and not realise the situation themselves:

> F: She used to take him back [to hospital], see, and then we got to know like – kind of gradual then, see. [How did they tell you?] Well, they didn't turn round and . . . well, they didn't tell you at first like, you know . . . our own doctor used to say 'He'll be backward, but in time, he'll come – in time.' He's about 2 or 3 years behind the ordinary child, see . . . and we knew then, I suppose, by putting a bit here and a bit there, see, we were putting it together like, see . . . We knew before a twelve-month that he wasn't an ordinary child.   (1972)

These parents thought the child was spastic because the specialist kept looking at the child's hands.

Another mother had been told at 6 months that the child would 'come in a year's time'.

One parent was not told anything at all, and two others were only told officially when they asked themselves after 2½ years:

> Nobody mentioned nothing to us he was different from any other child. My own doctor told me nothing. I wasn't told nothing till I came to L, but of course there was no need for them to tell me – I knew. But the health visitor that used to call on me said [at 4 years] 'Oh, there's a little mongol like Raymond up in C.' and that was the first word anybody had told me he was mongol and it hurt me, though I knew he was.   (1972)

> It was in a cafe actually – somebody who'd had a child herself . . . the woman said, 'Don't worry, I had a little girl like yours but your child is beautiful compared with mine – she died when she was 13' – and of course it was such a shock. I'd never suspected anything was wrong . . . I just got up and walked out and I couldn't take it in at the time what was the matter, you know. My mother said, 'Oh, don't listen to her, she must be a crank or something, you meet these people in towns', you know. But of course it was in my mind when I came home and I got my husband to take me to the doctor's that night and he said, 'Yes', she was a mongol, and I said 'Why didn't you tell me?' and he said 'It isn't the thing to tell, we don't normally tell parents.' Well, she was 2½ then, you can imagine the shock.   (1972)

> Well, I thought there was something wrong . . . a couple of months after he was born because he was slow doing things like, but I never really found out 'til he was 2½ years old. They knew he was a mongol when he was born because the midwife who delivered him told me – later on like – 'We knew but we didn't tell you because we thought it might upset you.' It upset me more knowing at 2½ than it would have then . . . I went to my own doctor and he said 'He's a bit slow picking up' – you know . . . and that's what they all pointed out . . . you know . . . just let it go. I even went to the clinic – 'Oh, he's a bit slow, he'll pick up.' Well, I got fed up of that and went down to the hospital and saw the specialist and I didn't have to ask

him. He took one look at him and said 'Oh yes, I know what you've come to ask me: yes, he's a mongol baby' . . . he was the only one who was definite, you know – who would tell me. I think they all knew but they just wouldn't tell me. (1972)

It was in the rural, Welsh-speaking areas where parents were least likely to be told officially. In contrast, in the capital city parents were usually told early. It should be said that the fact parents were not told was not necessarily a careless policy in these matters. The policy in the rural areas seemed to be *not* to tell the parents and it must be said that several parents saw nothing wrong with this and seemed to imply that a bald statement would have been tactless: 'They didn't turn round and [say] . . . '; 'It hurt me to hear the word though I knew that he was'.

There were others who were easily persuaded that delay was for the best: 'You get annoyed really but, if I'd known in the beginning, I wouldn't have done the things I did, you know – he was toilet trained at 5 months,' said one mother. And another:

I asked the paediatrician to tell me and he did . . . well, I felt cross at the time [that they hadn't told me] but when they explained they *had* to see how mothers cope – well, perhaps they do because they say some reject them on sight and that's the end of it, they don't bother with it at all. Well they weren't to know I wouldn't do that, I suppose. (1981)

Since policy nowadays clearly is to tell parents about their child, these comments are of interest. In fact, not to tell parents was perhaps a sensitive response to meet the needs of an area and, excluding those who saw their notes, only one parent in a secretive area thought she had grounds for complaint. On the other hand, while some parents who were not told felt they should have been, no one who *had* been told said the news should have been withheld.

Spontaneous criticism was expressed by 18 (34%) mothers about other things that happened when their child was born. In the one or two cases where parents had made formal complaints hospitals were very ready to apologise and, it is to be hoped, improve procedures.

Seven mothers criticised the way in which they were told. They felt a lack of interest, concern or sympathy on the part of the staff involved:

The doctor followed my husband and sister-in-law down the corridor and told him behind his back . . . he just followed him down and said 'Your child is a mongol' and my husband said 'Well, if you're talking to me I'd like you to tell me to my face and in an office, not in the corridors' . . . the doctor just walked off and left them standing in the corridor. (1972)

One mother was told during a routine ward round and was offered no further explanations:

Nobody offered even to draw the curtains round my bed and let me have a good cry. I was left in the ward, nobody mentioned it again. I felt that they could at least have let me have some time on my own, or somebody come and talk . . . there was one person on the ward and she said, 'Well, let's go down to the bathrooms and have a good cry and get it out of your system' . . . which I did. But this was another *patient*, you know – it wasn't a nurse. (1972)

This contrasts with another hospital where one of the doctors sat with a mother all night.

For seven couples the main criticisms centred around delays in having their fears confirmed, or initial denials that anything was wrong. One woman had to wait two days before the paediatrician saw the baby:

I went into the nursery while he was examining him and he just – he didn't look at me – he was just walking out – he wasn't going to tell me. I just stopped him, 'Well, is he or isn't he?' and he said, 'Well, it looks as if he is' . . . I suppose it upsets them to tell the mother, you see, but why don't they say? (1972)

Of the mothers who saw their own notes two expressed dissatisfaction. One mother had taken the baby to the routine baby clinic:

> I went in to the lady doctor and I said, 'What's wrong with the baby?' 'What do you mean, what's wrong?' she replied. I said I'd looked at the paper. 'Naughty girl', she told me. She said to cross my bridges when I came to them. She didn't explain much.   (1972)

These parents were in no doubt that they should have been told as soon as a question about the child arose. As one father said:

> When a woman is pregnant there's 40 weeks of safety valve growing inside you, whether you know it or not, isn't it and if at the end of the 40 weeks there is something wrong, well, fair enough, that valve has built itself up and you can accept that better. But then, after you think everything is all right, then they tell you it's not – it's a real body blow then, isn't it?   (1972)

Two of the mothers who had not been told felt that they should have been informed.

With the increasing emphasis on community care and community services it is perhaps worth while to mention the role of the general practitioner. Where the general practitioner was involved there was often great consideration shown towards parents and no time or trouble seemed to have been spared:

> I couldn't see anything wrong with her at all – a little girl, you see, it was lovely, and then the doctor came after about 4 days and he told me about some friends he's got down in North Wales and they've got a little mongol boy, and how they took him to dances and everything and I thought – well – fancy you telling me all this, what's it got to do with me . . . it was the farthest thing from my mind, you see – it was so funny. Well, I felt so happy, everything in the garden was rosy, you know. I had this little girl, and then the doctor told me about her being a mongol child, and I said 'You're a liar' – Oh dear, fancy telling a doctor that.   (1972)

> My own doctor came up to tell me. The baby was still in hospital. She was very, very nice. It took her about one-and-a-half hours to tell me. She said she didn't know what she'd have done if it had been a little girl . . . but she's been wonderful since the time he was born.   (1972)

In the case of one 18-year-old mother living in a small village, the general practitioner told the girl's own mother first so that she could break the news. This was presumably because the father was scarcely older than his wife. In fact, the young mother had already guessed.

It seemed that parents had high expectations of their general practitioners and they were usually not disappointed. Where general practitioners fell short of expectations the parents were not slow to criticise: 'Mind you, I do blame our own family doctor. I think he should have told us . . . Oh, he *did* know – *yes*, of course he knew.'

From what parents said it seemed that they were angered most when questions and doubts were pushed to one side or when the issue was treated as if it were trivial. There was an implied, though not explicit, feeling that this was so when they were told by 'a young gynaecologist' or a 'doctor on the ward'. In this context the paediatrician in his role as 'specialist' or 'expert' and the general practitioner in his role of 'family friend' made mothers feel they had been treated with due consideration.

Genetic advice given to parents

One important area where parents of Down's syndrome children need advice is on the likelihood of having another Down's baby. This is especially important for younger mothers, both because they are more likely to have additional children and because the risk that an inherited factor is involved is greater. For mothers with this risk there is a 1-in-3 chance of having another child with Down's syndrome, though with spontaneous abortion the real risk is probably 1 in 5. (A low risk is taken to be 1 in 30.)

It has already been said that most mothers in this study did not actively want more children in any case, and so it could be argued that the risk was hardly important for these women. However, some parents did want more children, some went on to have them, and it seems likely (judging from mothers in the original sample who did not plan to have the Down's child) that a proportion of mothers who did not actively want children would be likely, in spite of this, to have them in later years if unaffected by the Down's syndrome issue. A further factor is that the normal children of those mothers at risk could have an increased likelihood of bearing a Down's child themselves.

Possibly because the question of additional children was unlikely to arise for many mothers, it was found that advice was not always given to them, that it was not always given effectively when it was given and was not always given to those mothers (in their twenties and thirties) who were most likely to need it.

Information was available for 34 mothers in the original sample and 17 in the new sample. Mothers were divided into five categories of which a summary is given in Table 8.3.

Table 8.3 *Genetic advice and number of additional children after the Down's syndrome birth*

	Additional children		No additional children		
	Original sample[a]	New sample[b]	Original sample[a]	New sample[b]	Total
Tests & advice	6	2	2	2	12
Tests, no results	2	–	1	–	3
No tests, advice	1	–	3	2	6
No tests, no advice	4	2	8	7	21
Sterilised	–	–	7	2	9
Total	13	4	21	13	51

[a] Three not available
[b] Two not available
Excluding 9 sterilised women, $n = 42$.
Those with additional children compared with those without; those given 'tests and advice' compared with the rest: $\chi^2 = 3.38$; df = 1; not significant (χ^2 value for $p < 0.05 = 3.84$).

Genetic advice given to mothers in the five categories

Group one. Twelve mothers were given genetic tests and advice. Eight of these mothers did go on to have more children, two initiated the tests themselves before considering a further pregnancy. Only one still felt she had to be sure of having the amniocentesis test before having more children. One of the mothers who made arrangements for genetic tests herself had been advised after the birth of her child and without having any tests, to 'put him away and forget you had him and have another child, this couldn't happen again'.

Another mother, a teenager, had been given tests and advice but she interpreted the advice as follows:

> They told me in the hospital I had a 50:50 chance I'd ever have another like him – it would be a chance in a million. [They said 50:50?] Yes, a chance in a million that we'd have another like him. I was afraid to have another but we decided to have it. (1972)

Another was told not to have more 'for a while', but it was not entirely clear whether this was for health or genetic reasons.

Group two. Three mothers in the original sample had genetic tests but no results. Two of these mothers went on to have more children. One assumed that since she had not heard anything all must be well, but in any case she felt 'it didn't matter'.

Group three. Six mothers had been given advice but had been given no tests (or so they thought) on which the advice was based. One mother was told not to risk the chance of having another baby and two mothers were told they could have an abortion if they conceived again. One mother had another child. A mother who was 35 years at time of the birth with Down's syndrome on both her mother's and father's sides of her family reported: 'The GP told me to have another one straight away. I don't know where I'd be if I had.'

Another mother (23 years at the time of the birth) said: 'The doctor said there was a thousand to one chance against it [happening again]' and one more mother was given positive encouragement to have more children; advice she did not take.

Group four. Twenty-one mothers were given no advice or tests. Six went on to have more children. One of these mothers was over 40 years at the time and had asked to be sterilised but had been refused. Another is the mother of two Down's syndrome children and her history is quoted at some length since she is clearly of interest in this context. Her eldest son (D) had Down's syndrome, her second son (E) was normal, her third daughter was Maralyn (part of this population) and her youngest son (F) was normal.

> After I had D they told me it wouldn't happen again, have another baby. So I went in the way for E and he were all right. Then I had Maralyn and I had the shock of my life. And then we tried for F because they had the test out – but it wasn't, it was the test for German Measles, so the doctor left it up to me then to decide if I wanted an abortion or not – I asked him about it because I wanted company for E, see, and he said 'No, it's only if you've had contact with German measles'. Well, I was going on 3 months and so he said 'You'll have to make your mind up quick if you want an abortion – after three months they don't like doing it.' I decided not to – I thought I'd take a chance for E. Mind, I'd never do it again . . . Oh, God, terrible . . . When I had E I was quite confident that he was going to be all right. They'd told me and, you know what it's like, I was young and they said it wouldn't happen again. Well, you believe them . . . They couldn't work out that I was so young. When I was having F they took tests from me, and my husband and the three children.   (1981)

In fact, before F was conceived this mother had considered sterilisation, as the following quotation shows:

> I nearly had a nervous breakdown . . . I couldn't go out, I couldn't manage the three of them, you know. D was just starting to walk, E was a toddler and Maralyn was in my arms . . . I had the three of them in napkins together. D and Maralyn didn't come out of napkins 'til they were 5 and I went to see about being sterilised and they didn't think I ought to be done – they didn't think, because I was young – 24 – Well, Dr N said yes I should be, but whatever happened I don't know . . . I kept 'phoning and 'phoning – they'd lost all my files [from the maternity hospital]. Well, anyway, I thought 'Oh, bugger' and I went on the Pill. I was on the Pill for 6 years then I felt pains in my legs . . . and I had a coil fitted.   (1981)

Group five. Nine mothers were sterilised after the birth of the child. (Two were sterilised *after* having additional children and so are included in the other section.) One of the mothers (45 years at the birth) was offered tests 'to see which side she came from' but her husband 'wasn't willing' since 'there was no point in it'. Another was sterilised straight after the birth and before she knew about the child. She was advised not to be sterilised. With hindsight she felt the advice was given in case the Down's syndrome child did not survive.

The most important question, since not all were receiving advice, is how far advice was going to those who needed it. Table 8.3 shows that the relationship between those who had adequate advice and those who had more children just falls short of significance.

Seventeen mothers had more children. Almost half of the mothers could be said to have had adequate advice (although this includes the mother who interpreted her chances as a 'chance in a million'), but 9 of the 17 mothers could be said not to have had adequate advice. This means that 9 out of 30 (30%) mothers who did not have adequate advice had gone on to have more children: 14 additional children were born to these women.

The mothers considered above were those who had run an actual, rather than

Table 8.4 *Genetic advice and age of mothers at Down's birth (% in brackets)*

Age of mother	Under 29	30–39	40 +	Total
Tests and advice	6 (50)	6 (50)	–	12 (100)
Tests, no results	2 (66)	1 (33)	–	3 (99)
Advice, no tests	2 (33)	3 (50)	1 (17)	6 (100)
No tests, no advice	6 (30)	6 (30)	8 (40)	20 (100)
Sterilised	1 (11)	3 (33)	5 (56)	9 (100)
Total	17 (34)	19 (38)	14 (28)	50 (100)

Excluding one mother, age not known, 3 from original sample and 2 from new sample.

potential, risk. Table 8.4 shows the age of those who had advice. The question is, were the younger mothers (that is, those more likely to have yet more children) those who were receiving advice and could the small percentage having proper advice be accounted for by the fact that older mothers were considered by professionals to be unlikely to need it?

The younger mothers were those who had advice and tests rather than the older mothers, but there was still a substantial proportion of mothers under 40 years who were not having adequate advice (56%). All the genetic counselling done was directed to the younger mothers.

It should be said that although women over 40 were unlikely to be having more children (although one mother, in spite of making a request to be sterilised, went on to have two more) and were less likely to be affected genetically, a mother's plight, had she had another Down's child at that age, would possibly have been more critical than that of a younger mother. In any case, judging a woman's family planning intentions by her age is, obviously, likely to lead to error.

Amniocentesis

Only two mothers in the sample had amniocentesis tests on subsequent babies. Four siblings, or their wives, had this test when they became pregnant, although one who requested it was told it was 'not necessary'. Only one mother said she would have considered adding to her family had she known of the test.

OTHER EARLY SERVICES

Advice given to parents about Down's syndrome

When parents were told about the child they were not usually given a great deal of advice at the same time. Many would agree with the mother who said 'I don't think anyone was interested, quite frankly.' They were often told – usually by the paediatrician – the child would be 'slow' or 'backward', that he would walk and talk eventually, and that his life span would be short (usually the age given was in the twenties but sometimes it was younger). Sometimes the advice was more pessimistic and parents were told 'He'll never walk or talk,' and several parents were delighted when the child did both.

Understandably, a great deal of advice would not have been appropriate when parents were first told they had a Down's syndrome child. It is of interest to see, however, how far the advice was supplemented afterwards. It seems from what parents said in 1972 that no one had an embarrassment of advice or help, and, in fact, for many the reverse was true:

No, I was surprised at it when he was born. Being as he is I thought I'd have people knocking on the door all about what to do with him and how to care for him and all that, and nobody came and I thought it looks like we've got to get on with it . . . When we saw they weren't coming . . . well, we just done what we could then.   (1972)

Well, I got over the shock and I was left to carry on as best as I could.   (1972)

Nothing, no. No help, no nothing, no. Just that was that and – you know . . . I did feel at one time I was taking her to the clinic and not getting anywhere . . . We're all paying enough tax and insurance and [to put her in a home] would cost more – and yet there was no help to keep her myself . . . they just don't seem to be interested in this type of child.   (1972)

Parents suspected that there were no answers given in some cases because the answers were sometimes known neither by the professionals nor anyone else. Though mothers were pleased to be told they were doing well and should carry on as if the child were normal this did not always answer their questions adequately. As one mother said: 'The more I know about it, the more I know how little he knew about it.'

Sometimes parents were given conflicting advice when attitudes on a subject changed: 'The Social Worker said no, not to let her out. She said J. [a handicapped child nearby] was let out too much. Now she's changed her mind.' On questions such as these there is no 'right' answer and such decisions were left very much to the parents. Those who had sought advice themselves and received it sometimes felt it was not sufficiently encouraging, was inaccurate, or would have been better left unsaid:

I told him [Medical Officer] about [hitting his sister], what could we do? 'How old is she?' 'Ten'. 'Oh, she can take it' he said to me. Well! I said we were interested in these Trust villages. 'Well, you know,' he said, 'you can't make a silk purse out of a sow's ear.' So I thought, 'Well, I don't want to see *you* again.' It's surprising what you have to put up with.   (1972)

I found before that I was taking her to clinics and she was given tests that really – you might just as well have put her in a corner and forgotten about her – no question of her coming to do anything – she was only then – well, you know – I think it was a question of there's no hope so don't bother . . . I sent away for the book issued by NAMHC and I was no wiser after reading it – in fact, it depressed me more than helped me . . . it was a very bleak outlook . . . they didn't suggest any *degrees* of handicap – it was a bad case and that was it.   (1972)

The attitudes of professionals were commonly criticised. One mother felt she was treated as if she herself were mentally handicapped. Another said people were only prepared to talk to her in detail when they realised she knew something about the subject.

Only one mother felt authority was rather too much involved with her child over schooling:

I want permission [in fact she wanted money as well] to do what I want to do with her instead of them telling me what they think I ought to do. It's our decision and we should be allowed to make it and not have to get on our bended knees and say, please give us permission.   (1972)

In babyhood parents largely turned to medical staff – usually at the routine paediatric clinics. A few had contact with other professionals. Three mothers in one area, for instance, spoke of helpful contacts with a mental welfare officer.

Only a very few mothers felt they were able to obtain advice themselves if they needed it and so did not need it thrust at them. Most parents would have liked more advice particularly on the progress that could be expected of the child, on his upbringing and how to encourage his development. The type of parents' workshops and home teaching that is more commonly offered nowadays would, without doubt, have been popular. This very specific advice was exactly what parents lacked. Most could almost certainly have been able to appreciate more sophisticated advice and consequently they were simply irritated by the general statements they were offered.

SUMMARY

Early services for parents in the 1960s were very variable. Undoubtedly there were parents who were told early and sensitively about their baby's condition and who received prompt, accurate and intelligible genetic counselling, but those who received all these services were in the minority. While the quality of the service that broke the news largely depended on area – those in bigger hospitals receiving a more standard and less idiosyncratic approach than in rural areas – the quality of genetic counselling depended to a greater degree on need. Although not all who needed advice received it, there was some evidence that advice was focused (in a rough and ready way) on the mothers most at risk of having more children. Advice on risks for siblings and other family members was non-existent.

Early advice was poor for everybody. It was either not available at all or was unduly pessimistic, vague, general or conflicting. There was no one universal or automatic source of advice for parents.

9 Later Help for Families

A somewhat grim picture of early services for families with a Down's syndrome child in the 1960s emerges from Chapter 8. Despite the fact that there were examples of good – even excellent – practice, satisfactory overall help reached a minority of families. Services for Down's syndrome babies have certainly improved in South Wales (see Appendix 2) but this does not help parents with Down's teenagers. This Chapter examines how far the very early services were later supplemented for the population, and how far better help reached more families. Chapter 10 will consider how far the call for financial helpthat was being made generally in the 1960s – and echoed by parents in this population in 1972 – was answered by the new provisions made in the 1970s.

SERVICES PROVIDED TO FAMILIES

Professional contacts

The families' earliest, and most intensive, contact was with professionals in the health service. For some families this was widened later as the following accounts show. The chief characteristic of professional contact for these parents was its idiosyncratic nature: there was variation in who visited them, the frequency of such contact and the content of such encounters.

Professionals who visited homes

A variety of professional workers visited families at home. Significantly, and illustrative of the lack of planning and clear responsibility for mentally handicapped children, there was no one professional who could be relied upon to have visited all families.

Health visitors, who could be expected to maintain regular contact with families, did not figure largely in mothers' accounts. One mother felt she had less contact with her health visitor than did families with ordinary babies.

Specialisation within social services was discontinued for a time in 1970, but, before that, three mothers in one area had helpful visits from a mental welfare officer. In another area a similar function was served by a home visitor attached to the local ESN(S) school. It is not clear whether she was a health-care professional or a social worker.

One head teacher of an ESN(S) school made home visits herself – even visiting those who were on the waiting list for her school. She did not confine her help to educational matters but advised on allowances and other services.

In the late 1970s social services departments began to specialise again. In 1981 30

(57%) families had some existing contact with a professional who was probably a social worker; five had had some contact in the past. What help did they offer families?

Pre-Seebohm much social work was case-work orientated. Practical help for families with handicapped children was, in any case, severely limited and Younghusband *et al.* (1970), reporting parents' views, firmly stated that families wanted practical help more than they did counselling. Social workers seem to have responded to this and most family contact in this study was of an intensely practical nature. Indeed, the increased contact that families encountered largely resulted from the increase in short-term care facilities that social workers tended to arrange. This contact did not usually result in any substantially increased involvement in other spheres (or so it seemed to parents) and it must be asked how far social workers, at a time when there was little choice about facilities, should be used for this low-level, intermediary and administrative function. (Increased choice about alternatives – such as family placement schemes – could justify the involvement.)

Other more important tasks were sometimes performed. Social workers helped with information about, and with claiming, benefits, or provided access to other services. One arranged school transport, another mediated in a family quarrel and yet another gave lifts to a mother to visit her daughter in residential care. One social worker, apparently unexpectedly, visited a mother once, dispensed blankets, left and was never seen again. Another most importantly, and with great success, persuaded a mother that her health had deteriorated to the stage when she should relinquish the full-time care of her daughter. Had visits not been made to arrange short-term care this family could have deteriorated into further crisis and the chance of successful intervention would have been missed. Even so, breaking point had almost been reached. Again, a social worker, following much careful work, persuaded a mother to send her child to school after many years of absence. Unfortunately other services could not adapt to needs: the provision of weekly rather than daily transport meant that allowances were lost and the child's school attendance once again lapsed.

Mothers did not speak of the contact they had with social workers as vitally necessary to them, although the service offered by some was clearly important. The mother of two Down's syndrome children, who must have had substantial needs, said: 'I can honestly say I've never had a bit of help off any social worker'.

The emphasis on practical help seemed to be welcomed by parents, who complained when it was lacking. One father said social services departments, since they had records, should automatically inform parents of changes in benefit when children reached 16 years. In 1981 only one mother said she would have welcomed visits as a chance for a chat and moral support and she regretted the fact that, if she did not telephone, she was not visited. This was an unemployed single mother, of low social class and with a severely disabled child and it might have been expected that she would be picked out for help. Clearly she was not. Evidence from this study, would suggest that – especially in the early years – some form of counselling would have been helpful for a proportion of parents, even if, in 1981, parents did not express the need.

Other problems with social workers centred around the youth and inexperience of the officers, and the fact that staff changes prevented relationships being built up. This latter point was not a problem confined to social services departments; hospitals and their staff were also at fault here. In contrast, teachers and heads did not change often and this perhaps accounts for some of the satisfaction parents felt with schools.

It was suspected that one or two families had had contact with a community mental handicap nurse. It is argued that this profession developed rapidly because of the failure of social services departments, following reorganisation in 1970, to meet the needs of families. (Hall and Russell, 1985) From a mere handful of such nurses in 1970 numbers rose to about 600 in 1983 (Sines, 1985). Since families were not always clear about the profession of their visitors any account of their input must be speculative. It seems, however, that they worked with the more severely disabled children (so the association with the mental handicap hospital did not seem inappropriate to the parents) and helped with very specific problems using a goal planning orientation.

Speech therapists

Down's children are particularly likely to be disadvantaged in language (Lyle, 1959, 1960a, 1960b) and this obviously has important implications for their relationships with others and is an important barrier to integration. Buckley (1987) points out that even if a child is understood by his family he may be unintelligible to those outside.

Mothers were concerned about speech and also felt that their own relationship with their Down's child suffered because of difficulties in communication and, consequently, it was an area where parents were anxious to see improvement. One mother described her son's language in the following way: 'He hasn't got a lot of conversation, the words he's got are necessary to him. He hasn't got any spare words.'

Another spoke of 'word-by-word' contact. The following mother said her daughter's speech had improved – for instance, it was no longer possible to have a 'secret' conversation using a complicated vocabulary – but poor language skills still presented problems:

> One of the daily things is the difficulty of dialogue – more now because she's growing up. She can't really articulate her needs – over and above only the practical things – food, etc. It's easy to tread on her emotions because there's a change happening now. You still regard her as a child because of her limitations but she's not any more, she's an adolescent – I'm having to rethink a bit on how we treat her and what to expect. Even her mode of dress, the rules we put on her – I haven't adjusted to her in adolescence and you'd like to be able to have some conversation with her, as with her sister, but it's very difficult.
>
> (1981)

These were very typical problems and, for many, lack of communication was a major worry, and not only because of the way it could make relationships lack depth. Mothers considered their children very vulnerable because they were unable to explain that they were unhappy, or that they had been ill-treated, or taken advantage of, outside the home.

For all these reasons, speech was an area where parents would have liked improvement and many felt that a speech therapist could help. Sign languages (e.g. Makaton), which schools were introducing, were not felt to be a substitute and, indeed, some viewed such moves as divisive, as likely to create more barriers with the normal population and further reduce the use of ordinary speech. There are, of course, several factors that militate against good communication skills and clear articulation, (e.g. low mental development, poor muscle tone, large tongue and hearing problems) and not all of these can be solved by speech therapy. Equally, some of the difficulties can be improved, if not remedied, by sensible home training such as extending the vocabulary, encouraging the use of longer sentences and discouraging 'showing' rather than 'asking'. In fact some parents benefited from contact with a speech therapist simply through becoming aware of goals and simple methods to use themselves.

In this population only 20 children (38%) had definitely had speech therapy at some time. Of them 13 were known to have had therapy at school and possibly more parents were unaware of therapy their children had at school. Seven had had therapy arranged at various places outside school hours – at hospitals, clinics and at home. Two of them had only one session. Most parents had pushed for these sessions themselves and one had paid for private tuition. Three more had asked for help but been refused it. There were parents who had been discouraged from using speech therapy because their children were too good to need help ('It's only for those who are really bad') and others had been told that, where there were problems of mental retardation, improvement would be limited and so therapy was of little real help.

On the whole, parents of children who had therapy were pleased and noticed an improvement, but two found it unsatisfactory.

Psychologists

Contact with psychologists had increased for the children over the years, but even so only in 11 families had parents themselves had meetings with these professionals. Nine more knew that there had been visits at school and it is possible that more children had contact in this way. For some parents, the contact had been limited to meetings about changes of area or school. Others had more routine progress checks at school but no one spoke of any specific outcome from these checks, e.g. advice on the next stage of progress, or programmes to be tackled at home. Two mothers did have more concrete help in the home: one with toilet training and the other with moving a boy out of the parental bedroom into his own room, but it is not known for certain that the professionals involved were psychologists.

One psychologist had regular meetings with parents and seemed very ready to tackle emotional problems in the family. It was one of the few examples of intensive professional contact but a mother who received this care showed ambivalent feelings about it:

> I saw him every 3 months. Yes, it was a help – just to know things were going all right. [Did he give any advice?] No – just used to look at her and say she was looking well or – I think he was trying to get into your mind more than anything else and I'm not very good at things like that. I used to be glad to get away. I don't know why. He was very very kind – well you could tell when he looked at her and talked to her. Obviously he knew his job well ... But I used to get into such a knot answering questions.
>
> (1981)

Physiotherapy

Only four children had had physiotherapy, two of these at school.

Later advice

The generalisation that can be made about the early advice given to parents is that is was not readily accessible, was in short supply, dealt in stereotypes and was sometimes inaccurate.

By 1981 there had been a general improvement in both services and advice. One or two mothers spoke of the marked changes that had taken place in some areas. Two of the following speakers came from the capital city. The first lived in an area where a planned expansion of community services was taking place.

> There are so many people coming along I don't know who they are. It started in April – we've got a child psychologist and a speech therapist. They are all going to try to help Pat one way and another. It will be a good thing when it gets going. It seemed to go on for years that no one wanted to know, there was no interest in these children.
>
> (1981)

> I wish we'd had more help when Pete was younger – from social services. I seem to be getting more help now than ever. Now he can do a bit more for himself I don't really *need* all they're offering. I wanted special taps and things for the bath – I couldn't get them. Now they're falling over me with the apparatus, and I wanted a special buggy, but I had to fight. I got it but, oh, I had to fight and fight.
>
> (1981)

Some parents spoke of specific problems that had received attention – sexual problems, self-care and behaviour problems. Only two mothers spoke of having had 'very good' advice and help – both, significantly, had had practical help and advice on a specific problem. In spite of these comments, however, there was not universal satisfaction. The subjective opinion of 21 mothers (40%) was that they had had some advice, but another 30 (57%) still considered they had had none at all. There was a felt need in some quarters for more guidance and information. One father gave a vitriolic attack on the guidance he had received over the years.

> Everybody falls down. The family falls down, the education system falls down and the social services are the main cause of complaint. They should know about it and they should inform us. Nobody can know everything but there are people getting paid by the government who are supposed to know these things and it's their job to come to tell us when we're making mistakes. But they're afraid to do so and the mistakes then are discovered by me too late. [What sort of mistakes?] Well, my boy should be able to cross the road, he should be able to go next door and fetch a pound of butter. But the blame has got to be put – you don't blame this mother or that mother because these mothers don't know that there are people paid by government and it's *their* job and the failure of these people has meant some deficiency in [my son's] life . . . Look at all the disabled children being deprived of a better life because *we* don't know at 3 he should have done such and such a thing. At 5 he could have done better. He could have crossed the road now and had a better life, but you know, we didn't know, we didn't think it was possible . . . so she [mother] mothered him like a little baby till he was about 12 and we suddenly started to realise what my boy was missing. Mothering of children is natural, isn't it – especially with children like him who are loving and attentive, he's mother's boy. But the thing is when I went over and saw these other children and I realised I should have been told I was wrong . . . and you can't make up years in a boy like him. What you've lost you can never make up with them.   (1981)

The father was clearly making a plea for unsolicited advice and this perhaps is not always forthcoming. One mother remarked that the paediatrician preferred to be asked rather than volunteer information – but it is difficult to ask about a problem one does not recognise. It is impossible to ask for details about an allowance unless its existence is known. There were other predictable crises that were ignored. For example, one woman who had taken over the care of her Down's syndrome sister had expected to have advice given and interest shown or, at the most negative, some element of supervision, but none was forthcoming. Other mothers, especially if the child was not progressing well, would have welcomed confirmation that they were doing all they could.

Parents still lacked one obvious and available source of assistance. Advice was available from various quarters and its quality depended on the individual skills of the worker.

> We're looking at all the possibilities [for after school] but there's not a lot of advice for people – you don't know where to go. I suppose you've heard that before.   (1981)

There was also objective evidence of lack of advice. Not all who should have received allowances knew of them and there were, generally, services or rights about which parents were ignorant.

Advice was most lacking where there was no obvious service available to meet a need. In the early days, given the pessimistic outlook on what Down's syndrome children could achieve, there was probably little that professionals felt able to say to help. When there was no choice of schools, when there was little choice of employment, there was little discussion. Parents in these circumstances were possibly left on their own more because professionals understandably hesitated to interfere with parental choice when they had little confidence that they had a good alternative to offer.

Numbers are very small and so a table is not included, but advice did seem to be related to area to some extent. At the extremes, 85% of parents in one local authority area claimed to have had no advice compared with only 33% in another area who felt that this was the case.

Short-term care

Whether or not, and how often, parents took advantage of offers of short-term care for their children depended on the availability and acceptability of the provision, how far the children were considered able to adapt and enjoy a stay away from home and how important it was considered for the parents to have some relief from caring for the child. Table 9.1 shows how many children had experienced short-term care in 1972 and 1981.

Table 9.1 *Offers and acceptance of short-term care 1972 and 1981 (% in brackets)*

	Original sample (1972)		Original sample (1981)		New sample (1981)		Total population (1981)	
Accepted	14 (38)	19 (51)	26 (77)	29 (86)	4 (21)	10 (53)	30 (57)	39 (74)
Not offered – would accept	5 (14)		3 (9)		6 (32)		9 (17)	
Refused	2 (5)	18 (49)	3 (9)	5 (14)	5 (26)	9 (47)	8 (15)	14 (26)
Not offered would refuse	16 (43)		2 (5)		4 (21)		6 (11)	
Total	37	(100)	34	(100)	19	(100)	53	(100)

In 1972 there was less short-term care available for children although, even so, 14 (38%) children had already experienced some form of care away from home. Provision was mainly in local authority hostels attached to schools and in a charity holiday home in the area. For two families the local authority hostel was taking over a good deal of the term-time care of the child. Two children had been in mental handicap hospitals for brief spells when family circumstances had made care essential.

Attitudes of mothers to short-term care in 1972 ranged widely. There were those who considered these 'holidays' essential so that they could have a rest from the child, and those who would not have considered short-term care for their normal young children and so would not for their handicapped child either. Others would perhaps have considered care if it were presented in the form of a treat or holiday for the child but not if it were suggested as a break for themselves. Some parents, who did not like the idea of sending the child away, had been forced to accept care when they had had to go into hospital themselves. This could cause great resentment when no one in the family would have the child. In other words, by some it was considered to be a 'last resort'.

Not all parents who had accepted short-term care in 1972 would repeat it. One mother said the rest for her was not worth it because he was such a 'naughty boy' when he came back. Another had a very upsetting experience when her own ill-health forced her to accept care when the child was three-and-a-half. She had wanted daily care for the child:

> They kept him in for one week and they advised me not to see him. When my husband and mother went to fetch him he was crying and absolutely changed – he was whimpering on the floor of the car. He was in a terrible state and of course I said 'He's not going back there.' There was such a change in him from then on. He was frightened of the dark and frightened of cupboards in particular. (1972)

This child was then given a much gentler introduction and gradually was able to be left for longer periods.

By 1981, not only were more facilities available, both in the range of what there was and the number of places on offer, but parents themselves were more inclined to feel their children could cope with leaving them, or indeed could benefit from it. Thirty (57%) teenagers had been away at some point in their lives but 13 of these did not go away until after 10 years of age and six of these not until 14 or 15 years old. The average age at which children took their first stay away from home without parents was 9.1

years. By 1981 seven of the teenagers were having regular care up to four or five times a year and one of these was away 15 weekends a year. For the other 23 teenagers the average number of stays away from home was 3.7 a year. Table 9.1 shows the increase in take up over the years.

The type of provision being used in 1981 varied. Hostels attached to the schools were very popular for weekend stays and one country school had a cottage where pupils could go and stay. The charity holiday home continued to be available and was much appreciated. One severely retarded boy stayed frequently at a mental handicap hospital nearby, but two other families, who had had experience of the hospital before reforms had been undertaken, had been dissatisfied with this and one father had withdrawn his child instantly when he saw the bare ward containing 30 children left to do pretty much as they pleased. The other parents had complained that their incontinent daughter had been left without knickers. Three local authority areas had had new short-term hostel accommodation built since 1972. One was too new to assess, but one of the others was felt to have too restrictive a regime and was considered to be more suitable for younger or more severely retarded children. Short-term care was sometimes liable to be rejected by parents if it was felt the facility was intended primarily for the more severely retarded (especially if their own child was more able), or if it was felt to be intended primarily for the socially disadvantaged. Both of these considerations were disincentives for parents of those attending ESN(M) schools.

Some mothers expressed a fear that after their children reached 16 years provision would be reduced, although one mother, who at the time had to pay for care from her daughter's non-contributory invalidity pension, felt that the reverse would be true. One mother, regardless of the issue of age, felt that cutbacks in services had already affected provision in the area.

Table 9.2 *Sex of teenagers who had experienced short-term care 1981 (% in brackets)*

Short-term care	Boys	Girls	Total
Taken	21 (70)	9 (30)	30 (100)
Not taken	7 (30)	16 (70)	23 (100)
Total	28 (53)	25 (47)	53 (100)

$\chi^2 = 6.67$; df = 1; p < 0.01

Turning to those who had taken up offers, the majority of boys had been away whereas it was a minority of girls who had had care (Table 9.2). This was probably because of the higher abilities of the girls, rather than because the parents were less willing to send girls away. Table 9.3 shows the relationship between offers and acceptance and the Gunzburg scores of the teenagers.

Table 9.3 *Teenagers who had taken short-term care and Gunzburg PAC scores, 1981*

Short-term care	Number of teenagers	Average Gunzburg score
Accepted	30	50.6
Refused	8	72.6
Not offered	15	77.9
Total	53	61.6

It seems that those with the more severely retarded children were having the greatest help with short-term care although it was not invariably these children who presented most problems. Fewer children at ESN(M) schools had offers of places than those at ESN(S) schools. Although some mothers who had not received formal offers of care made it clear they knew they could have had it ('I could have made enquiries – I heard of others going, but she wouldn't like it') at least one mother did not know how to set about it: 'We don't know how to approach these things, what to do, who to ask'.

The paramount consideration for most parents was not the freedom which a holiday for their teenagers gave to them, but whether or not the teenager himself enjoyed going away. Those who did not enjoy it were not sent again and two children were brought home early from unsatisfactory holidays.

Future plans

Table 9.4 shows parents' expectations or wishes about future care for their children in 1972 and 1981.

Table 9.4 *Future-care plans 1972 and 1981 (% in brackets)*

	Original sample		New sample	Total population
	(1972)	(1981)	(1981)	(1981)
Residential care ⎫		15 (44)	5 (26)	20 (38)
Farm ⎬	15 (41)	–	3 (16)	3 (6)
Hospital ⎭		1 (3)	–	1 (2)
Siblings or family	13 (35)	12 (35)	7 (37)	19 (36)
Don't know	9 (24)	6 (18)	4 (21)	10 (19)
Total	37 (100)	34 (100)	19 (100)	53 (101)

In 1972 most parents felt their children would need some form of protected environment when they grew older. This was a major worry for parents. Fifteen (41%) felt they had no alternative but to consider residential care because they did not think any of their own family would take the child. They were not complacent about the care given in 'homes' and it was seen very much as a last resort.

> Look how many cruelties there are in the homes . . . Well, that's it all over – who wants to look after the mentally handicapped? There's *no one* – I can say sincerely, willing to look after mentally handicapped children – not that I've come across. No one would say to me now – not even my sisters, not even my brothers – if anything happened to you, we'd look after Megan. They don't want the responsibility . . . and *why should they*? (1972)

Only four mothers, three of them from social classes I and II, had made enquiries or thought seriously about care away from home while the child was still young, although more had thought about it straight after the birth. Generally, thoughts turned to schooling rather than to permanent care in a mental handicap hospital:

> At first I said no, I don't think I could, but I look at it this way – people send their normal children away to boarding school and they just come home for holidays – if one can look at it that way it becomes acceptable. (1972)

This was perhaps why mothers in social classes I and II were more likely to consider the idea. In social classes IV and V homes the reaction was firmly against it, perhaps because in some of these homes (two in the original sample) taking children 'into care' was not unknown. Children were 'taken away' not 'sent away' by parents.

Where parents had wanted a full-time place immediately after the birth there was some suggestion that those responsible for finding a place would do all they could to deter parents. One mother asked for a place because of her own ill health. She was advised to have the child home for 6 months 'and then see how you are'. By the time the 6 months was over, this mother said, 'I was too ill to go'. Another mother thought she had been offered a place at the school hostel if she agreed to take the child's name off the waiting list for full-time care.

By 1981 for nine families 'the future' had already come and their teenagers were no longer living permanently at home. Two were in local full-time establishments for adults but both maintained regular contact with home. Three were in boarding schools and were at home for the half- and full-term holidays. Four were at more local residential schools and were home at weekends, although this intensity of contact was only because of the private efforts of the parents, the school having less liberal arrangements.

In all, seven of the nine teenagers who were in boarding schools or hostels were there primarily because care at home was becoming difficult for some reason: family stress (four); mother no longer at home or dead (two); mother's ill health (one). Parents who needed this help were understandably becoming apprehensive as school-leaving age drew near. The use of residential schools primarily to provide care rather than education is, of course, of interest. In one case care was only needed for a few hours a day while the father finished work.

Four boys had been away from home in the past. One had left the residential ESN(M) school (the only suitable school available) and now attended the local ATC. Another lost his place in the children's hostel when he left school and he was on the waiting list for an adult place. This was causing great problems at home and was one of the more obvious examples of inadequate service provision. Two severely disabled teenagers had been weekly boarders at school, but this was discontinued by their mothers, almost certainly because they lost allowances when their children were absent. One of them now spent all day at home. Aside from these was another boy who was due to go on to further education away from home as part of his mother's long-term strategy to settle the boy into a realistic adult lifestyle.

Table 9.4 shows the future provision being considered in 1972 and how little change there was in 1981. However, attitudes towards residential care had softened in 1981. Parents increasingly saw that acceptable provision was becoming available – albeit in short supply – and that residential care was no longer inevitably synonymous with mental handicap hospitals. The two families who had teenagers in adult hostels were delighted with the accommodation and others could see hostels that they considered to be satisfactory. In view of this, and especially since it was realised by some that expecting siblings to shoulder the responsibility was unrealistic, it is surprising that the number opting for residential care remained so stable. The fact remained however that, for most parents, residential care was still a second-best choice and very few viewed it as a goal in itself. Those who did tended to envisage accommodation and employment as linked and taking place within a sheltered community, preferably rural. Indeed, a number of parents cherished romantic notions of farms and country life as being ideal for their children. The popular modern notion of integrated housing was rarely discussed, but this was more because parents did not view this as being on offer, rather than because they rejected the principle.

Table 9.5 *Parental expectations about siblings' involvement in future care, 1972 and 1981 (% in brackets)*

	Original sample		New sample (1981)	Total population (1981)
	(1972)[a]	(1981)		
Hope siblings will take child	13 (48)	13 (42)	10 (56)	23 (47)
Siblings will not take child	14 (52)	15 (48)	7 (39)	22 (45)
Don't know	–	3 (10)	1 (6)	4 (8)
Total	27 (100)	31 (100)	18 (101)	49 (100)

[a] Seven mothers omitted.

Four mothers remained profoundly pessimistic about residential care and hoped their child would die before such services were needed. No doubt improved provisions would have encouraged them to revise their opinions.

Five mothers had more optimistic views of their teenagers' capabilities and their needs in the future. Three looked for further improvements that would mean only minimal supervision would be needed. Two felt that their Down's syndrome offspring would be able to stay at home and indeed, by acting under instruction, would be able to help them when they themselves were physically less active. As one said, 'She'll look after us.'

As before, carers were asked in 1981 if they would expect siblings to take care of the Down's syndrome adult (see Table 9.5).

In both 1972 and 1981 expectations about whether siblings would (or should) take responsibility for their mentally handicapped brother or sister was related to social class (see Table 9.6).

Table 9.6 *Siblings' involvement and social class 1981 (% in brackets)*

Social classes	Expect sibs to take Down's child	Not expect sibs to take Down's child	Don't know	Total
I and II	2 (18)	9 (82)	–	11
III	13 (50)	10 (39)	3 (12)	26
IV and V	8 (67)	3 (25)	1 (8)	12
Total	23 (47)	22 (45)	4 (8)	49

Excluding those with no siblings
Excluding 'don't knows': $\chi^2 = 7.05$; df = 2; p < 0.05.

This relationship possibly reflects the fact that those in higher social classes were likely to find caring for a mentally handicapped person more damaging to their way of life and so were less likely to think it fair to impose this sort of restriction on their other children. Not only this, but they were more likely to be in a position to make satisfactory alternative arrangements. When rejecting the idea of immediate residential care those in social classes I and II tended to add 'as long as her sister doesn't suffer' or that residential care would be considered 'if the family was suffering'. No one brought up the alternative (that has been discussed in Jaehnig, 1975) – that to exclude an unsatisfactory family member could make the siblings feel they, too, could be pushed out if they were deviant.

Three sisters were already taking over a good deal of the care of their disabled brothers and sisters and so expecting siblings to take over is not perhaps unreasonable. A minority of parents seemed unrealistic and had high expectations of siblings who had, to date, shown little interest in or concern about their handicapped brother or sister. In other cases parents felt that it was the siblings who were unrealistic in that they made extravagant offers but had little understanding of the difficulties they would encounter. As one father put it, not many would tolerate 'a man stuck in the corner'. Very few parents seemed to *expect* their other children to take over automatically although one father felt that with six children problems could be shared and so absorbed. His wife was less confident. One mother commented, 'You need a dozen children really.' Other parents simply expressed the hope that siblings would keep in touch, watch their brothers' and sisters' interests and have them home for holidays.

In contrast with 1972 when only one mother had made positive moves towards providing for adult care and only one family had made financial arrangements, by 1981 there was some evidence of more concrete planning. Three or four wished to settle their youngsters into acceptable accommodation before a crisis forced an unsuitable and unplanned 'solution'. About a fifth of the families had begun to make financial arrangements. A common strategy was to leave the house to the Down's syndrome child or to the siblings (or in one case, nephew) who would then care for him.

Self-help and voluntary associations

When services are not available parents must do without or look to themselves to fill the gaps. Not all found that there were gaps and one mother had continued working after her child was born in case extras were needed but, by 1981, found it had not been necessary. More, however, would agree with the mother who said, 'I'm using the attendance allowance for all the things she's not having.' The help mothers mobilised themselves was mainly concerned with improving their children, rather than helping relieve the burdens on themselves. They used private speech therapy, private nurseries and investigated schools, future care and employment prospects outside the normal provisions. One mother had started a local club for the handicapped and this helped other children as well as her own son. Two mothers had hired private teachers to supplement school lessons, and another had employed students to visit her son at home and take him out. Other activities included dancing lessons, riding and guitar lessons. One mother invested much effort in fund-raising to provide a swimming pool for the ESN(S) school. Some families had become expert both at understanding what their children needed and organising the system to meet these needs. Their all-round knowledge of their children gave them skills and a balanced viewpoint which professionals, with their narrow specialisms, could lack. One mother, for instance, said that by the time her child was 6 months old she had a broader knowledge than the paediatricians advising her, because she had read books and had visited families and schools.

On a more formal basis parents could turn to the NAMHC (now Mencap) for help and guidance. In 1972 there was little alternative to this because the Down's Children's Association (DCA) had only recently started and there were no local contacts. The fact that there was no alternative until then may reflect the fact that it was only in the 1970s that there was popular support for the idea that Down's syndrome children were able to be helped to make significant achievements in independence. The growing support for the DCA may also reflect the increasingly middle-class backgrounds of parents (Shepperdson, 1985a).

In 1972 only eighteen mothers (49 per cent) were actually members of the NAMHC, although several would have been willing to join if they had been approached. Five parents could be said to be very active members (four mothers and one father) and some had had or were holding official positions in the society. It was obvious that some of these parents played a very active role helping others and giving advice, even on topics outside the scope of the Association. As one mother said, 'I think they think I'm a social worker.'

At least three mothers, far from joining the Association, avoided it. One mother felt she would be upset be seeing all the handicapped children, but two others had other reasons:

> It doesn't interest me at all, I just want to get away from it. I don't want to go further into it or to – you know – the idea of going to a club and sitting down with somebody who perhaps has the same problems as me – I don't want to discuss it. I just want to live my life – an outside life – you know – away.
> (1972)

> I just don't want it to become our life bringing up Tom. We want to integrate him into the family, not to make him the main one.
> (1972)

There was some indication that mothers in rural areas would also avoid the Association, in this case because of a wish to hide their children. One mother, very involved in the work of her local branch said:

> They pay their money, but they don't attend. Most members haven't got handicapped children . . . We're wonderful at raising money, they'd give, but the ones with handicapped children keep themselves to themselves and the children likewise.
> (1972)

In 1972 one of the most important aspects of help given by the society was the relief parents gained from meeting others in the same position. Some, seeing the plight of others realised, perhaps for the first time, that there were things to be thankful for. Several mothers said they were able to relax more fully with mothers who had the same problems. For one or two joining the NAMHC proved a turning point:

> My insurance man who calls, his wife was on the committee for the B. society and she called this particular week for her husband and she asked what was the matter. She said to me . . . 'Come to the society . . . ' and I went on Thursday evening with her and from then on I never really looked back, you know. I met all the mothers. I was there 'til 11 o'clock but I was talking about my problem and I wasn't the only person. 'Til then I'd felt I was on my own. (1972)

Apart form this major function of meeting other parents the society organised trips, outings and activities for the children. This was not always wholly approved of:

> I used to go a lot – it's rather personal really but I don't support their aims. Their aims seem to be a social life for the children and I'd rather be doing something more constructive . . . all they do is have these club meetings – which is delightful for the children, I'm glad they've got it, but there should be more with it. From what I can see of it, money that's collected is spent on the social side – trips and things like that for the children . . . I think there should be more of an effort made, building a dormitory where childen could stay a night or two if necessary, something like that, something nearby where they might know the people. (1972)

Sometimes more ambitious projects were attempted by some branches. The mothers made no mention of achievements at national level.

In 1981 only 3 families did not know of the Society, 8 (15%) were members and attended meetings and 14 (26%) were inactive members although some took advantage of clubs or outings. Eight parents had been members in the past but had left; four did not agree with the aims of the local groups, which were seen as mainly providing a social life for the children rather than changing or providing services or giving advice. Two dropped out when their children went to residential school, and one mother, in an isolated area, found it impossible to get to meetings. The 20 who did not join gave similar reasons: a social life was not needed or their children were not considered to be 'bad enough' to benefit from the activities.

The Down's Children's Association had less support – four mothers were members, but only three attended meetings. Nineteen (36%) others had heard of the association; most were discouraged from joining because the DCA was perceived as being more concerned with younger children and, indeed, of those who had joined two did feel that this was the case. Most mothers were in sympathy with the approach although one preferred her own methods and did not want to be 'brainwashed'. It is possible that more mothers will join as the groups become more concerned with older children and as more local, accessible branches begin to thrive.

DEFICIENCIES IN SERVICES

Problems with providing adequate services

The problems that arose with meeting parents' needs were predictable. Above all, services that would have helped were simply not available in some places, and parents who had moved between areas were quick to spot the differences.

An extremely common problem, which no doubt stemmed from this inadequacy of provision, was that parents were made to feel services were granted as a favour, rather than a right, and so had to be pleaded for. Parents felt it to be humiliating to be forced into the role of supplicant for services to which they were, after all, entitled and for which they had paid. Not only this, it meant that allocation could be based on who shouted loudest, rather than where there was greatest need. This rationing approach, without question, deterred parents from using some services or forced others to exaggerate their problems:

> He used to wet the bed and dirty it when he started having fits. [Did you have any help with that?] No, do you know I'm still waiting for a plastic sheet – but he's great now so I never bother, but I've never ever had any help with his bed. In fact I don't ask, I struggle myself, you know, because you always have a lecture – 'You have this' or 'You're having that.'   (1981)

The following quotation is from a single mother wanting residential care for her son:

> We've had one call from the social services since we were here – that was 3 months ago. 'Everything OK?' sort of thing. I said 'No, it's the same as it always was,' but that's as far as it goes. I think from what I can understand you have to be on the 'phone every day, screaming down the place, going completely berserk, knocking hell out of the other children. But if you try to live and keep yourself sane and try to carry on – well, they're quite happy to let you do so. It's the old story, people who are helpless are the ones who get helped. I suppose that's how it should be but you wonder how long am I going to go on with this strain – not knowing? If they'd turn round to me and say 'Look, in a year's time we've got a place for him' – you go on coping, but at this stage it's going on and on and on and it's never going to be different, you know . . . and I do realise the only way I'd get any action will be by going into a mental home. This is where I feel so frustrated because the number of hours I've sat talking like this to a social worker and telling them all the problems and they write it all down and it's going to be stored away somewhere and nobody's really interested. In other words you're keeping them in a job . . . I know it's not their fault, they're doing the job they're meant to but, when it comes to the crunch, they're obviously told there's no place.   (1981)

> F: There was a period when we were desperate to get her into short-term care and the local social worker was obviously of the opinion that her place was at home and not anywhere else and made this abundantly clear to us. Well [my wife] was desperately in need of a break, even of just two weeks and I had to resort to the point of getting on the 'phone and saying 'I'm going to beat my daughter if you don't come and take her.' I wasn't going to do it, but 'you can't take the risk that I don't mean it'. And they came and she was gone in 20 minutes. They were saying there wasn't room, it was scandalous one had to go to that length.   (1981)

Services had undoubtedly improved but it was repeatedly stressed by parents that provision had come too late and at the wrong time. As one mother said: 'It was when I had £13 unemployment and four children, that's when I never seen anyone'.

Even when services were available, lack of information about them could mean they were not used. This was a particular problem for those with teenagers in ESN(M) schools who did not meet other, similarly placed, parents. Such schools, too, were often dealing chiefly with the problems of the socially disadvantaged and 'solutions' were less appropriate for the Down's syndrome teenagers.

The problem of advice and information being given only when requested has been touched upon earlier. If information is to reach everyone and deal with all possible problems, it must be given consistently and universally, that is, to all about all possible areas of difficulty. The burden of responsibility must be on professionals to inform, rather than on parents to ask.

Another difficulty was that provisions tended to be for the standard child in the standard two-parent family. The lack of flexible care arrangements that would allow a parent to continue work and also continue the care of his or her child has been noted. The use of boarding-school placements as a substitute for a few hours of daily care must be inappropriate. One mother, who needed a few hours of help daily, was told she could only be helped if her son was taken into care!

Similarly, the very severely retarded and, at the other end, the more mildly affected, could find provision that was intended for the average inappropriate. The ATCs were a particular problem in this respect and were not felt to cater adequately for the extremes of the ability range. Although with the extension of school-leaving age only one boy had been left without a placement of some sort there were fears that others would be in this position in future. For parents who had had worked hard at improving their child it was discouraging to find that, because of their success, less help was offered to them.

An important issue is how far services do, or should, interfere in family life and decisions. There were certainly examples where, had the child been of normal intelligence, there would have been intervention. The withdrawal of children from school by their parents is an obvious example. Another is that of the child who was given unprescribed medicines by his mother. In the section on advice one father clearly called for more directive advice on upbringing. There were certainly others who would have benefited from a more vigorous approach in this sphere from professionals.

In 1981 services seemed still to be activated in response to crisis, rather than before a crisis arose. There were several families who had experienced problems that they had coped with alone, or that had received help after the event. In 1981 it was possible to identify families with potential crises – the single mother quoted earlier in this section, those families where parents were suffering ill health, families in complete ignorance of what might be offered at the end of boarding school placements – who seemed at the time to be receiving little positive help or guidance or promises about future help. The assumption that parents can be kept in a state of uncertainty about how to order their lives smacks of contempt.

Cutbacks had not at the time begun to bite hard. Most concern about them came from one area where ATC places were particularly short and there were fears that the promise of extra places would not be fulfilled. Others spoke of short staffing at the ATC, and in schools and of under-equipped hostels. Two mothers feared short-term care would be restricted and another was worried about transport. One club for the handicapped had not received a local authority grant because of cuts. Others were concerned that all provision would deteriorate for those of post-school age.

A more general worry arises from cutbacks. Although in the 1970s there were few provisions, aims were clear and there was a general feeling by those providing services that more should be offered. Now that cutbacks are so widely accepted as inevitable there may become more tolerance and fatalism about the provision of poor services both from those providing them and from those receiving them. A lowering of expectations will inevitably result in a lower standard of service.

What parents felt they needed

Many of the needs parents expressed in 1972 were met, in part, by 1981. Services were more evenly distributed; early services (telling the parents, help for the under 2s, school places before and after 5 years) had all improved, advice and short-term care were better and more available. There was some financial help. It was sad, though, that improvements for older children and adults had not kept pace with those for younger children and that, for many of this cohort, their main experience of services continued to be a negative one.

Some of the needs identified in 1972 were not met and continued in 1981 to need attention. Certain services were still not easily available, e.g. speech therapy. The future – both accommodation and employment – remained uncertain. Help was still inflexible with parents expected to fit in with what was offered rather than finding that the services responded to their needs. Practical help in the home – home helps, laundry services, incontinence services, sitters – was still rarely available. Parents still, in 1981, stressed the need for better information about services.

There were also new needs in 1981. Some of these could be said to centre loosely around the wish to integrate and normalise the teenager, although parents did not voice it in these terms. Parents wished for fashionable teenage clothing that would fit awkwardly-sized teenagers and shoes were a special problem. Companionship with others of the teenagers' own age was a need even the most willing parents could not meet themselves. Provision of work – touched upon in 1972 – was far more frequently stressed in 1981. Few ATCs were seen as providing adequate stimulation. Parents of the more able teenagers were uncertain which alternative was worse – the ATC or unemployment.

There were also unmet needs for which parents did not seek help. The wish expressed by some parents to be able to lead their own lives was not followed up by a request for services to help. Although parents could see their teenagers had missed out on early stimulation programmes there was no call for special compensatory programmes. Parents could see that allowances did not pay for 'attendance' or 'mobility' or, sometimes, the cost of keeping a teenager, but satisfaction with the allowances was still high. Parents paid lip-service to the idea of integration but did not over-stress the need for services that would actually bring this about or provide opportunities for independent living. It is, in fact, not at all certain that parents would welcome an independent life for their children if it was at the expense of the high standard of physical care they themselves gave the teenagers.

SUMMARY

Services for Down's syndrome children have improved over the years but in 1981 there were still variations and inequalities in the quantity and quality of services to the various age groups of those with Down's syndrome, to children within the same age range and between the services offered. For instance, early services improved during the 1970s but those for teenagers had not kept pace. There were also those whose needs remained unmet because services were inadequate e.g. residential care. Some services were more readily available e.g. short-term care, others were not available at all or were not sufficiently well staffed to meet all needs e.g. speech therapy.

There were more services available by the 1980s, and generally they were directed at the most severely handicapped children. This is perhaps judged a proper allocation of resources but it could mean the more able child who had problems, could miss out. Parents understandably, then, felt they were penalised for their efforts with their children.

Within service provision it was possible to pick out speech therapy as a particular weakness. This was unfortunate for Down's syndrome children because it is an area where they are likely to be particularly deficient and chances of integration are severely endangered if communication skills are not mastered.

10 Financial Help

In the 1960s, when the population was born, there were no allowances for disabled children. In the 1970s, beginning with the attendance allowance, new financial help became available. This section outlines how these provisions affected the Down's syndrome population: how far they were applied for by the population and how far those who applied qualified for the allowances. The 'border line' and ambiguous status of Down's syndrome people in relation to other mentally handicapped people is illustrated in the difficulties they have encountered in the introduction of the attendance allowance and the Family Fund.

The attendance allowance

The attendance allowance was introduced in 1971 and was intended for 'people who are severely disabled, physically or mentally, and who need a lot of looking after by day and night' (Disability Alliance, 1981).

In 1973 two rates were introduced: a lower rate for those who needed frequent attention connected with bodily functions or continual supervision through either the day or night and a higher rate for those who needed either of these attentions both day and night. The rate was £4.80 when the attendance allowance was introduced in 1971 and by the end of 1973 the higher and lower rates were £6.20 and £4.15 respectively. In 1981 when the second period of fieldwork was carried out the rates were £21.65 and £14.45 (Disability Alliance, 1981).

In 1972, 32 (87%) mothers knew of the allowance but 7 of them did not apply because they did not consider their children were sufficiently handicapped to warrant it: 'Oh, she's not handicapped or anything – she's just backward, slow in picking things up.' When the allowance was introduced there were many anomalies in how it was granted and this further discouraged applications since parents could see some 'with real disabilities' apparently failing to qualify.

Most of those who knew of the allowance did feel they should qualify and, at the time of the interviews in 1972, 25 (68%) parents had made an application. The results of 23 of the 25 applications were known, including 3 in which the decision was being appealed against (see Table 10.1).

To some extent parents selected themselves and, of the seven non-applicants, four children scored over one standard deviation above the mean on the Gunzburg PAC and so, arguably, were less dependent than others. The decisions made by the Attendance Allowance Board on those who did apply showed no such reasonable rationale. The intention clearly was to base decisions about eligibility on a functional assessment, that is, 'people who need a lot of looking after' (Disability Alliance, 1981), rather than on a clinical label. In the application of this principle, however, either the functional criteria

Table 10.1 *Results of applications for the attendance allowance 1972*

	n	%
Successful	12	32
Successful after 2 appeals	1	3
Unsuccessful	5	14
Unsuccessful after appeal	2	5
Appeal result not known	3	8
Application result not known	2	5
Did not apply	7	19
Did not know of allowance	5	14
Total	37	100

were not sufficiently precise, or (as it seemed from what parents said) decisions were being made, in practice, on the basis of a clinical label with no agreement between the assessors on the implications of such a label. For whatever reason, the decisions made for the original sample were unsatisfactory.

Of the 23 applicants about whose applications the decisions were known 12 had qualified without difficulty and one did so after appeal; a further 10 were refused. The successful children were not, however, invariably the most severely disabled, as Table 10.2 shows. Rather, successful applicants tended to be of high social class or have mothers who had responded negatively and felt their child presented a major problem. No doubt these feelings made them put their case very forcibly.

Table 10.2 *Success of applicants for attendance allowance and Gunzburg PAC scores 1972*

Gunzburg PAC scores	Successful	Unsuccessful[a]	Total
1 SD above the mean	1 (100)	—	1
Average	10 (59)	7 (41)	17
1 SD below the mean	2 (40)	3 (60)	5
Subtotal	13 (57)	10 (44)	23

[a] Three under appeal

Had the children been distinguished from each other accurately the decision to treat Down's syndrome children differently from each other would have been acceptable, but there were obvious ambiguities. One of the most severely disabled boys in the sample did not qualify. Of the nine children who scored one standard deviation below the mean on the Gunzburg PAC in 1972, and who presumably needed most care, three mothers did not know of the allowance, one did not apply and, of the five who did apply, only two qualified. (See Shepperdson, 1973, for a fuller discussion.)

In 1981 it was possible to ask all families how their applications had fared. Some parents had encountered unreasonable difficulties in qualifying (see Table 10.3) and an initial rejection meant that some parents received help very late, two not until 1977 and one as late as 1979. The problems were all encountered in the early days of the allowance and all who applied after 1974 obtained the allowance with no difficulty.

In spite of these difficulties, by 1981 the situation had been transformed and 87% of the teenagers were receiving the allowance. With one exception all who applied for the allowance were granted it (see Table 10.3).

Of the six who did not apply (see Table 10.3) only one mother rejected the idea of applying at all because it meant 'playing on someone's health' and 'making them out worse than they are'. Three girls were very competent and their mothers had not felt justified in applying and, in any case, all families were comfortably placed financially. Two other girls attended residential school and their parents did not realise they were

Table 10.3 *Results of applications for the attendance allowance 1981*

	n	%
Successful	32	60
Successful after appeal	5	9
Successful after 2 appeals	3	6
Successful after 4 appeals	1	2
Refused, later application successful	5	9
Refused, no later application made	1	2
Not applied	6	11
Total	53	99

entitled to the allowance when their daughters were at home on holiday.

Most of the teenagers were granted the lower allowance (Table 10.4) and this caused dissatisfaction among a minority of parents. It has been shown that few teenagers were left alone for any appreciable length of time and not one was left alone overnight. Since all that is required for 'attendance' is 'continual supervision . . . in order to avoid substantial danger to yourself or others' a few parents argued, with some justification, that they should be entitled to the full rate since they were not free to leave the Down's teenagers in the way they could have done with others. Since the mental age of the teenagers was much younger than their actual years parents were probably not being unduly cautious in the close supervision they gave their teenagers. It is a criticism that is likely to gain support from more parents as the gap between the young people's expected and actual independence increases. Some parents still regarded their teenagers as children and so had not begun to consider the 24 hour supervision as anything unusual.

Table 10.4 *Receipt of attendance allowance 1981*

	n		%
Higher rate	15	} 17	32
Increased to higher rate	2		
Lower rate	19	} 29	55
Reduced to lower rate	10		
Applied and refused, did not reapply	1		2
Did not apply	6		11
Total	53		100

Quite apart from this general criticism, six teenagers' allowances had been reduced from the higher to the lower rate in spite of them still presenting specific problems at night and, for half of them, the problems were persisting in 1981. Unusually, one mother was receiving the full allowance even though there were no night-time problems.

Turning to the use families made of the allowance, the Disability Alliance (1981: 10) states the intention of the attendance allowance is:

> to make it easier for you, the disabled person to obtain the care you need. But you are free to spend it, whether as a contribution to general household expenses, as a payment for services, or to buy anything else you need.

The amount obviously falls short of any attempt to pay a realistic price for actual services or care that is undertaken. The allowance would buy very few hours of care in the open market. In fact, in 1972 and 1981, only one mother was buying care. The poorer families tended to use the allowance simply to help make ends meet and most others to meet the extra expenses resulting from disability (e.g. clothing, transport, extra toys).

However, although the amount was inadequate in terms of truly paying for care or compensating families for the losses arising from the constant attendance necessary, there were few expressions of dissatisfaction and few of the complaints made in 1972 that parents were saving the country money by keeping the children at home. Indeed, in some of the poorer areas, the allowance was regarded as excessively generous by outsiders.

> I mean people do think I get the attendance allowance for him – 'Oh it's good money.' I do tell them, – 'I tell you what, you take him for a fortnight and I'll give you his fortnight's money.'   (1981)

On the same theme one woman had been accused of taking over the care of her Down's syndrome sister simply because of the handsome allowances that came with her.

An unfortunate consequence of the loss of allowance for children staying in residential schools, was that it seemed likely two poorer families withdrew their children from residence because of this. For one, who was not offered daily transport as a substitute for weekly care, this meant the boy's total withdrawal from school. Since neither home was providing a background comparable with a good residential place, the very teenagers most needing extra stimulation were denied it. One mother continued to receive the full allowance in spite of her son's weekly boarding place. The extra money was used to bring him home at weekends since the school transport was provided only fortnightly.

The Family Fund

The Family Fund was established by the government in 1973 in the aftermath of the Thalidomide crisis. The Fund makes grants to families with a very severely handicapped child for specific, named purposes, (e.g. holidays) or for items that ease the burden of caring for the child (e.g. washing machines). The aim of the Fund is to relieve the stress that is assumed inevitably to arise from caring for a severely disabled child. The intention of the government in 1973 was to help families quickly and flexibly and so the administration of the Fund was freed from government restrictions and given instead to an independent charity – the Joseph Rowntree Memorial Trust. Even though it is an unorthodox way of disbursing public money (Bradshaw, 1976) and in spite of considerable freedom of action, the Fund has encountered few criticisms from parents.

As time has passed guidelines have been issued to clarify the criteria on which decisions are based. One of these guidelines has concerned Down's syndrome children, to their disadvantage. The guideline issued in August 1976, when most of the grants under discussion here were allocated, recognised that Down's syndrome children are not invariably 'very severely handicapped' and so should not automatically qualify. Few would wish to quarrel with this. More controversially a distinction was made between Down's syndrome children and the rest of the severely mentally handicapped population. Down's syndrome children needed an IQ below 35 to qualify for consideration unless further specified difficulties were present. Other children had only to have an IQ below 50 to qualify for consideration.

In 1980 further guidelines altered the position slightly but the clear intention was still to make the average and uncomplicated Down's syndrome child ineligible.

Both sets of guidelines suggested that the award of the attendance allowance could help to show that there were 'marked problems of care, or difficulties of management.' However, in practical terms this is largely irrelevant, since in this Down's syndrome population, once over initial difficulties, all who applied for the attendance allowance received it, regardless of mental (or IQ) status, and so the introduction of attendance allowance entitlement as a guide to distinguishing between Down's syndrome children cannot be regarded as useful. Parents who did not apply for the attendance allowance would be unlikely to apply to the Family Fund and no one in this population did so.

Table 10.5 shows how these guidelines worked out in practice for the population. The Fund is intended for those who are 'severely disabled' and consequently it is not surprising that most applications were from families with less able children and those at ESN(S) schools. Parents with children at ESN(S) schools were more likely to know of the Fund than others (64% compared with 21% of those receiving education elsewhere). Sixty-one per cent of those who could remember how they found out about the Fund said they were told about it by the child's ESN(S) school or by other parents.

Table 10.5 *Applicants to Family Fund and type of school attended (% in brackets)*

	Attended ESN(S) school	Attended another type of school	Total
Applied	29 (97)	1[a] (3)	30
Did not apply	4 ⎫ 13 (57)	3 ⎫ 10 (44)	7 ⎫ 23
Did not know of fund	9 ⎭	7 ⎭	16 ⎭
Total	42 (79)	11 (21)	53

Applicants compared with non-applicants:
$\chi^2 = 10.4$; df = 1; p < 0.01.
[a] At ESN(M) school when application made. Attending ESN(S) school in 1981.

Applicants to the Fund are not means tested, but the 'social–economic circumstances' of the families are taken into account. In this population, those in social classes I and II were less likely to apply (33% of social classes I and II, compared with 57% in social class III and 77% in social classes IV and V). In fact, who applied and who did not, was the only major sorting of the children that took place since, with one exception, all who applied to the Fund were helped. It is possible that the single exception would have succeeded with a later application.

Table 10.6 shows the success of applicants who applied to the Family Fund. It is of interest that the three who were refused initially were all in social classes IV or V. Although one of these teenagers could perhaps have been assessed in her youth as too able to qualify there was nothing to distinguish the other two from those who had been successful and, indeed, both children had below-average abilities compared with the rest of the South Wales Down's population.

Table 10.6 *Success of applicants to the Family Fund*

	n	%
Granted	26	49
Granted after appeal	2	4
Refused, later application successful	1	2
Refused	1	2
Did not apply	7	13
Did not know of it	16	30
Total	53	100

It has already been said that, with one exception, all those who applied to the Fund were helped. Since the Fund guidelines operating at that time would seem to intend to exclude an average Down's syndrome child with no additional problems, either it was recognised that average Down's syndrome children would all have additional problems and so would qualify, or the guidelines have been interpreted too generously. The question, then, must be how far the children met the criteria laid down by the Trust.

Looking at the most competent teenagers in this population (i.e. those who scored one standard deviation above the mean on the Gunzburg PAC), only two families of these nine teenagers had made an application. One presented some behaviour problems. The other still needed help with cleaning after a bowel movement and was still wetting the bed. Three mothers did not know of the Fund.

Turning to the least competent children, eight out of ten of the families with children who scored one standard deviation below the mean on the Gunzburg PAC in 1981 applied to the Fund. The two families who did not apply were not in great financial need but one, in any case, did know of the Fund.

Of the 34 families with teenagers who fell between the two extremes, 20 applied to the Fund (1 unsuccessfully), 2 did not apply and 12 did not know of the Fund. The average Gunzburg scores of these three categories of average-scoring teenagers did not differ substantially from each other.

It is clear that in this population the average Down's syndrome child did qualify if the application was made. The guidelines state that Down's children can qualify if they have 'disabilities not usually present in mongolism' (although the list that is given includes heart malformations and deafness, both of which are commonly associated with Down's syndrome) or must have 'behaviour more disturbed than the usual pattern'. It is recognised that all are 'difficult to manage' because they need 'close supervision'. It will be considered whether the more detailed guidelines explain how average and above-average children managed to qualify. The full details of circumstances surrounding applicants cannot be known, but using the most generous interpretation of ill health and poor behaviour and assuming that all below-average children would qualify, there remain about eight children whose qualification would seem to raise a doubt that their success was justified *within the criteria laid down*. This is not to say their claims for help were in any way frivolous but, rather, that attempts to distinguish the children on these criteria leads to anomalies. For instance, a child with a heart malformation is not necessarily more difficult to bring up than one without. The guidelines have little relevance if the aim of the distinctions is to select and help only those who are under stress. Those who qualified according to the criteria were coping no less well than those who had more questionable claims and vice versa. No doubt Family Fund social workers, in attempting to relieve all too obvious stress and difficulties, are presumably left with little alternative but to draw attention to behaviour and health 'complications' that are, in fact, more typical than atypical of the Down's syndrome population.

Satisfaction with the Fund was extremely high, with only one criticism – incredibly enough – 'You do not get what you want'! Most, however, would agree with the mother who said: 'Whoever paid it, we're grateful and it's made *my* life easier!' Apart from the straightforward appreciation of washing machines, holidays, help with cars and so on, satisfaction was high because for some families it was their only chance of buying items that needed a lump sum. One single mother brought up the problem of not being able to obtain a hire–purchase agreement. Apart from this, many parents were unaware that the money came from the government and so regarded the money as something to which they had no automatic right. This discretionary, and supposedly charitable, status both discouraged some from applying and also meant others limited their claims. One mother refused the offer of a holiday because she felt she should not make excessive claims on a charity.

Discretionary benefits in social security matters are increasingly unpopular (Donnison, 1982) although recipients may see their abandonment as a cut in benefit. Despite the fact that an annual lump sum to be paid to all classified as disabled, which would meet some of the costs of disability, might be fairer and less paternalistic, it would undoubtedly not produce the same level of consumer satisfaction. On the face of it the Family Fund statement made in 1976 that

There is no entitlement and because we are using discretion flexibly we cannot be called upon to show

> our grants are equitable. Whilst we should always be prepared to explain to families our reasons for giving or refusing them help, we should not worry about the demands of other people for explanations about how circumstances have been assessed

could lead to discontent, but it has not done so. This may be because, as with this population, discretion errs on the side of a generous interpretation, which few would wish to criticise. With all other benefits for which families applied the burden of proof seemed to be firmly on them so that they were made to feel like supplicants, or as if they were making unnecessary claims. Paradoxically, with the Family Fund, where they had no rights at all, this was not the case. Although the Fund is examined by auditors from the Joseph Rowntree Memorial Trust and the Treasury, freeing the benefit from too much public scrutiny may, in fact, allow administrators to act more generously than when they are fully accountable. It needs to be considered if dispensers of public money are more likely to encounter (or consider they will encounter) greater criticism when found to be acting too generously than when their interpretation is too stringent.

To sum up, in practice, in South Wales, the guidelines for Down's syndrome children did not seem to have much relevance. The handful of healthy, 'high grade' children, or those from better-off families, did not apply to the Fund anyway. The others all seemed, somehow, to qualify. This implies the average Down's syndrome child (who probably has an IQ between 35 and 50) does place his family under stress, like all others with a similar IQ. Policy should follow practice and the additional criteria should be reserved for the few above average Down's children who apply to the Fund. The 1980 guidelines include a clause on problems at puberty, and this is likely to make it even easier to succeed but, since most applicants, in South Wales at least, were qualifying anyway with the old, tougher guidelines, it seems unnecessary to go to the trouble and expense of trying to determine the exact physical and mental status of all except the most able Down's syndrome children. The able could be identified by the type of school they attend. This would not lead to perfect discrimination between the two groups but would be no worse than the ambiguities that no doubt occur with the IQ of 50 definition for mental handicap as a whole.

The mobility allowance

The mobility allowance was extended to children over 5 years old in 1977. To qualify, a person must have been unable to walk, or virtually unable to walk, for 6 months because of physical disablement and be likely to remain so for at least a year. Those who can walk but who, for practical purposes, may need help to go to places (e.g. mentally handicapped or blind people) do not qualify. The rate in 1981 was £14.50 per week plus exemption from road tax for car owners.

After the Robert Edmund case in 1977, which ruled that Down's syndrome was physically based, Down's syndrome children should have been able to qualify, but, in spite of the mobility problems of many of the children, most did not. In the population only two teenagers qualified without difficulty. Both were largely immobile. Two more did qualify, both after three appeals. One boy had a severe heart condition and the other was a wheelchair user.

Eight other children were refused, one twice. Two parents seemed to misunderstand the allowance and one applied because her son could not go on buses alone and the other because the boy enjoyed the car so much. Two others had heart problems, one severe vision difficulties, another had fits and had been advised not to go on buses and two others had behaviour problems that made outings difficult. One application from an overweight girl and with severely restricted mobility was pending.

The allowance is not intended to help all those with mobility problems, only those with mobility problems that arise from not being able to walk. Without any question there were families who did not qualify for the mobility allowance but who were considerably disadvantaged by their teenagers' lack of mobility. Problems included difficulty in walking anywhere, and the expense of having to pay double fares or of needing taxis for outings. Those who could afford cars were relieved of a considerable everyday difficulty (although one mother would not drive alone with her son) and, equally importantly, the children derived much positive benefit and an improved quality of life from the ease with which journeys and outings could be undertaken. Those who lacked this advantage were negatively influenced.

As it stands, the allowance purchases little actual mobility unless it makes the difference between buying a car or doing without. Of the four who were granted the allowance only one actually owned a car and there was little evidence for the others that the allowance was used to buy extra mobility. Six of eight who were refused the allowance were not limiting their teenagers' mobility in any way.

Non-Contributory Invalidity Payment (NCIP)

The Non-contributory Invalidity Payment (NCIP) has now been replaced by the Severe Disablement Allowance. NCIP was a weekly payment for those unable to work because they were sick or disabled and had been unable to work for 28 weeks or more. Those over 16 years who were still at school could qualify if they were receiving special schooling or training. The rate in 1981 was £16.30 per week. As an alternative, supplementary benefit for 16- and 17-year-olds was £13.10 per week and £16.65 on the long-term rate. The best course for an individual to follow depended on their own circumstances and entitlement to additional requirements payments. The Disability Alliance (1981) recommended that those at special schools should consider claiming NCIP for one year and, using that year to qualify, then switch to long-term supplementary benefit. Only one family had adopted this strategy. The position of the 19 boys and 11 girls who had reached 16 years at the time of the interviews is shown in Table 10.7.

Table 10.7 *Benefits received by those over 16 years*

	n	%
NCIP	17	57
NCIP and Child Benefit	1	3
Application for NCIP pending	4[a]	13
Supplementary Benefit	3	10
Child Benefit	5	17
Total	30	100

[a] One mother was receiving neither NCIP nor Child Benefit; it is assumed her son would qualify and be paid arrears.

The mothers of the five teenagers who were still receiving Child Benefit thought that because their children were still at school they could not qualify for anything else. The three teenagers who were receiving supplementary benefit all had different reasons for this. One was waiting the 28 weeks needed to qualify for NCIP, one had attended comprehensive school and was following the example of the other schoolleavers, and the third thought supplementary benefit would be more beneficial than NCIP.

One problem that arose was that some teenagers had to wait 6 months to qualify for NCIP whereas others were able to use the period from $15\frac{1}{2}$ to 16 as the qualifying period. One or two mothers were afraid (wrongly) that receiving the attendance allowance would affect their children's entitlement.

Invalid Care Allowance (ICA)

Invalid care allowance is for people of working age who cannot work because they have to stay at home to care for a severely disabled relative who receives the attendance allowance or constant attendance allowance. (This was the position in 1981; now the person need not be a relative.) In 1981 women living with their husband or partner could not claim, nor could divorced or separated women claim if they were receiving more than £16.30 per week maintenance (1981 rates), but this has now been changed to allow married women to claim. The basic rate in 1981 was £16.30 per week. ICA is deducted from supplementary benefit but it preserves pension rights for applicants. In one sense the existence of ICA recognises that the attendance allowance does not pay adequately for attendance since, if it did, there would be no loss of earnings except for the highly paid. As it is, both ICA and the attendance allowance together would not buy much care on the open market or compensate for the loss of a full-time job.

No one in the study knew of the allowance. Ten women were living on their own. Three were working and four were on supplementary benefit and so would have had no immediate financial advantage in claiming. For the remaining three the financial situation of one was not clear, but two were widows living on pensions. Both of these women were under 60 years and possibly they could have benefited. Ironically, one of these widows had been told 'very rudely' by someone in social services that she was young enough to work but had not been told of the existence of the invalid care allowance.

It has been pointed out that these allowances were most often used to help in the general running of the home or to help meet the extra costs of disability. Mothers were asked if they considered that they did incur extra expenses because of their children. There were 37 (70%) who said they did and only 15 (28%) that they did not. One mother said her son was less expensive to keep than the average teenager. Nineteen (36%) teenagers were said to be heavy on clothes either by wearing them out, or pulling threads, or making small holes worse. Bedding and sheets suffered in the same way. Incontinence obviously exacerbated the problem. Two lost or threw away clothes. The need for larger sizes or to be specially measured for clothes made 10 teenagers difficult and expensive to dress. Shoes were a particular problem. Four mothers emphasised that they were excessively careful to dress their children smartly in order to avoid negative comment. For instance, one mother dressed her other children in clothes from jumble sales but would not do this for the Down's teenager. Transport was another major difficulty: two fares were always needed, and taxis or buses were taken for short distances that could normally have been walked. Extra journeys were needed to hospitals and residential schools. Buying items to improve their child's development and education was an additional expense.

SUMMARY

Although the introduction of the new allowances for handicapped children in the 1970s answered one of the major complaints of parents, Down's syndrome children experienced difficulties qualifying for some of the new provisions. Early attempts to distinguish applicants both for the attendance allowance and the Family Fund were not markedly successful. As the allowances became established the interpretation of the rules became more generous for Down's syndrome children, although the Family Fund's regulations were formally more stringent. Most who applied for these allowances were helped.

The remaining anomaly is the allocation of the higher and lower rate of the attendance allowance. As the teenagers become adults it is likely there will be increasing dissatisfaction with a lower allowance for any adults who need 24-hour supervision.

The mobility allowance was only granted to those with extremely severe mobility problems, but there were others with restricted mobility who did not qualify. The allowance does not attempt to help those who *can* walk but who, for all practical purposes, need a companion.

There was a tendency for families with more able children not to apply for allowances. By 1981 this was the only major cause of variation in the receipt of allowances for children. Ignorance was responsible for some lack of take up for ICA, for the Family Fund and, to a lesser extent, the attendance allowance. In spite of the fact that the attendance allowance and mobility allowance cannot meet any of the real costs of attendance or mobility, satisfaction with the allowances was high.

The extension of the invalid care allowance to married women is likely to be greeted enthusiastically by mothers although it will further exaggerate the disadvantage of those on supplementary benefit.

11 The Education Services

Under the Education (Handicapped Children) Act, 1970, provisions for the education of mentally handicapped children were changed. Until that time pre-school children of below average intelligence were assessed and those who 'failed' (usually those with an assessed IQ of below 50) were said to be 'ineducable' and so no longer the responsibility of the Education Department. Significantly (illustrating the perceptions that were then held that such people's needs were for medical care only) these children became the responsibility of Health departments. Authorities varied greatly in the provisions they made for the children. In some, the Junior Training Centres (JTCs), which catered for day care, provided as good an education as that available in many schools. Some also ran nursery sections. In other authorities there were long waiting lists for places in the JTC and the training given in some was felt by many to be inadequate. After April 1971 the JTCs became schools, administered by the local education authorities and no child was considered to be ineducable. This chapter shows how the population fared in the education system.

Length of time in school

Some of the children in this population, born in 1964–1966, had suffered the disadvantages of waiting lists for entry to JTCs and almost a third of them were late in starting their education (see Table 11.1).

Table 11.1 *Age of entry into JTC or school (% in brackets)*

Starting time (in years)	Original sample	New sample	Total population
Early (Under 4½)	12 (32)	7 (37)	19 (34)
On time (4½–5½)	10 (27)	8 (42)	18 (32)
Late (Over 5½)	14 (38)	3 (16)	17 (30)
Did not start	1 (3)	1 (5)	2 (4)
Total	37 (100)	19 (100)	56 (100)

Authorities in South Wales varied greatly in the number of places they provided. The factor determining the age of entry into the JTC was clearly not the needs of the child himself, but what was available in that area. Where places were available, although in short supply, again it was often the efforts of the parents themselves and their need for relief, rather than the needs of the child, that influenced the offer of a place. There was a lack of emphasis on educational needs in many placements. For instance, unlike the situation for normal children, there was little pressure on some parents to send their children to the JTC at all:

> He'd have been left if I hadn't asked.   (1972)

> I'd have had a heavy fine if I'd kept the [other] children at home. As I said to [educational psychologist], 'If I don't worry you, you won't worry me . . . if I keep Helen at home, nobody's going to worry me because that's a place for somebody else who *will* worry them.'   (1972)

Most parents who were denied a place for their children had a long and wearying battle. 'It'll be easier to tell you who we didn't see', said one parent whose list included her Member of Parliament, doctors, Medical Officer of Health and councillors.

At the end of the population's education, in 1981, these same parents were again finding that decisions were being influenced by what was available rather than by what was needed. The majority of teenagers were at the ESN(S) school and were allowed to stay on until 18 or 19 years, often because of the shortage of places at the Adult Training Centre (ATC) rather than because of assessed educational need. This was not invariably the case and three boys in one authority had gone to the ATC before the age of 18 years because it was considered they were 'ready' for the transfer. The ATC staff were expressing doubts that there would be space available for the next intake. Those not in the ESN(S) school were in a more ambiguous position and one mother had had considerable difficulty in persuading the ESN(M) school to offer her teenager a place after 16 years. The boy at the comprehensive school left at 16 years along with his school fellows.

TYPE OF SCHOOL

Early placements

The old procedure, which did not seem invariably to be followed, was to test the child to decide whether or not he was 'educable'. If he was not, parents were sent a letter saying the child was no longer the responsibility of the Education Department. Needless to say the decision about whether or not a child was 'educable' was a fruitful area for discord.

To begin with, not all parents said that their child had been tested or that they had had a letter. Certainly some of the children attending the ordinary school were not there because they had 'passed' a test. Most children did have some sort of test. Parents often felt the tests did not bring out what the child could do, even though they did not always disagree with the final placement. Dissatisfaction was expressed because of the way in which the test was administered (too hurriedly or when the child was tired), or sometimes because of the test itself:

> The doctor had a different language in Welsh. She's a North Walian or something and little Raymond didn't understand her and when I was trying to help Raymond she told me to be quiet . . . . There was a picture of an elbow – you know – arm. Well, it didn't look to *me* like an elbow – how did she expect Raymond to – and a small branch of tree – well, Raymond couldn't say – I couldn't make out myself what it was.   (1972)

Parents were angered, too, by the letter telling them the child was ineducable, both because the child was 'registered' as 'mentally handicapped' and also of the assumption the child would never change:

> I wouldn't waste my time [appealing]. I knew the child, I knew the psychologist would have to spend a day with him to get the child's trust first – but in any case I knew he wouldn't have passed those tests – I wasn't stupid about it, but that didn't mean to say he wouldn't improve in the future. It was drawing this line – here he is and this is how he's going to stay, I objected to . . . . I told them with the 11 plus, it's ridiculous for them to assume what a child will be like at 11, and for them to come to this conclusion at 5 was fantastic in my opinion. What right did they have?   (1972)

In 1972 the children were attending a variety of schools as Table 11.2 shows.

Table 11.2 *Type of school children attended in 1972 (% in brackets)*

	Original sample	New sample	Total population
ESN(S)	33 (89)	7 (37)	40 (71)
Specialist/observation class in primary school	2 (5)	5 (26)	7 (13)
Assessment unit	—	4 (21)	4 (7)
Normal primary school	1 (3)	2 (11)	3 (5)
No school	1 (3)	1 (5)	2 (4)
Total	37 (100)	19 (100)	56 (100)

In the same way that age of entry to school depended more on the area in which the child lived, or a mother's need for relief, or the amount of parental pressure, than on an educational need so too did placement sometimes depend on these sorts of factors. One mother described how her own daughter came to attend the village bilingual school. This semi-informal approach was more common in the rural areas.

> I didn't think she'd ever go to the normal school – I just didn't think they'd take her in – I don't really know how she got there because I never asked for her to go. My mother did take her to play in the school before she was school age – at playtime . . . . There was an old headmistress there and whether she put her name down to start next term I don't know, but the new headmistress stopped me on the road and said, 'Well, if you're going to send her, send her now because term has started.' I had such a shock . . . . Pleased, I was that pleased I forgot to make [my husband's] food that night . . . he didn't mention it because he was so excited himself . . . . This is the point, you see, people always say 'Oh, she's wonderful' and so on but she's never . . . no one who could ever do any *good* for her ever saw this, nobody who could do anything about it and I knew when she started school they would see what was in her for themselves. (1972)

Asked how she would feel if the child were transferred the mother said:

> Oh, I wouldn't mind. I think I could take it from this headmistress. She's been so genuine that if she said Clara couldn't advance at the school, then I would accept it. (1972)

Although this placement had been very successful it had hardly been arranged on the basis of a careful assessment of need. Other parents had wanted much the same provision but been denied the opportunity. 'I'd like her to try and have a go at T [village school] – I think she's sensible enough, I think she'd manage.' (This was a child who played happily with the other village children and did, in fact, seem 'sensible', and scored well on the tests.)

A further example shows how, even when educational need had been assessed, this could be pushed aside on pragmatic grounds. One girl had been assessed and an observation unit placement had been recommended for her. It was later arranged, by those responsible for transport, that she should go to the JTC instead simply because transport to the observation unit was not available. Her parents had to threaten strong action before the decision was reversed. Four or five mothers had battles with authorities who wanted to 'downgrade' their children from the type of school they as parents felt more appropriate. Most mothers, however, were inclined to accept the placement offered.

Parental satisfaction with early placements

However realistic parents were, and however much they thought the ESN(S) school was the most appropriate place for their child, many were disappointed that it was so. As one mother said, 'It's the lowest there is.' Mothers of Down's syndrome children, in particular, could see children at the school who were 'much worse' and this led to the feeling that education appropriate for these children could not be the most appropriate for their child. Several parents expressed the wish that the child could be with 'better' children, learning from them rather than from the 'worse' children at the ESN(S) school.

In 1972, mothers were asked which school they thought would be best for their child. Not all knew of ESN(M) schools, and so possibly results do not give a wholly accurate picture. Twenty-seven (73%) mothers seemed to think the ESN(S) school was best, although several qualified this by saying 'at present', and several were clearly aiming at the ESN(M) school for the future. Four mothers said they would prefer something 'in between'. Ordinary school seemed ideal to six mothers altogether; four of them were thinking in terms of a unit in the ordinary school. Many parents were against the idea of 'segregation' although a few saw it as a protection for their child. Some mothers were sure their child 'couldn't cope' at an ordinary school, but others would have liked the child to have tried the ordinary school first.

Later placements

By 1981 the teenagers were in, or had just left, the variety of schools shown in Table 11.3 and Table 11.4 shows the average scores of the teenagers on the Gunzburg PAC along with their final school.

Table 11.3 *Final schools attended by teenagers in 1981*

School	n	%	
ESN(S)	33	(62)	
Residential ESN(S)	7	(13)	77%
Special Unit ESN(S)	1	(2)	
ESN(M)	6	(11)	
Residential ESN(M)	4	(8)	21%
Comprehensive (Remedial)	1	(2)	
None	1	(2)	
Total	53	(100)	

The Gunzburg PAC, of course, is only one measure of ability and so can only be the roughest of guides to the educational status of the teenagers. Not only this, the higher average scores of those attending ESN(M) day schools over the average scores of the teenagers attending ESN(S) schools could result from the type of teaching they had been exposed to, rather than from their superior natural abilities. As it stands, it can be seen that there was some overlap between the scores of the teenagers at the various types of day schools.

The exact status of the residential schools was less easily defined and there was little difference between the scores of the teenagers in the severe and moderate categories.

Table 11.4 *Average and range of scores on Gunzburg PAC and final school attended in 1981*

School	n	Gunzburg: 1981 Average score	Range of scores
ESN(S) Day	33	67.2	2–94
ESN(S)Residential	7	50.4	25–91
Special Unit in normal school	1	57	57
ESN(M) Day	6	96.2	88–107
ESN(M) Residential	4	51.3	24–81
Comprehensive (Remedial)	1	75	75

Parental satisfaction with later placements

A high proportion of parents (64%) still believed the ESN(S) school was appropriate for their teenagers, although this was a lower proportion than in 1972 (73%). Fourteen parents (26%) felt the ESN(M) schools were appropriate and three the remedial section of ordinary schools. Two parents were unsure.

In all, eight parents felt their teenagers would have benefited from more demanding schooling. Their hopes were probably not unrealistic. Six of these teenagers were in ESN(S) schools and three of them were very able and could probably have coped with the ESN(M) school. There were other youngsters who scored equally well but whose parents felt they were appropriately placed in ESN(S) schools. The two who would have preferred ordinary schooling to the ESN(M) school had teenagers who both scored exceptionally well on the tests.

The issue of integration was somewhat confused: parents sometimes felt the ESN(S) curriculum was appropriate, but this was rarely offered in the ordinary school system. In 1972 integration was commonly considered to be desirable, especially for those with brighter children; in 1981 it was not invariably the choice for teenagers. Some parents again advocated special units attached to ordinary schools, although the mother whose son was in such a unit said that, in practice, integration was not very great.

There was certainly some lip-service to integration, but when seven children had the option of attending comprehensives, only two had taken advantage of it and one of them left after a year. One mother described the problems she had making the choice of school, and illustrates the fact that Down's teenagers may have special needs that are not met by simply diluting, simplifying or repeating what is learned in mainstream schools.

> I didn't know whether I had made the right decision for a twelve-month. I've got to be honest, I thought to myself – well – they have got a remedial class in the comprehensive – my son had found out all about it. But I thought – Well, you've got a lot of older children there, when they are changing classes they might bowl her over. There are a lot of things that we – you know – and it did have good points, I suppose, perhaps Judy would have really come on, but then, academically – it's the other things Judy wanted to learn, isn't it? That was the biggest decision I think we ever had to make. But now I can see after being in Y. I think we made the right decision, she's learning the everyday things, the things she needs to know, I think, the cooking – and, of course, there's only eight to ten in that class. I think there would have been 40 in the class in the remedial in the comprehensive. We did go out, mind, and look and ask a lot of questions . . . . The headmaster said, 'It's up to you entirely, see what you . . . ' She could have gone, yes, but what they had to offer Judy was not, how can I say, we thought there was a lot – they're there in that class, Judy would have been 12 years old going there, with bigger boys and bigger girls mixed up, and I wondered about menstruation – whether it would have been private enough, whether Judy could have coped without me all day over there, that much further away. So we talked it over as a family. My son was all for saying give her a chance to go to the comprehensive and see how she gets on, and then my daughter was thinking to herself 'Well, she's got to move around with the handicapped children some time in her life.' My husband thought that Y would give her confidence because she'd be helping other children a lot worse than herself – which she does. They had more to offer over there I think as regards – well, more individual attention. (1981)

Here, the only choice offered had been the ESN(S) school or the remedial section of a comprehensive. Those at the ESN(M) schools faced another problem in that the gentler Down's children could find it tough mixing with ESN(M) children, a high proportion of whom had social problems.

Residential school placements

Twelve children had been in residence during term time at some point. Seven of them were, or had been, in boarding schools and five were attending day schools while living in a nearby local authority hostel. Boarding places were offered to three more children but were refused. One child was not offered a day place and so did not go to school at all.

Only two youngsters went to residential school purely for educational reasons and here both parents spoke of the advantages of increased independence. The main difficulty for these parents was that transport between home and school was provided every third weekend only and so both sets of parents were involved in long, costly journeys to bring their children home every weekend. (This also applied to a family in another area.) Three parents pressed very strongly themselves for places away from home because they found daily care too much for them. Three others had help when they became one-parent families, although, for one mother, this help stopped when her son left school and went to the ATC, despite the fact that her own needs had not changed. One mother became too ill with arthritis to cope. Two others (including a bereaved mother) had discipline problems with their children.

One mother made a decision, which she later came to regret, to keep her son at home when she learned that he had serious heart problems. She described how this happened and how her son eventually went into boarding school.

> I wish that when I had decided – or we had decided – to keep Charles from school that someone had said 'Well, you know, you're not doing the right thing.' I might have resented it, I don't know at the time, but I was allowed to do and decide for Charles without help really and it was only when Charles had gone back to day school permanently that I was having a talk with the headmaster . . . and he pointed out that because of all the years that Charles had lost his schooling that it wasn't fair to *them* to start to cope now, you know. Because they found Charles hard, I think . . . . I was hurt about that and well – you know – to be criticised for something you thought you'd done for his good, and I felt a failure.

This mother then kept her son away from day school once again. She gave her reasons as follows :

> Well, I felt because I'd chosen to keep him from school to ask them to cope, that they'd lost the three years of not having him, and not knowing him – once he'd said *that*, I kept him from school. This was when they decided that Charles would go to [residential school]. Oh, I could have sent him to [the day school] but I felt I was being unfair to ask them to cope with Charles. You know I'm very sensitive to other people's feelings and I felt I'd chosen to keep Charles at home and have home tuition for three years and, because I just found it hard to cope and because I felt I'd made the wrong decision about keeping him home you know, he was getting harder to handle and not so well behaved as he should be – well, I'd made the wrong decision, hadn't I? . . . The Headmaster said that I'd kept Charles away from school because of his heart condition. 'Well we've got children here worse than Charles, if anything's going to happen it could happen at home or school – you should never have kept him home.' But he said that after I *had* kept him home, you know, probably if he'd said 'Well, in my experience of these children, I've dealt with them and you're making the wrong decision', I might have sent Charles to school then, but I felt if I had sent him and he'd died because of infections – they said don't expose him to too many infections, if he has pneumonia he won't survive it – you know.   (1981)

This mother admitted she might have rejected advice but her lack of guidance about this critical decision cannot be regarded as satisfactory.

Parental satisfaction with schools

In 1972 satisfaction with schools was high. Since this was the one service that was likely, eventually, to reach all parents in those days, this was fortunate and perhaps helps to explain why parents were so favourably disposed towards schools.

Twenty-nine of the 36 (81%) mothers whose children went to school were not critical and some were enthusiastic. Eight children had started too recently for the mothers to do anything but express their satisfaction 'so far'. Criticisms from the others centred around the lack of qualified staff and the fact that reading and writing were not emphasised:

> I thought she could be educated. I can teach her to wash and iron and cook and clean myself. I want her to read and write. (1972)

> I'd like to see her learning a bit of arithmetic now, spelling and that. She's not moving on. (1972)

> It's an occupation centre: I want an education centre, I don't want him just to be occupied. (1972)

Other parents were harsher in their criticisms of staff, size of classes and the teaching:

> They don't have the time or ability to teach the children anything. I'm glad he *is* there but he'd have progressed just as well if he'd never gone . . . I don't ask him what he's being taught, I know he's not being taught anything – well I suppose he's bound to learn something from them but not as much as I'd like – as far as education goes it's not very much to do with education. (1972)

Parents' expectations about the school and its aims could influence their feelings. Those who felt the school was simply a 'dumping ground' for the children were not surprised when nothing was achieved:

> In some cases it's just a case of keeping the children out of the way, isn't it. . . . Some children, they can't be taught a lot . . . it's mostly to keep them out of the way, that's all it's for really, isn't it, come to the truth of the matter? (1972)

Parents with low expectations were happy if the school was convenient. For instance, one mother was pleased her child was transferred from the local school to the ESN(S) school some miles away because now the child was collected by bus, where before she was involved in a long walk across the village to and from school. Transport was not uncommonly an area of complaint, either because of distances or because mothers with delicate children were often kept in the cold for up to 45 minutes waiting for the bus to arrive. One mother was concerned about the speed of the bus and clearly showed her feelings about the use of the school while she discussed it:

> And what *is* the point? They're all mentally handicapped, why *start* them at that time? It's not like the normal school, the children got to be in by 9 o'clock . . . for children of that nature half past nine would have been early enough. (1972)

Rather more mothers were inclined to complain that the hours were not long enough.

Perhaps because of the fact that most parents were satisfied with the school there were few parents with very strong views about the change from Health to Education, although most felt it was a 'good thing'. Several hardly knew of the change and said it would make little difference: 'If the money was short with the Health Department, why should it be more with the Education?'

For the most part, parents were still satisfied with school in 1981. Progress was deemed satisfactory by 73% and only ten (19%) were seriously dissatisfied.

The most common complaint was concerned with the limited teaching of reading. There were about a third of the teenagers who could read to some extent and so clearly had been exposed to the written word, but another third of parents felt that reading tuition should be given. Not all were of this opinion and one mother, at least, considered that learning to dress and wash were more relevant skills than 'scribbling' and so were more important for their children to master. Others felt resentful if teachers concentrated on teaching academic skills to the more able while ignoring their own children. Some simply expressed a more general dissatisfaction:

> She's been going to school since she was 4½ and coming back in the night the same way as she went in. (1981)

> All his generation's lost out. (1981)

It's only keeping them happy – there's not enough education.   (1981)

As in 1972 there were still complaints about the wide range of abilities in the schools, and about transport.

Cooperation between parents and school was, on the whole, good. As with most services, however, specific individuals could transform the situation, single-handed, for good or ill and some teachers and heads encouraged parents to participate, though others did not.

A common and predictable difficulty in maintaining contact with schools was distance. One mother in an isolated valley 'cul-de-sac' had been to her son's school twice in 10 years, although the distance involved was only about 10 miles:

> Well, you have letters, and they have parents' evenings but they don't start till 6.30 or 7.00 pm which means I go from her at 5.00 pm to get there and then if you're there two hours, by the time you travel back to M. there's the possibility that you've missed the last bus up here . . . They did a play at Christmas, but I never go down there.   (1981)

In some schools there were beginning to be signs of real cooperation and a continuity of teaching between school and home. One school, as has been mentioned earlier, encouraged parents to allow shopping for clothes to be done in school time. There must, however, be sensitivity and school aims can be rejected if imposed unilaterally on parents. One mother criticised the fact that some mothers were expected to continue to carry out deprivation of treats at home. Since the deprivation selected was missing Gateway Club, and since attendance provided relief for the parents, this was felt to be an unsatisfactory policy.

READING AND NUMBER

Whether or not Down's syndrome children should be taught to read and write is the subject of some debate (see Buckley, 1985), but in view of the importance parents attached to 'academic' work, and reading in particular, some details are included here on the teenagers' competence in reading and number activities. These details were supplied by teachers. In addition teachers were asked if the teenagers knew the words on the Schonell graded word reading test. The test was not administered in standardised conditions and so can be only a guide to reading age. The main intention was to differentiate between the children.

This account does not attempt to argue the rights and wrongs of teaching Down's children the 'three Rs' except to say that a few teenagers certainly could read well and with pleasure. One boy (estimated reading age 8.5 years) had his own tabloid newspaper delivered daily and read this with interest as part of his evening routine. A few educationalists were clearly against wasting time on an activity they felt would not be done well ('barking at print') at the expense of mastering everyday, useful and essential tasks. There were some parents who did not agree with this approach and, it must be said, their teenagers were generally among the more able. In other words they were not expecting more from their own youngsters than others, similarly placed, had achieved. As with so much else, parents were happier when the individual's needs and abilities seemed to be considered, and a stereotyped approach based on what was considered to be appropriate for a Down's syndrome child was avoided.

Tables 11.5 and 11.6 show how far the teenagers were able to participate in reading-related activities. Just over one-third of the youngsters had some reading ability.

Although there were some teenagers who were unquestionably incapable of reading, there were others for whom it seemed likely that they could only read little because they had not been exposed to the experience, rather than because they actually lacked the

Table 11.5 *Teenagers' reading activities*

Level of ability	$n = 51$	%
Listens to a 5 min. story	42	82
Answers questions about the story	25	53
Tells the story in his own words	16	31
Groups or matches colours	38	75
Groups or matches shapes	39	77
Reads any words at all	33[a]	65

[a] In 9 cases only their own name

Table 11.6 *Estimates of reading age based on Schonell graded word reading test*

Estimated reading age in years	$n = 50$		%	
6.0–6.11	9		18	
7.0–7.11	5	18	10	36
8.0–8.11	2		4	
9.0–9.5	2		4	

ability. The score of teenagers on the Reynell language scale who could read something was as low as 26.5. For those with more useful reading skills – a reading age of over 7 years – the lowest Reynell score was 48. The relationship was not wholly consistent.

Table 11.7 *Teenagers' number abilities*

Level of ability	$n = 51$	%
Counts to 10	36	71
Counts to 20	19	37
Counts 5 objects		
(a) in a row	40	78
(b) random	33	65
Counts 10 objects		
(a) in a row	30	59
(b) random	22	43
Counts 20 objects		
(a) in a row	18	35
(b) random	11	22
Recognises numbers 1–10	27	53
Writes numbers 1–10	21	41
Adds to 5		
(a) in head (using fingers, etc.)	15	27
(b) as a sum	17	33
Adds to 10		
(a) in head (using fingers, etc.)	13	26
(b) as a sum	16	31
Subtracts to 5		
(a) in head (using fingers, etc.)	12	24
(b) as a sum	9	18
Subtracts to 10		
(a) in head (using fingers, etc.)	7	14
(b) as a sum	6	12
Names		
circle	37	73
triangle	32	63
square	32	63
rectangle	15	27
Shares 10 objects between 2 people	18	35
Recognises numbers 11–20	13	31
Knows some coins	24	47
Knows all coins	13	26

There were six teenagers with scores in excess of 40 on the Reynell scale who could not read at all.

Table 11.7 shows the number abilities of the teenagers. Table 11.8 shows how many of the 26 number activities the teenagers had mastered.

Table 11.8 *Teenagers' total scores in number activities*

Total scores	n = 51	%
0	9	18
1–4	9	18
5–9	10	20
10–14	5	10
15–19	5	10
20–25	12	24
26 (Maximum)	1	2
Total	51	(102)

With one exception all who did well on reading (that is, had an estimated reading age of over 7 years) did well on number (that is, had a score of over 20 items). There were five teenagers who, in spite of doing well on number, had made little progress on reading. Not surprisingly, it was children who were from ESN(M) schools who were most likely to have mastered 'academic' skills.

AFTER SCHOOL

Although there were some criticisms of schools, most parents appreciated the service and considerable fears were being expressed about the future, when school ended. Table 11.9 shows the families' intentions or wishes about future employment. In 1981 four boys and one girl were already at the ATC, although the girl also attended a Further Education course three days a week. Eight others had offers of places although one had refused his.

Table 11.9 *Teenagers' work intentions 1981*

	n	%
Attending, or planning to attend, ATC	31	(59)
Special care unit	2	(4)
Stay at home	6	(11)
Job	7	(13)
Sheltered community	3	(6)
Don't know	4	(8)
Total	53	(101)

Those parents with average children were generally content if there was an ATC place available. There were considerable worries among them about the availability of places, especially in one authority. Only one mother of a teenager needing special care, though, thought there was a real possibility that he might not be accommodated.

It was the parents of the more able teenagers who were most concerned about the future. Most felt the ATC was an inappropriate setting for their teenagers although, in some ways, they had an advantage over their non-handicapped peers in that there was somewhere they could go. Generally mothers felt the work at the ATC was too routine – only one viewed it positively as real training – and parents of girls were worried about the lack of supervision there.

Some parents had revised their notions of employment over the years. One mother realised the family small-holding would not provide suitable employment and another began to see that, in spite of her daughter being very capable, she would not be able to work in the family shop on her own, partly because she could not work under pressure. Others were still optimistic about the capabilities of their children, although pessimistic about the state of the economy. Work which seemed suitable to parents included Remploy, filling shelves, waiting on tables, cleaning, factory work, shop work, gardening or animal farming.

Parents were very critical of the lack of advice available at this stage: one mother said she knew more about Pathway schemes than the school. Those who, in happier times, might have entertained hopes of employment were offered very little. Even when schools made an attempt at work training this sometimes simply raised hopes which were to be dashed:

> He did one day a week at the NCB . . . at the sign shop . . . which he was doing very well at, great. And the man said, 'If he leaves school get him a job here'. Well now he's left school the unions won't take him. The careers officer came and said, 'No way will I get him into the NCB because there are 12 points he's got to pass which he can't. He can't read and see "Danger" signs and all that business'. I said 'Good gracious, those "Danger" signs were there the 6 months he's been there. He couldn't read then, so what's the difference?' They'd no right to take him in the beginning. But up here he worked so well, they reckoned he was wonderful. He was ripping off the backs of paper and putting the names, and then the men were putting it straight for him and he would put them under the machine and pull it down – marvellous . . . I'll put his name down for the Remploy.   (1981)

SUMMARY

The importance of appropriate education for children does not need stressing and the disadvantages for those who, like a third of the population here, are denied early access to school are obvious. It should also be remembered that the children in the population had no access to home teaching schemes that could have helped to compensate them for the lack of a school place.

The education the children received – its length and its type – was to a great extent determined by chance, that is, where families happened to live. One or two families took this into their calculations and moved or did not move house according to provisions available in the area, but families with these opportunities were clearly in the minority.

The type of school the teenagers attended was not invariably related to ability and some of the more able children attended ESN(S) schools.

While the children were young, parents tended to welcome the idea of integration but the choice became less clear cut for them as the children grew older and only one boy continued in the ordinary system until he left school. Others, although given that option, and in spite of current debates about integration, chose the protected environment of the special school where the teenagers could learn tasks for daily living rather than 'academic' skills.

With such important problems for parents to contend with, more detailed considerations of activities in school – the subjects covered, the lack of integration and classroom organisation – tended to receive less attention. Since Down's children nowadays will certainly be given a school place at 5 years at the latest and parents are more likely in the primary years to be happy with the placement, issues concerned with the daily life in school are likely to come under closer scrutiny. In particular the social and financial relationships between main schools and the special units attached to them are likely to need investigation.

Conclusion

This monograph has been concerned with variations between families and the help they have received. It is apparent that the responses and experiences of families differed, but a common factor was that all the Down's youngsters had lived with ordinary families in the community for most of their lives. Consequently their experiences illustrate the strengths and weaknesses of such living patterns and indicate the strengths community care policies can build upon or the weaknesses they should attempt to rectify.

The teenagers in the population are not representative of all Down's people, and the picture presented is not definitive of all families with Down's children. In particular it is possible to point to two general disadvantages that have affected this population.

Even apart from individuals and families who lie outside the range of families in South Wales, people with Down's syndrome (as well as everyone else) differ according to their year of birth. Down's children born in the 1960s have grown up in a period of transition. To their disadvantage they were born at a time when most professionals held a strongly negative 'mongol' stereotype and when there were few services to help parents. Services were largely confined to a limited number of places in mental handicap hospitals. On the other hand, during their early childhood changes in the education system occurred and other services began to improve. These factors have affected the life chances of this cohort and, to an extent, their experiences are unique and distinct from those born in either an earlier or later decade. (In particular, younger Down's children are likely to be doubly advantaged. Down's syndrome is an increasingly middle-class phenomenon and younger Down's children are likely to reflect this advantage. So, for these younger generations, improved services plus advantaged home background are likely to place them in a fortunate position compared with their older peers.)

There is a further unique factor in the lives of this 1960s cohort. These youngsters have spent all, or part, of their lives in South Wales and this is an area unlike some other regions in Britain. Even within South Wales it would be misleading to speak of the region as if it were homogeneous. Within it there exist relatively affluent communities and strata together with those which, by any Western standards, are not. The fact of the matter is that there are some communities that are pockets of disadvantage so great that even the relatively privileged within them find problems arise simply from living there. Indeed, those who are fully privileged will not go there: for instance, it is no inexplicable accident that the majority of general practitioners in some Welsh valleys are not British by birth. (This is not to imply a worse service results in this case.) Disadvantage begins with the uncompromising terrain, which isolates communities from each other and makes travel on foot difficult, and progresses to the personal poverty of many of the inhabitants whose livelihood has gone and to the public poverty that results in poor services (in health, education, social services, transport and housing) in spite of the greater needs of those who live there. Voluntary services are similarly underdeveloped. It is not surprising that it is an area of outward migration. It will be difficult for the reader in – for instance – the south-east of England to understand the grim realities of life in some of the more isolated and run-down valleys of South Wales.

These factors have produced some extremely disadvantaged Down's children in this area. Arguably, it is the disadvantaged who are most important in that their needs are greater and because they are more likely to be neglected. Neglected partly because of their social and geographical isolation from the rest of the population, but also because they are less likely to have people among them who will recognise such relative disadvantage and draw attention to their situation. There may also be another reason. The deprivation of these socially and economically impoverished areas, which negatively affects the lifestyles, opportunities and achievements of their Down's syndrome members (as well as those of everyone else), may seem to present unpopular and unpalatable facts for those who, in these times of rising optimism for the Down's population, wish to overturn the old-fashioned Down's syndrome stereotype. It should not do so, rather it should lend strength to the argument that Down's children do well if they are given the opportunity but, deprived of the opportunity, they dramatically highlight the limitations that are imposed on all people's lives when they live in impoverished communities. The disabled encounter the same sorts of problems as everyone else but, for the disabled, the difficulties are exacerbated (Open University, 1982). Down's people may illustrate this effect even more than other populations. Lyle (1960b) points out that Down's syndrome children may be particularly vulnerable to a deprived environment and other findings from the studies in South Wales would lend support to this view (Appendix 1). To this extent, then, the disabled are already integrated members of society, bound together with their normal peers in common disadvantage. Certainly variations within the region accounted for some of the differences in lifestyle found between the Down's syndrome families in this study.

Community care and the All Wales Strategy

'Community Care' is currently the popular clarion call of policy makers. It is presented as a new policy and ignores the fact that most mentally handicapped people have always been cared for in the community. Wilkinson (1985) points out that the 120,000 patients awaiting discharge in mental handicap hospitals represent only 10% of those already in the community. Although, so far, the running down of such hospitals is depressingly slow (see Wertheimer, 1982 and 1986), these ex-patients will compete for resources with those already in the community. Doubts about the adequacy of services in the community are beginning to be expressed and Ayer and Alaszewski (1984) suggest that community care is a 'policy based more on the limitations of institutions than on the proven advantages of the community'.

The move to community care as the ideal for disabled populations has also taken place in Wales. The national policy for mentally handicapped people has been set out in the *All Wales Strategy for the Development of Services for Mentally Handicapped People* (AWS) (Welsh Office, 1983). The AWS has provided for additional resources to initiate or improve services that will enhance the lives of mentally handicapped people and their carers. This provides the opportunity to redress the balance in favour of a section of the population who, in spite of having increased problems and needs, have traditionally suffered from inadequate provision. There are two fundamental aims in the AWS for mentally handicapped people:

1. To encourage as independent a life as possible.
2. To promote their integration into patterns of normal life to which the non-handicapped have access.

Unfortunately the contribution of the education services to the AWS is confined to two rather bland references, although the fundamental role of the education services in promoting both these aims will be readily apparent.

This study describes the reality of community care for Down's syndrome teenagers in South Wales. In many ways, the teenagers had the ideal of community care insofar as they were brought up in the bosom of their natural families exactly like most other children. So, what are the implications of this study for the AWS's aims of independence and integration?

The importance of the two aims of independence and integration for community care policies are obvious. The aim of promoting independence will present few problems. Promoting independence in self-care skills and the development of the person's full potential have been the aims of several services and programmes over the last 20 years. It is when independence moves on to the next stage and decisions need to be made about when a handicapped person becomes able to live more independently, or even on his own, that the issue will become more controversial. The South Wales study shows that independence at this level was still some way off for all the teenagers. Even the most able were not, as yet, using public transport, managing a budget or cooking for themselves. (This is not atypical. Jeffree and Cheseldine (1983) found only 2% of their sample of mentally handicapped adolescents were using public transport, 6% could count money and notes and 3% could cook a simple meal.) The mid-teens are not, of course, adulthood and further gains will undoubtedly be made, but independent living demands an element of risk. As yet few parents in the South Wales study were facing up to this notion. While the issue has not been addressed in this study, parents may well resist independent living for their offspring if this means a lower standard of living than they themselves have provided.

There is a further point. The important role parents play in initiating and encouraging independent activities for their own teenagers is clear from this study. It must be asked how far mere professionals will undertake this painstaking and individually orientated task for *all* the mentally handicapped people in their care.

The issue of integration is more difficult. Integration demands not only efforts from the mentally handicapped person and his carers but, unlike developing independence, demands a response from others. Integration is not a one-way process and difficulties for the disabled arise from barriers that are not merely physical (CORAD, 1982). This is particularly true for mentally handicapped people and attitudes of ordinary people shape expectations about what is possible for the mentally handicapped population to do, and so influences what they actually achieve, the type of services that are provided (e.g. custodial care in hospitals) and the rights that are given to them (e.g. Bicknell, 1983; Shepperdson, 1983b). Above all, attitudes determine the value placed on people and the dignity that is accorded to them.

Attitudes, particularly towards mentally handicapped people, may be exceptionally resistant to change. Negative attitudes towards mentally handicapped people are easy to understand. We live in a society where, increasingly over the years, people have been judged and valued according to their economic usefulness. It is tempting to blame this on a long period of Conservative government with its stringent and single-minded application of economic return as the paramount consideration, but the outspoken defence of this policy by its adherents is simply the reflection of a trend that has possibly gained momentum over the years but has always been generally accepted. Indeed, it is an economistic trend that may have even greater force in socialist countries, such as the Soviet Union (Ryan, 1978). Pinker (1971) points out that services in the United Kingdom are provided on the basis of what the recipient has, or will, contribute to society rather than on need and there is no evidence that this approach lacks popular support. So, an injury sustained by a soldier in a war attracts more compensation that a similar injury sustained – say – on the ski-slopes. Many would feel this a wholly just allocation of resources. The Disability Alliance, however, constantly argues for a distribution of resources according to the needs arising from disability rather than, as now, on the original cause of the injury.

Paradoxically, however, governments that advocate the supremacy of economic success above all other criteria may provide the climate in which such values do, at last, begin to be questioned. Now that so many people (indistinguishable from the economically active population by age, sex, race or disability) are unemployed and so have been deprived of their economic standing in society, the sense of loss normally attached to this may diminish and lead to people being judged and valued according to other criteria. It is arguable that this can only augur well for mentally handicapped people who are the antithesis of the 'go-getters' many would have us become (see, for example, Mrs Thatcher interviewed by Robin Day on 'Panorama', 9 April 1984) and they are unlikely to make massive economic contributions.

There are signs that traditional views are in fact changing. Families often point out the advantages that they derive from the experience of having a Down's syndrome child. Similarly, moves towards the use of mentally handicapped people as Community Service volunteers (i.e. as givers rather than recipients of help) may be particularly useful in shaping attitudes and suggest that traditional views are being questioned.

However, this study in South Wales demonstrates that, as yet, there is little integration of Down's people into the community. Firstly, there was little community help given to families and care largely fell onto one family member (see also Grant *et al.*, 1984; Pahl and Quine, 1986; Wilkin, 1979). Secondly, the Down's syndrome teenager was involved in few activities that were not dependent on his family. Thirdly, most importantly, simple physical integration may mask the fact that social integration is minimal and there was some indication that a few of the Down's teenagers who were physically integrated were not integrated socially. This is a recurring problem, as several studies show. For instance, the location for this sort of socially engineered physical integration is frequently in playgroups and schools. Sinsen and Wetherick (1981) show that physically placing children into integrated settings does not inevitably lead to interaction. (This study is criticised in Booth, 1985). Hegarty and Pocklington (1981) describe the use of 'peer tutors' in schools, indicating that new methods of educating the normal population may have to be considered if true integration is to take place. The spirit, as well as the letter, of integration needs to be considered. It is implicit in the work of Hughes and May that seemingly acceptable activities and practices can conceal meaningless rituals: they describe the 'occupation' of patients on long-stay wards (1983) and interviews about job placements by careers officers (1981). While there are several examples of successful integration of living accommodation into the community (e.g. Feinmann, 1983), Eastwood (1983) reports the findings of a survey by the Campaign for Mentally Handicapped People that shows that hostel residents had mainly formal and organised contacts with others in the community and that even sustained contact with tradesmen was limited.

To sum up – there was variation in how far Down's syndrome teenagers in South Wales were integrated into the community, but few people approached full integration. Can we be sure that paid (albeit trained) professionals will do better in providing opportunities in the community than loving and caring parents who have only one child to consider? Some of the best schemes to be started for mentally handicapped people have been initiated and implemented by parents precisely because professionals have failed to make progress in difficult service areas e.g. Welsh Initiative for Specialised Employment (WISE) in Swansea, West Glamorgan; M H Forestry Projects Ltd., Hexham, Northumberland. Both have attempted to provide access to more normal job opportunities for mentally handicapped people.

Integration should not be pursued without consideration of into what it is intended people should integrate. It has been said that deprivation in some areas in South Wales has operated to the disadvantage of some Down's syndrome teenagers. The implication of integration into local communities must be that those who live in privileged communities will be relatively advantaged by that integration, whereas the reverse may be true for those in areas of public and private poverty. This accepts and solidifies regional inequality. Will it always be to the benefit of mentally handicapped people to integrate into the community, regardless of the opportunities that are offered there? Paradoxically, in South Wales, there were signs that, in poor regions, London-rated allowances were making families who benefited somewhat privileged compared with their neighbours. Whether this truly fosters integration is uncertain.

There is yet another aspect of integration to be considered. It is intended that mentally handicapped people should have access to the same services as everyone else. It is recognised that, as yet, some service providers lack the skills to meet the special needs of the mentally handicapped population. However, it is argued that if professionals are never exposed to these populations, they will never learn to cope (Bicknell, 1983). This is a persuasive argument but, at present, parents clearly find that it is specialists rather than generalists who are of most use to them. There will be overlap in the needs of all babies – normal or mentally handicapped – but there are likely also to be highly specialised needs for those with individual categories of handicap, e.g. spina bifida, cerebral palsy and PKU. For instance, Cunningham *et al.* (1982) showed that health visitors needed a period of additional training if they were to deal adequately with the problems of mothers who had Down's syndrome babies. Cunningham and McArthur (1981) illustrated how the routine hearing tests for all babies were inadequate in picking up the problems of Down's syndrome babies. There will be those with even more rare conditions who are likely to be particularly disadvantaged by non-special services e.g. those with cri du chat syndrome or tuberous sclerosis. How realistic is it for generalist workers to have a detailed knowledge of all conditions? As it is, specialist workers feel somewhat under threat – particularly those with a health background such as the mental handicap nurses (Jones, 1981) and consultant psychiatrists in mental handicap (Heginbotham and Day, 1983).

Rather than abandoning people with needs to inadequately prepared services, it would seem that ways must be found of meeting needs within an integrated setting. Here the community mental handicap team may find one of its major roles is educating non-specialist workers and acting as a resource for those workers who encounter problems beyond their own immediate expertise. It seems likely that different services require a different degree of integration. Those dealing in advice and which are, anyway, in contact with mentally handicapped people and their families for only brief periods in any 24 hours, need to have professionals with very specific skills. Because of the brief contact they are unlikely to promote segregation to any marked degree. Services that are in contact with consumers more intensively – schools, employment, accommodation, leisure – and where a segregated service provides a segregated way of life, need to consider how to make specialist skills available within an integrated setting.

The consumer

The idea of consultation with those who use services gains momentum. The Court Report (1976) considered it valuable to identify consumers' own priorities and the value they placed on services. The AWS, as a central theme, has provided for consultation with parents at all levels of implementation. Although this is a welcome move away from the assumption that consumer opinions are usually biased towards the vocal middle classes and so can be justifiably disregarded (e.g. see Shepperdson, 1983a) consultation in the context of mental handicap must face the awkward fact that the real consumer – the mentally handicapped person himself – is rarely consulted. The most vulnerable members of this population cannot speak, much less formulate demands. Sometimes they are not consulted even when they are able to contribute. Increasingly the real consumer voice is being heard (e.g. APMH Annual Congress, Cardiff July, 1985; EEC Bureau for Action in Favour of Disabled People, 1985) but it is only the most able who can participate at such public events and they may be far from representative of the total population.

To avoid this dilemma parents are usually asked to represent their children. Is this wholly acceptable? Parents have been presented in this conclusion as providing the best of care but, of course, not all do so and, besides this, there are specific aspects of care where they are particularly likely to be deficient in what they offer. For instance, this study, as well as others, shows that parents do not always push for independence in their offspring as vigorously as they could. This is an especially pertinent problem for parents of teenagers and adults who have few examples to follow in the field and who may not realise the efforts that are still required. Again, parents can become so involved with the day-to-day struggle to provide care, education and leisure for their youngsters that the implications of what they are doing may escape them. As May and Hughes (1986) point out:

> Parents . . . were so occupied with the immediate task of ensuring continuing care [for their teenagers] that they had little time or patience for such elusive concepts as emerging adult identity . . . these concerns do eventually intrude once the issue of care has been resolved. (p. 296)

The future also presents difficulties for parents – understandably in view of the poor services available – and Buckle (1984) shows how inadequately parents had prepared even their very elderly offspring for inevitable future separation from home.

In any case, reaching parents may present problems. For instance, the AWS has set up 'Parents' Forums' but it needs to be considered whether they are truly representative of parents. In the field of mental handicap it may well be that those who are most under stress and weighed down by the burden of their responsibilities, and who have consequently the greatest needs, may be least able to attend such functions and put forward their own point of view. Certainly, in the South Wales study, several mothers with very severely disabled children would have been unlikely to attend such gatherings. Their views needed to be solicited actively. Opinions must also be regarded: there are signs that Parents' Forums are seen by parents as rituals, unrelated to the actual provision of services (Down's Children's Association meeting, Swansea, in June 1986).

Consultation with consumers runs into the further difficulty that satisfaction – be it with the quality of life or the quality of services – is strongly linked with expectations. One reason why those in higher social classes are in danger of responding less well to the birth of a mentally handicapped child is almost certainly associated with their expectations about what are acceptable roles and an acceptable quality of life for themselves and their children (Farber, 1968; Tizard and Grad, 1961). Turning to satisfaction with services, there may be a danger that the AWS will raise popular expectations to a level that cannot be met. What satisfied in 1980 may not do so in 1990 and the publicity surrounding the AWS may contribute to this discontent. Satisfaction with services is only partly related to what is available. One mother in the South Wales study who had a 1-hour journey to hospital, a 3-hour wait, a 10-minute consultation with the doctor and a 1-hour journey home was well pleased with the service. Not all mothers would feel the same, and perhaps fewer will do so in the future. It is certainly not suggested that educating people to discontent is undesirable, indeed improvements are unlikely to take place without it, but it does present problems for those who wish to meet and satisfy expressed needs.

Parents are not invariably the best people to speak for their children, and recent court cases illustrate this dramatically (*Re B (a minor)* (1981); *R. v Arthur* (1981); *R. v Brown* (1985)) but professionals may not do any better. Leaving aside major hospital scandals, there are numerous examples of inappropriate intervention by professionals e.g. the sterilisation of a girl with Soto's syndrome (Loxley, 1976). This issue was raised again (with a different outcome for a more severely disabled girl) in *Re B (a minor)* in April 1987. (It may well be that on this question – as in the euthanasia debate – Down's syndrome will be the 'borderline' condition about which opinion becomes extremely divided. If so it will not be possible to avoid the genetic issues.) Again, a television programme ('Brass Tacks', November 1986) discussed the discharge from hospital of a woman who had spent much of her life there. The professionals spoke of 'informed consent' but it became apparent during the programme that this was a totally unrealistic notion for that particular woman. A professional worker admitted this later on. Discharge went ahead despite the doubts of the mentally handicapped woman's mother. This is introduced, not to argue the rights and wrongs of this case, but to express concern that professionals can, if unchallenged, deceive themselves about 'consent' in this way. When the views of others are being imposed on vulnerable populations particular care should be taken that not only is it to their advantage, but it should also be very clear that professionals *are* imposing their own wishes, albeit with the best of intentions. They should be very wary of using their power to manipulate the opinions of those they are meant to protect, so gaining consent in this way.

On a similar theme, in order to pursue integration, parents and professionals may in fact distort or frustrate some of the spirit of the AWS. To foster integration efforts are made to make mentally handicapped people behave in ways that are acceptable to the general public. There were examples in this study of a narrow range of behaviour being imposed on the Down's teenager, in order to make him conform: in other words individual choice was restricted rather than expanded. Not only this, but a few of the more desirable characteristics of some of the teenagers were seen as unhelpful in the outside world. Those teenagers who were gentle and lacked aggression were felt to be very vulnerable. Logically, to hold their own, they should be encouraged to be nastier! Again, the current emphasis on achievement for Down's people may place undue emphasis on this aspect of life, at the expense of other desirable goals, such as happiness.

As it is, placing the onus on the handicapped person to change, without similar requirements being put on everyone else, compounds the disadvantage from which mentally handicapped people already suffer. It also avoids asking people in society to begin to exercise tolerance and acceptance towards those who are unable to present a conforming and standard image. However successful Down's people are in making progress and – rightly – overturning the old sterotypes, there will still be left those who are unable to 'succeed' in these terms. Real change for mentally handicapped people demands much more sweeping and fundamental reorganisation of society than simply providing specific help and services for the people themselves. It demands a more equal sharing of resources (regardless of a person's personal attributes) followed, it is to be hoped, by a person's standing in society not being judged by their economic position. Such changes would produce benefits for a wider section of the population than simply those who are mentally handicapped.

Appendix 1

The Attainments of the Teenagers

There is a wide range of abilities between Down's syndrome people. In this population in South Wales some of the teenagers were only mildly mentally handicapped and were able to care for themselves and make a contribution to running the home. The majority were more severely mentally handicapped and so were more dependent, but only a minority were almost totally dependent on their carers for all activities. This appendix examines the differences between the teenagers in the areas of social competence and language. How far differences between the teenagers are due to their inheritance cannot be dealt with here but consideration is given to whether differences are due to chance or, more optimistically, due to differences in their environments.

There is already ample evidence to suggest that environment influences the attainments of normal children (e.g. Jackson and Marsden, 1962; Nisbet, 1963; Douglas, 1964; Bernstein, 1971), handicapped children (e.g. Baumeister, 1968; Pringle and Fiddes, 1970) and Down's syndrome children (e.g. Centerwall and Centerwall, 1960; Stedman *et al.*, 1962; Shotwell and Shipe, 1964; Lyle, 1959, 1960a, 1960b; Francis, 1971; Carr, 1970, 1975). Many studies concentrate on the gross differences which occur between children brought up at home and those reared in institutions, but it would be wrong to assume that all institutions and all homes are the same, or that all institutions lower achievements or that all homes enhance them. Whilst it is probably easier to provide desirable care in a family home (e.g. a high ratio of adults to children, with continuity, warmth and intensity in adult–child interactions, and so on – see Goldfarb, 1954), an institution need not necessarily provide bad care. As early as 1963 Wolfensberger *et al.* suggested the time had come to 'discard the fashionable stereotype of the ''bad'' institution' and suggested instead that the factors distinguishing 'good' from 'bad' should be studied. Not only this, but the environment of both institutions (Tizard, 1964) and homes (e.g. with home support programmes) can be changed for the better, with consequent improvements in the child's attainments. The issue is complicated, however, for mentally handicapped children at home. Ryan (1973) suggests that patterns of parental behaviour towards the mentally handicapped child are more varied and less predictable than those adopted towards normal children (see also Jeffree, 1968). In addition, it is difficult to disentangle the causes of differences in attainment since they may be due to variation in environment or differences in natural endowment. Fraser and Sadovnick (1976) found that the IQ scores of Down's syndrome children living at home correlated significantly with those of their parents and siblings. Gibson (1979), in a useful review of home versus institution studies, casts some doubt on how far it has been shown conclusively that home care does inevitably ensure superior and long-term gains for the Down's syndrome child.

This study sets out to determine if the same factors which influence the attainments of normal children affect Down's syndrome children too: namely, social class and stimulation.

THE CHILDREN IN 1972

In 1972, 36 of the children in the original sample were tested. One parent refused testing for her child. Children were tested for social competence using Gunzburg's Progress Assessment Chart, Form 1 (PAC 1). Teachers were asked to complete a form for each child although certain items, which not all teachers could be expected to answer confidently, were excluded. This reduced the maximum possible score from 120 to 107. The children were also tested for language using the Reynell Developmental Language Scales. This test is designed for use with normal babies and children under 6 years and it is a useful test to use with handicapped children because even those with limited abilities can expect to score. In 1972 in two instances, and in 1981 in one instance, the test was administered in Welsh through a teacher.

In 1972 it was found that, for all tests, age and sex were not related to differences in scores. Those in social classes IV and V, however, scored significantly lower than those in the higher social classes both on the Gunzburg PAC and the Reynell scales. These results are not consistent with those of Carr (1970 and 1975), who found no significant differences between the social classes in the scores of her younger sample of Down's syndrome children. Possible explanations are as follows:

1. Different tests were used in Carr's study. Carr used the Bayley Infant Scales of mental and motor development, because 4-year-old Down's syndrome children rarely scored on the Stanford-Binet test. However, the correlation between scores on most tests in the South Wales study were high and it seems likely that children in 1972 would have had a similar pattern of results even using different tests.

2. Carr used a manual/non-manual division for social class. Had this sort of division been used in the South Wales study, the high-scoring and more numerous social class IIIb children would have cancelled out the very low scores of those in social classes IV and V. This would have been less likely had the whole population been available for testing in 1972 but, even so, it was the low social class children who scored most differently from the rest of the children.

3. It is possible that Carr's younger sample (up to 4 years) would not have been sufficiently influenced by environment to show measurable differences. Differences between normal children emerge increasingly with age (Douglas, 1964). Bayley (1954, p.5) says, 'Differences in parental economic status are related to the child's scores after two years but not in infancy.' It may be that for mentally handicapped children it is mental age that must be considered in this context and that social-class differences appear at a later stage.

In 1972 homes were rated as providing 'good', 'average' or 'poor' stimulation according to an assessment of activities inside and outside the home. While the children in those families given 'good' stimulation had higher average scores than those in 'average' and 'poor' homes, the most dramatic differences were between the scores of those in 'poor' homes and the rest. These differences were significantly lower using the Reynell scales but, while the scores were lower for the Gunzburg PAC, they were not significantly so.

THE TEENAGERS IN 1981

In 1981, 33 of the 36 children who had been tested in 1972 were re-tested on the

Gunzburg and Reynell tests. The 19 children in the new sample were also tested. It was also possible to test the child from the original sample who was not seen in 1972. His results are included with those of the new sample, which thus consists of 20 – rather than 19 – teenagers in this appendix. Results in 1981 are for the 53 teenagers in the population. It was explained in Chapter 1 that able children were over-represented in the new sample.

It was considered that the Reynell test, while useful for distinguishing children in the lower ability ranges, did not allow the brighter children to show their abilities. Consequently, the English Picture Vocabulary Test (EPVT) was also administered. The EPVT is a measure of 'listening vocabulary' which correlates highly with IQ measures. Its use as a measure of general mental ability is suspect, however, particularly with mentally handicapped children (Leeming *et al.*, 1979). While no one scored full marks on the Reynell, the EPVT did allow some teenagers to reach higher scores. The highest score on the EPVT was 101 months compared with 74 months on the Reynell. In contrast, 10 of the poorer children failed to reach an adequate score on the EPVT and had to be discounted as 'untestable'. Even so, in spite of excluding these children (who for the most part scored unusually badly on all tests), the correlation between the Reynell and EPVT results was high (Pearson's $r = 0.64$).

The test results in 1981

Age

As in 1972 there were no important differences between the year in which the teenagers were born and their test results (Table A1).

Table A1 *Year of birth and average test scores*

	n	Gunzburg	Reynell	n	EPVT
1964	19	56.5	36.4	14	50.6
1965	13	65.4	42.2	11	53.4
1966	21	64.0	40.5	18	51.9
Total	53	61.6	39.4	43	51.8

Sex

In 1972 there were only small differences between the average scores of the girls and boys. In 1981, however, when the whole population was available for testing, the average scores of girls were higher (Table A2). It is possible that differences were due to the fact that more of the girls came from higher social classes. Studies of small numbers are particularly vulnerable to this sort of chance distortion. However, both Carr (1975) and Cunningham *et al.* (1985) find sex differences in the scores of Down's syndrome children.

Table A2 *Sex and average test scores*

	n	Gunzburg	Reynell	n	EPVT
Girls	25	68.0	42.1	20	54.1
Boys	28	56.7	37.1	23	49.9
Total	53	61.6	39.4	43	51.8

Social class

Differences between the social classes and average test scores were maintained in 1981

Table A3 *Social class and average test scores*

Social class	n	Gunzburg	Reynell	n	EPVT
I and II	12	78.6	43.4	10	59.9
III	28	65.4	41.3	24	53.5
IV and V	13	41.6	29.1	9	40.5
Total	53	61.6	39.4	43	51.8

(Table A3). While the major differences continued to be between those in social classes IV and V and the rest, in 1981 differences between social classes I and II and those in lower social classes also appeared. This was due to the fact that the whole population was available for testing in 1981. Differences between social classes I and II and social class III were small in 1972 and 1981 on the Reynell Language Scale.

Stimulation

Homes were again rated on the stimulation they provided. The rating was based on outings, holidays, club membership and an overall assessment of opportunities provided in the home. The amount of stimulation given in the home was shown to be as important for the teenagers as it had been when they were children (Table A4). The greater differences were between the disadvantaged and the rest rather than between the advantaged teenagers and the rest.

Table A4 *Stimulation levels and average test scores*

	n	Gunzburg	Reynell	n	EPVT
Good	19	76.7	48.3	18	55.6
Average	22	62.8	41.9	19	50.6
Poor	12	35.8	20.9	6	19.0
Total	53	61.6	39.4	43	51.8

Having found some variation it was necessary to test this for significance.

An analysis of variance on these test results for sex, age, social class and stimulation showed that, for all except the EPVT, the variation between cells was significant (Table A5). It seems likely that the failure to produce a significant result for the EPVT was due to the exclusion of the teenagers who were untestable. This weakened the differences between the various categories since it was those teenagers who failed to score who showed the most marked differences from the rest of the population.

Table A5 *Analysis of variance for Gunzburg, Reynell and EPVT*

	n	df	F value	Significance level
Gunzburg	53	30,22	2.56	0.05 ($p < 0.01 = 2.58$)
Reynell	53	30,22	2.06	0.05
EPVT	43	8,17	1.03	Not significant

A more detailed examination of the relationship between social class and average stimulation scores for the three tests is given in Tables A6, A7 and A8. (See also Figures 1 and 2.)

Tables A6, A7 and A8 and, in graphical form, Figures 1 and 2 illustrate that the social class of parents and the stimulation Down's syndrome teenagers received at home both exerted an influence on their achievements. The most powerful influence was stimulation. Good or average stimulation given in homes of low social class could raise the

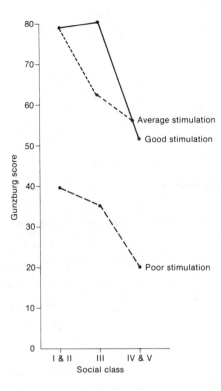

Figure 1 Relationship between stimulation and social class. Average scores on Guzburg PAC (Form 1).

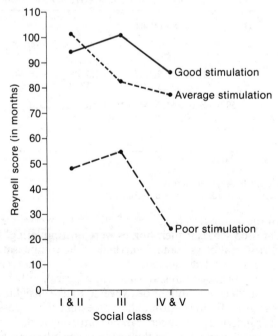

Figure 2 Relationship between stimulation and social class. Average scores on Reynell developmental language scales.

Table A6 *Social class, stimulation and Gunzburg scores*

Stimulation	Social class				Difference between highest and lowest social classes
	I & II	III	IV & V	Average	
Good	77.75 (8)	80.89 (9)	53.5 (2)	76.7(19)	24.1
Average	78.0 (3)	62.69(13)	54.83 (6)	62.8(22)	23.2
Poor	39.0 (1)	35.17 (6)	20.4 (5)	33.8(12)	18.6
Average score	76.8 (12)	65.4 (28)	41.6 (13)	61.6(53)	
Difference between best and worst stimulation levels	38.8	45.7	33.1		

Number of teenagers shown in brackets
$F = 6.3$; df $= 8,22$; $p < 0.01$.

Table A7 *Social class, stimulation level and Reynell scores*

Stimulation	Social class				Difference between highest and lowest social classes
	I & II	III	IV & V	Average	
Good	94.75 (8)	100.56 (9)	86.0 (2)	48.3(19)	8.8
Average	101.67 (3)	82.69(13)	77.33 (6)	41.9(22)	24.3
Poor	48.0 (1)	55.0 (6)	24.0 (5)	20.9(12)	24.0
Average score	46.3 (12)	41.3 (28)	29.1 (13)	39.4	
Difference between best and worst stimulation levels	46.8	45.6	62.0		

Number of teenagers in brackets
$F = 3.94$; df $= 8,22$; $p < 0.05$.

Table A8 *Social class, stimulation level and EPVT scores*

Stimulation	Social class				Difference between highest and lowest social classes
	I & II	III	IV & V	Average	
Good	61.6 (7)[a]	55.8 (9)	34.0(2)	55.6(18)	27.6
Average	56.0 (3)	49.9(12)[a]	42.8(5)[a]	50.6(20)	13.2
Poor	—[a]	51.5 (4)[b]	42.0(1)[b]	19.0 (5)	9.5
Average score	59.9(10)	53.5(25)	40.5(8)	51.8	
Difference between best and worst stimulation levels	5.6	4.3	−8		

Number of teenagers in brackets
Not significant
[a] One teenager excluded because untestable.
[b] More than one teenager excluded because untestable.

average scores of the children to the levels of others. Conversely, even high-social-class children had depressed scores if their homes were unstimulating. It follows that some teenagers from low-social-class homes, who lacked the compensation of good stimulation, suffered extreme disadvantage and this was reflected in their scores.

It is possible, using average scores, to show these overall influences on performance. Looking at individual teenagers might be expected to give insights into the processes at work behind these gross figures. Although to an extent this is possible, it must be said that the picture for individual teenagers can be confusing and, for some teenagers, it is not possible to account adequately for their superior or inferior scores, or for their high or low gains over the years.

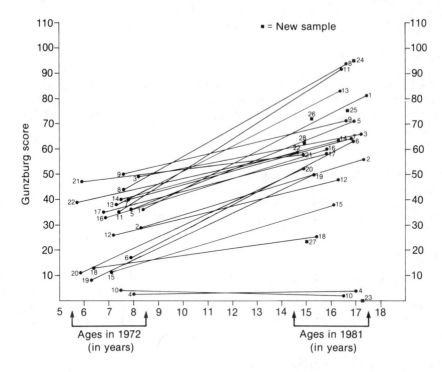

Figure 3 Gunzburg PAC (Form 1): ages and scores of boys, 1972 and 1981.

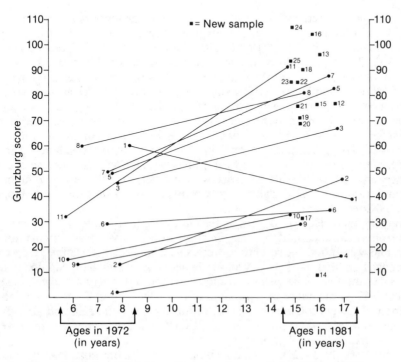

Figure 4 Gunzburg PAC (Form 1): ages and scores of girls, 1972 and 1981.

Results for individual children and their changes from 1972 to 1981

Figures 3 to 6 show the changes in the performance of the teenagers from 1972 to 1981. Details are also included in Figures 3 to 6 of teenagers in the new sample, although they were tested only in 1981. The following discussion concentrates on the top and bottom five places for scores (the 'scorers') for the whole population and for changes in scores from 1972 to 1981 (the 'gainers') for the original sample only. Individual children are referred to by numbers in Figures 3 to 6.

The Gunzburg results (Figures 3 and 4)

On the Gunzburg PAC changes in performance from 1972 to 1981 varied from an increase of 59 points to a deterioration (for one girl) of 31 points.

High scorers

The five teenagers with the best Gunzburg scores in 1981 (Boys 24 and 8; Girls 24, 16 and 13) tended to show the predictable advantages of either high social class (Girl 13) or high stimulation levels at home (Boy 8; Girl 24). Only one boy (24) – the highest scoring – had both advantages. One girl (16) was from social class IIIb and had only an averagely stimulating home. However, she had many normal friends and did go out, if not in a wholly unrestricted way, quite extensively. Consequently she had abundant opportunities for stimulation outside her home setting.

High gainers

Similar influences affected those teenagers who had made most gains since 1972 (Boys 11, 8, 6, 1 and 13; Girl 11). The 'top' six teenagers (two teenagers tied for fifth place) tended to be of high social class (Boy 1; Girl 11) and/or from stimulating homes (Boys 11, 8 and 1). Boy 1 particularly had been encouraged since childhood and had been allowed to take risks. Three of the four children classified in Chapter 2 as having 'unrestricted local freedom' were in this group of high gainers. The teenager (Girl 11) who made the most gains was not wholly advantaged. She was of high social class and had good stimulation at home, and these factors obviously compensated for some potential disadvantages. These were that she was brought up by a single parent (but with the advantage of resident grandparents), and, most importantly, her freedom outside was classified as 'very limited'. She was a weekly boarder at school. She was also one of the top gainers on the Reynell scale. She was (with another) the youngest child in the population and it may be that her gains partly resulted from a spurt in her development after the 1972 tests.

One boy (6), who made good gains on the Gunzburg test, is something of a surprise. He was from a social class IIIb home which provided only average stimulation. His Reynell gains were poor, the seventh lowest gains of the original sample. He was also disadvantaged in that he had developed epilepsy and had had additional health problems. His mother, while caring and concerned and with a very supportive husband, was still in 1981 considerably saddened by her son's disabilities. There was no obvious explanation of his good Gunzburg gains. A further boy (13) again had an averagely stimulating home and was from social class IIIb. His health was good and there were no negative features in his background.

Two other boys (19 and 20), whilst not among those with the most superior gains, are worth mention because they had made good progress from 1972 to 1981 (seventh and eighth highest gains). Both were from low-social-class homes. One (19) was from a home rated as unstimulating and the other (20) was the son of a single parent and his home was merely average. Both were young children compared with others and so, again, perhaps they were relatively immature in 1972. While their gains were good, their relative scores compared with others in 1981 were not exceptional.

Low scorers

Of the five lowest scoring children on the Gunzburg PAC (Boys 23, 10 and 4; Girls 14 and 4), three were from social classes IV or V (Boys 23 and 10; Girl 4), and four were from unstimulating homes (Boys 23 and 10; Girls 4 and 14). Two were looked after by a single parent and one had been in this situation for most of his childhood; another had a father who worked away from home (Boys 23 and 10; Girls 4 and 14). The mother of one child had herself been classified as mentally handicapped – probably wrongly – in earlier years.

One low-scoring boy (4) was an exception. His home was perfectly adequate and his mother was extremely thoughtful and responsive to his needs. In spite of this all his scores in both 1972 and 1981 were very low. A handicap additional to that of Down's syndrome was suspected but had not been identified. His behaviour was disturbed.

Low gainers

Those who made low gains tended to belong to the group of severely retarded teenagers who normally clustered to the bottom of any measure (see Cunningham and Mittler, 1981). For the six slowest gaining teenagers (two tied for fifth place), two boys (10 and 4) who made low gains were also low scorers. Two teenagers (Boy 21; and Girl 6) were of low social class but from averagely stimulating homes. The score of Boy 21 was puzzling. Had the Newsons' (1963) classification of social class been used, which takes into account the mother's occupation, this boy would have been given a higher class rating (see too Jackson and Marsden, 1962). He was one of the ablest children tested in 1972 and was one of the best gainers in the Reynell test in 1981. (Unfortunately it was the test where the teacher translated questions into Welsh.) In 1972 he had been fortunate in that he had a great deal of adult and individual attention. The one negative feature in his background was that his parents were somewhat protective towards him and this perhaps helps to explain his lack of progress on the Gunzburg PAC between 1972 and 1981. The final boy (18) had been withdrawn from school at one point in his career and so his lack of progress can be explained.

The performance of one girl (1) among the six lowest gainers warrants further comment. She was a child who performed extremely well in 1972 and, on both tests, she was the highest scoring girl. Not only this but she was open, bright, friendly and responsive. In 1981 her scores and behaviour showed a marked deterioration. It was difficult to attract her interest during the Reynell test. Throughout the test she was grinding her teeth and making repetitive hand movements. It was very hard to break through to establish any rapport with her. New teachers at the school found it difficult to believe that she had been so able in her younger days. There was no adequate explanation given. Her mother associated the deterioration with an incident when she was on holiday away from home when she had an accident which damaged her teeth. Deterioration can be expected in some Down's syndrome adults because of Alzheimer's disease (Jervis, 1948) or other problems (Thase, 1982). Although this girl was rather young for such problems to appear, she had not been tested for any physical explanation.

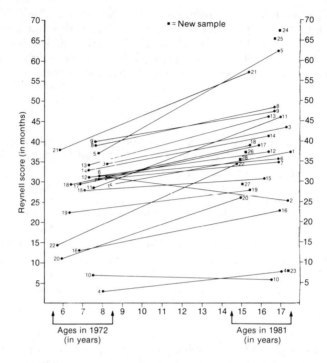

Figure 5 Reynell Developmental Language Scales: ages and scores of boys, 1972 and 1981.

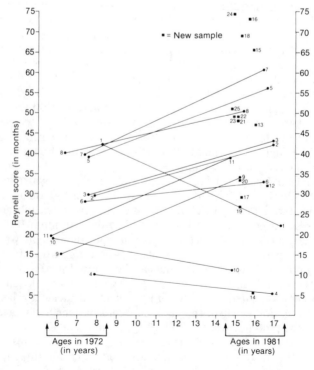

Figure 6 Reynell Developmental Language Scales: ages and scores of girls, 1972 and 1981.

The Reynell results (Figures 5 and 6)

Changes in the Reynell scores ranged from an increase in 25 months in one teenager to a deterioration in five teenagers, who did less well in 1981 compared with 1972.

High scorers

The six best scorers on the Reynell test (two tied for fifth place) were all from the new sample (Boys 24 and 25; Girls 24, 16, 18 and 15). Two of the six were of high social class (Boy 24; Girl 18) and only two did not have highly stimulating homes (Girls 15 and 16). One of these (Girl 16) has been mentioned already as having a wide circle of friends but it was difficult to account for Girl 15's success. She was from social class IIIa and had average stimulation at home.

High gainers

Among those teenagers who made the best gains in the Reynell test, five scored equally well in fourth place making a total of eight high gainers (Boys 5, 22, 11 and 21; Girls 7, 5, 9 and 11). Social class and stimulation were again important. (Boy 5 was high social class; Boy 11 and Girls 5 and 7 had high stimulation; Boy 22 and Girls 9 and 11 had both advantages.) However, two teenagers were from social class IV. One was mentioned earlier (Boy 21) and the other was Girl 5. Positive features in the girl's background were that she had always played with the village children and was brought up with several adult siblings who were still living at home. One sister had taken over her care when her parents died. The Down's girl was friendly and personable and was given 'limited' freedom. She was, however, becoming more, rather than less, restricted in that she had left her village and was also giving rise to concern as she became more sexually attractive. As a child she had been a poor attender at special school because her mother resented the fact that she could not attend the village school.

Low scorers

The lowest scoring children on the Reynell were all severely retarded children (Boys 10, 23 and 4; Girls 4 and 14). They were the same five who were low scorers on the Gunzburg PAC. Three were from socially deprived homes. Boy 4 has been discussed earlier and Girl 14 was one of the most disabled children in the new sample. Her mother reported a deterioration in her early childhood but it is difficult to know if this was a dramatic decline because she was not seen in 1972.

Low gainers

Five children did not only fail to gain but actually deteriorated (Boys 2 and 10; Girls 1, 10 and 4). It is possible that the scores reflected a poor response to the testing situation rather than ability. Most of the teenagers who deteriorated were low scorers anyway and it may be that testing of such young people is subject to the same difficulties as the testing of very young children. One boy (2) from social class IIIb and with a home rated as giving 'good' stimulation still deteriorated between 1972 and 1981. His mother suspected he had epilepsy but this had not been confirmed. There seemed little else to account for his very poor progress.

Influences on achievements

The implication of these findings would seem to be yet more confirmation that environment does influence the attainments of Down's syndrome children. Examples through-out this book will have made it clear to the reader that home conditions for the teen-agers varied considerably. Some aspects of family life and upbringing were obviously helpful for children's development while others were less than optimal. Chapter 7 gave a more detailed account of some of the family and environmental reasons for poor stimulation levels. Some problems arose from the teenagers themselves if they were un-responsive, uncooperative or difficult to take out because of mobility or behaviour problems. The situation can be more complicated. Spradlin and Rosenberg (1964) found that fluent mentally handicapped children received more stimulation than those who were not. This means that it becomes difficult to state categorically that poor stim-ulation *causes* a teenager to do badly, since it may be this very low level of development which leads to less stimulation being provided. It seems likely, however, that for what-ever primary cause the situation may well become one of self-perpetuating deteriora-tion. At the higher end of the scale, a similar beneficent spiral may be set up, but the gains at this end are less spectacular than the losses at the lower end of the scale. Francis (1971) and Lyle (1959; 1960a) suggest that Down's syndrome children may be part-icularly vulnerable to poor environments. It seems likely that they are more susceptible to the effects of a poor environment than to one that is enhanced.

There are also other characteristics which affect Down's syndrome children. It is well known that they are vulnerable to physical problems. Cunningham (1985a) found that severe additional handicaps affected scores of Down's syndrome children adversely. Barrera *et al.* (1987) showed that Down's syndrome children with heart defects received poorer caretaking at home (on various measures) than those without. In the South Wales study, children who scored well on the Gunzburg PAC were more likely to be rated by their mothers as enjoying good health and vice versa (see Chapter 1). Actual or perceived ill-health also affected the opportunities given to the child. One child was re-moved from school because of a heart defect (Boy 18); one child stopped using public transport because of epilepsy and the family had no car (Boy 12); one boy was unavoid-ably severely restricted in his early youth because of a heart defect (Boy 7). Others had severe physical problems, e.g. heart defect (Girl 4) and visual problems (Girl 2). All these children except Boy 7 had scores below the mean on the Gunzburg PAC and all except Girl 12 scored below the mean on the Reynell.

Three boys (including the one mentioned above) missed several years of school. All scored badly (Boys 18, 23 and 27).

Cunningham (1985b) points out the danger of secondary handicap resulting from poor parental expectations. Cunningham and Mittler (1981) also suggest that changes in attitudes towards Down's syndrome children and their potential took place in the late 1960s and early 1970s and that this positively affected the achievements of many Down's children, even for those without the specific help of formal early intervention programmes. The poor prognosis given to many parents in this study in South Wales has been discussed. While some disregarded this gloomy forecast, others were clearly influenced by it and consequently were under-motivated. The lack of advice available for parents in the population has been pointed out earlier in the book. It should be remembered, too, that some children did not have a school place until they were well over 5 years of age.

There were other reasons for stimulation levels that were lower than optimal. Parents could be disinclined to make the effort, they could choose other priorities or they could be unsure about useful methods of intervention. Three quotations (all from 1972) will illustrate these various problems.

> Well, this lady in L said for us to teach him [to speak]. Well, I mean, I've got other work to do. I haven't got time to go studying how to teach a child to speak.   (1972)

One mother, far from being encouraged by the story of Nigel Hunt (1967) as other mothers had been, saw it as a complete waste of time. She said:

> Oh, I don't know I'm doing my best for him at all . . . . We know there's nothing else really we could do rather than give our whole attention and energy and this wouldn't be fair on the other children – or to ourselves. I mean what is the point . . . . Well, I feel there are limits to what he'll ever do.   (1972)

> Before I took him to speech therapy I was trying to teach him myself. When he said a word I made him sound it out, but apparently I was doing wrong. She said, 'Don't bother with that, get his vocabulary first.'   (1972)

It is worth pointing out that, while these attitudes would seem not to be optimal for the child, none of the children mentioned in the quotations above were low scorers. In contrast, parents of children in deprived homes who scored badly never engaged in such debates. It is a generalisation, and necessarily speculative, since direct questions would have seemed like an accusation, but most of such parents did not seem aware that they might be limiting their children. It is apparent from examples in this study that a minority of parents had little knowledge about how to bring up children at all and their Down's children – who were particularly vulnerable – suffered because of it. It is important to realise that the deprivation in some homes (albeit a minority) could be very great and was certainly in some cases an interaction between poor parenting skills and an undemanding child. The following approach to upbringing could not have occurred with a mother who was more aware of the needs of a child or with a more demanding child. It was the combination that proved harmful. One family was visited in 1972 but the child (Boy 10) was left alone in his cot for the whole of the interview. Since his mother was got out of bed for the interview, and was not disturbed by the child during it, the child must have spent a night and almost a whole morning unattended. Very few normal children would tolerate this level of social deprivation and, indeed, his normal siblings did not. The mother declined the offer to delay the interview while she attended to him because she felt the child was quite all right. To illustrate his contentment and his lack of need for attention, she said that she frequently left him in this way while she went to the shops. The boy was felt to be no trouble at all to bring up. In 1981 the youngster was extremely retarded, but not nearly so biddable; he displayed abnormal behaviour patterns. The following quotation from another parent again illustrates how the interaction between the child's characteristics, the parents' ignorance of a child's needs and poverty which meant a lack of alternative strategies (here, a car) operated to the child's disadvantage.

> If you take her out she won't walk far, she likes to be carried. Well, she's a bit heavy to carry around, so we just stay here.   (1972)

In this context of parental effort there is some reluctance to imply fault to parents when they do make choices not to make maximum efforts. It must be considered how far it is reasonable to place additional burdens on parents who already have the difficult responsibility of learning to negotiate the tangled web of allowances and services for disabled children and adults. How far, too, does this approach, yet again, single out and segregate parents of handicapped children from those who have non-handicapped children? Enabling a handicapped child to lead a normal life may imply a very abnormal life for the carer. It is also worth speculating how far a teaching role is compatible with a parental role. This becomes particularly important when a child is handicapped and aspects of parent–child interaction are already in danger of distortion.

Priorities for services

The priority group for help must clearly be those vulnerable children in social classes IV and V who also suffer from under-stimulation. It is particularly to be regretted that, when some of such children have been offered residential placements, potential loss of allowances has prevented their acceptance. For one child this resulted in no school attendance at all, and no compensatory programmes were offered in the home instead. It is particularly important that services play an active – and even aggressive – role because simple offers of services to parents are less likely to attract the very parents who need most help (see Cunningham, 1985a, on lack of take-up and drop-out from intervention schemes). Such parents may be ignorant or apathetic but they may well also have practical problems such as poor transport facilities. Consequently, services must actively reach out to these families rather than wait passively for them to take up services.

Appendix 2

The Comparative Study in 1981*

In 1981 a study was also made of a new young cohort of Down's syndrome children. The children were living at home in South Wales and born in the years 1973, 1974 and 1975. The methods used in 1972 with the 1960s cohort were repeated. The purpose of this study was to enable a direct comparison to be made between two cohorts of Down's syndrome children and their families at the beginning of their school careers, but at two different points in time. Down's syndrome children born in 1964-66 were seen in 1972 and those born in 1973-75 were seen in 1981.

It has been explained earlier in the book that, for a variety of reasons, it was impossible to see the whole of the 1964–66 cohort in 1972 and that, by chance, the less able were disproportionately represented among those who were seen in 1972. Consequently, comparisons are not wholly satisfactory. In 1981 the whole of the 1964–66 cohort was seen and so, where appropriate, information about the earlier years which could be obtained from those who were not seen in 1972 is used.

In this Appendix 'the original sample' refers to those 37 Down's syndrome children who were seen in 1972 and the 'new sample' refers to those 19 teenagers who were seen only in 1981. 'The 1964–66 cohort' or 'the older cohort' refers to the 56 children who were born in those years. 'The 1973–75 cohort' or 'the younger cohort' refers to the 26 children born in those years who were seen in 1981.

1. CHANGES IN THE CHARACTERISTICS OF FAMILIES WITH DOWN'S CHILDREN

The use of amniocentesis to screen older pregnant women became common in the 1970s. There have also been changes in the intervening years in how parents plan their families. These factors have influenced the characteristics of the families of the younger cohort.

The parents

Marital status

There were no substantial differences in the marital status of the parents of the two cohorts. Twenty-three (89%) of the 1973-75 cohort had two parents living together compared with 82% of the older cohort in 1972.

Divorces and separations were more common among the older cohort's parents in

---

*The information in this appendix is based on material that first appeared in the *Journal of Epidemiology and Community Health* (1985), Volume 39, no. 4.

1972. There were four divorced women and one who was separated from the father of the Down's child (14%) in that year. Three of the divorces were directly related to the birth of the Down's syndrome child. In contrast, the two (8%) separations among the parents of the younger cohort were less clearly attributable to the child. There were no divorces by 1981 among the younger cohort's parents.

There were four parents (7%) who had died in the 1964–66 cohort by 1972, compared with only one (4%) parent in the 1973–75 cohort in 1981.

Age of parents

Mothers who had their Down's syndrome babies in 1973–75 were younger on average at the birth than mothers who had given birth nine years earlier (an average age of 29.8 years compared with 33.5 years for the 53 women whose ages were known). There were significantly fewer mothers giving birth in the 1970s who were over 40 years of age (11% compared with 49% in 1964–66). Fathers, too, followed this pattern. The average paternal age at the birth of the 1973–75 cohort was 32.0 years compared with 35.0 years for the 54 fathers of the 1964–66 cohort.

Employment

In 1972 only 69% of the original sample fathers were in full-time employment compared with 81% of fathers of the 1973–75 cohort. This is probably the result of the younger average age of fathers in the latter cohort. Fewer mothers of the younger cohort worked in 1981 compared with the original sample mothers in 1972 but differences were small. (23% of the 1973–75 mothers compared with 27% of the original sample mothers.) Of those in the younger group who did work, fewer worked full time. Only one mother (4%) worked full-time and five worked part-time (19%) in contrast to 1972 when five (14%) of the original sample mothers worked full time and five (14%) part time. This may reflect the younger mothers' greater family commitments as well as changes in job opportunities.

Size of family

The younger cohort tended to come from smaller families (an average of 2.7 children) than those born in 1964–66 (an average of 3.4 children) although the differences were not significant.

Position of the Down's syndrome child in the family

Children in the younger cohort were significantly more likely to be a couple's first-born child than was the case for their 1964–66 peers. Only 21% of the 1964–66 cohort were the first child in a family compared with 50% of the 1973–75 group. Similar proportions in the younger and older cohorts were only children (8% compared with 7% respectively).

Social class

The finding that the Down's children born in 1973–75 had younger parents, came from smaller families and were more often the eldest child in a family than Down's children born nine years earlier was, because of amniocentesis, not surprising. A more unexpected difference between the cohorts concerned the social class of the parents. While the social-class composition of the 1964–66 cohort did not differ substantially from the rest

Table A9 *Social-class composition of the two cohorts by father's occupation (% in brackets)*

Social classes	1964–1966 cohort	Wales (1966)	1973–1975 cohort	Wales (1971)
I & II	13 (23)	(20)	12 (46)	(22)
III	30 (54)	(46)	11 (42)	(48)
IV & V	13 (23)	(35)	3 (12)	(30)
Total	56 (100)	(101)	26 (100)	(100)

Difference between proportions, $z = 2.099$; $p < 0.05$.

of the population, that of the parents in the 1973–75 did diverge significantly from that of the earlier cohort and from the rest of the population. Among them social classes I and II were over-represented and social classes IV and V under-represented (Table A9).

The most likely explanation is concerned with differences in fertility between the social classes. Nowadays, those in higher social classes marry later and have a longer interval between marriage and the birth of their first child, making such mothers older, and so at greater risk from the Down's syndrome point of view, at the commencement of child-bearing. Women in lower social classes marry earlier, begin child-bearing sooner after they marry, but they no longer continue child-bearing or have larger families as they once did. There is now little difference in size of families between the social classes (Dunnell, 1979). Consequently the child-bearing of women in lower social classes takes place at a 'safer' age. It is worth noting that two of the mothers of the 1973–1975 cohort were over 40 years of age at the birth of their children. Both were from social classes IV and V. They had not been offered amniocentesis. (For a fuller discussion see Shepperdson, 1985a.)

The children

Sex

There were 12 boys and 14 girls in the 1973–75 cohort, compared with 29 boys and 27 girls in the older cohort.

Health

The health of the 1973–75 cohort was certainly not better than that of the original sample children. While only 35% of the younger cohort were in hospital during the first year of life (compared with 46% of the original sample), by the time the children were interviewed in 1981, 65% had been in hospital compared with 59% of the original sample in 1972. The only major changes in problems were that none of the older children had had bowel operations compared with two of the younger children who had had this done. Also none of the younger children had been put into hospital for purely social reasons compared with two who had in the original sample. Pahl and Quine (1985) suggest that more severely ill mentally handicapped children are being kept at home nowadays.

Excluding the almost universal respiratory problems, serious conditions which still existed among the younger children in 1981 were heart problems (4 children), bowel difficulties (2 children), eye problems (1 child) and feet problems (3 children). The original sample suffered in 1972 from heart problems (4 children), fits (2 children) and eye problems (1 child).

In the 1973–75 cohort 9 children had severe difficulties with mobility and 10 had some problems. This leaves only 7 (27%) children whose mothers considered them to be as mobile as a non-Down's child. Indeed, some of the 7 had outgrown earlier problems. Problems arose from heart conditions (2), easy tiring (11), refusal to walk (6) and feet problems (6).

It is possible to say that Down's syndrome children born in the early 1970s were likely to experience a family life more closely resembling that of their normal peers in contrast to the 1964–66 cohort, who were not only distinguished from their peers by handicap but were also more likely to have older parents and siblings. However, the younger cohort were more likely to have a high social class background and this is likely to be a positive influence on their achievements.

Both younger and older cohorts had a similarly high proportion of health problems.

2. CHANGES IN HOW FAMILIES RESPOND TO THE BIRTH OF A DOWN'S CHILD

The mothers

Thirty-five per cent of mothers in the original sample responded negatively at the birth of their Down's child. In the younger cohort six (23%) reported severe difficulties in adjusting to the birth of their children, two others were ambivalent.

Service provision for mothers who were uncertain about whether or not they wanted to keep their children had changed by the 1970s. Several mothers in the original sample emphasised the lack of any alternative to home care. A few were put under pressure to keep their children at home, and others were simply ignored and their misery not discussed as relevant, or of concern to anyone except themselves. This was not the case for mothers of the younger cohort and it seems highly probable that one or two children may have been lost to this study because they were fostered or adopted. Of the six mothers who experienced severe shock, or a feeling of outright rejection at the birth, four considered fostering for the baby and two of them went ahead with fostering for two and three weeks respectively. The possibility of an escape route for these four women seemed to make a remarkable difference to them. As one said 'They didn't put any pressure which, give the hospital its due, they did allow me more or less to sort it out for myself, you know.' The mother who was least helped was the one who was not given this unpressured time. She said 'Nobody believed I wanted him fostered. "Pull yourself together" [they said].' Not only this but she cut the fostering short herself not because she felt ready to cope but because she was told she would have to pay towards it. All told, when mothers were given the chance to learn to care for their children in an unstressed and unpressured situation, it did appear to help.

A mother's response should not be viewed in isolation. She is very much influenced by how her husband responds, and also how the grandparents respond. The grandparents exerted a greater influence with the younger cohort than with parents of the original sample, possibly because both grandparents and parents were younger. Fewer grandparents were elderly, infirm, or dead.

By the time of the interviews in 1981 no mother in the younger cohort could be classified as wholly negative. Six (23%) were classified as ambivalent (average Malaise score 8.7) and the rest as positive (average Malaise score 6.8). Again, circumstances played a part and if 'negative indicators' (see Chapter 3) are considered (i.e. high social class, negative relatives, one-parent family or unsupportive spouse, child ill, extra work, unwanted child, older mother) then the ambivalent mothers had an average of 3.1 indicators compared with 1.2 for others (1.7 for the whole cohort). The two mothers whose responses deteriorated after the birth (from positive to ambivalent) had an above-average number of negative indicators (3 and 4 respectively) while those whose responses improved (from negative to positive) had, on average, fewer negative indicators (0, 1, 1 and 3 respectively).

It seems that nowadays mothers who have their Down's syndrome children living at home with them are less likely to be unhappy about their situation than was the case with those whose children were born in the 1960s. Mothers of the younger cohort were far more optimistic about their children and also found that the attitudes of others were more tolerant towards mentally handicapped people. Several parents found the medical problems more trying than those arising from mental handicap. Indeed, some mothers were at pains to point out that the Down's child enhanced family life rather than detracted from it.

It is possible to speculate that situations of real unhappiness and stress that were found among mothers in the earlier study were avoided because of the improvement in services. To begin with, parents of the younger cohort no longer had to keep their children at home and the alternatives offered to them were more acceptable. The majority who wished to bring their children up themselves were no longer left to battle alone, but were given help with practical problems. Advice and training schemes were more readily available for the under fives. Down's syndrome children were treated more flexibly, e.g. in school placements. The attendance allowance and the Family Fund helped with financial problems and acceptable short-term care was more routinely available for the few who needed it.

The fathers

Five fathers of the original sample had problems of adjusting to the birth of their Down's child and three of these had subsequently divorced their wives.

None of the fathers of the younger cohort reacted with such finality. Two fathers experienced very severe problems in health and in work after the birth, but it was less easy than with the divorced parents of the 1963–65 cohort to associate the Down's syndrome child with the subsequent problems.

By 1981 most fathers of the younger cohort seemed to have come to terms with their child's disability. Only one father seemed totally unreconciled and his feelings were an important contributory factor to the unhappiness of the whole family. His patience with his child was limited. Of course, many fathers, used to hiding feelings of weakness, may have simply maintained a façade to their wives. One father, who was very active in service improvements in the area, described his feelings at the birth and subsequently as follows:

> Heartbroken. He was the boy I'd wanted all along – he'd play for Wales . . . . In those two weeks [before
> I knew] I had all my plans made. I broke down for a couple of days [and now] – Oh – I could start crying
> now if anyone talked about it for a couple of minutes. (1981)

On the whole, fathers were more involved with their children than those who were in the original sample. There is, of course, a general trend towards fathers in Wales being involved in child rearing (Cleary and Shepperdson, 1980). This perhaps is one reason why fewer mothers of the younger cohort reported that their husbands were unrealistic about their Down's syndrome children.

The siblings

The 1973–75 cohort had 44 siblings compared with 132 for the 1964–66 cohort. Understandably, since mothers of the younger cohort stressed the normality of their children, they were less likely to present having a handicapped sibling as a disadvantage. Several said the Downs's child had made siblings more sensitive to disability and generally more understanding of other people. Only one sibling was considered to have suffered to any major degree. The mother attributed the problems to the attention she had been forced to lavish on a much younger, handicapped child. Two siblings were said to be slow with speech but obviously a definite causal connection between that and the Down's syndrome child could not be made.

Problems that did arise were similar to those found for the original sample. Some arose, not because of the Down's child himself, but because of the effect of the birth on parents. As one said, 'I don't think he'll ever get over the early time – having an ordinary mother and then one who was crying morning, noon and night, for years.'

Parents also mentioned the problem of giving attention to siblings when the demands of the Down's syndrome child were so great. Minor jealousies were often attributed to this. Young children often assumed the role of elder brother or sister at an early age. A problem less common in the younger cohort than in the original sample was that fathers were not always even handed, tending to excuse faults in the Down's child but not in the others. A new problem for the 1970s siblings was that the Down's child, far from being deprived of school and activities, had now often more opportunities and activities than the normal sibling and this could create petty jealousies.

Although there were exceptions, a more universally happy picture emerged of family life for the younger children. This was perhaps partly due to changing family patterns. The Down's child was fitted more comfortably into family life when he was no longer 'the baby' as well. Parents had been given a happier picture at birth, were more optimistic, and practical help was available. Finance was less of a problem and the extreme isolation of parents had passed.

3. CHANGES IN UPBRINGING

General upbringing

Mothers

It was expected that in a cohort with younger mothers of higher social class there would be changes in upbringing. While fewer mothers were inclined to be lenient there were also fewer who were strict (Table A10).

Table A10 *Approach to upbringing by mothers of the original sample and 1973–75 cohort (% in brackets)*

	1964–1966 original sample in 1972	1973–1975 cohort in 1981
Strict	11 (30)	6 (24)
Average	12 (32)	14 (56)
Lenient/Variable	14 (38)	5 (20)
Total	37 (100)	25 (100)

Asked to consider the ideal approach, far fewer mothers of Down's syndrome children recommended a more lenient approach (8% for the younger cohort mothers compared with 35% for the original sample mothers). Similar proportions in both 1972 and 1981 (56% and 57%) felt strictness was the ideal policy.

Mothers were anxious to reduce differences with siblings but often felt the Down's syndrome child was less able to understand what was being said, was inclined to be stubborn and was confused by any inconsistency in approach. Consequently, firm and clear rules of behaviour were thought to be 'kinder and fairer'. It would be wrong to present all Down's children as needing a firm hand. At least one mother found her Down's child far more biddable than her other children. As she said, 'You've only got to say, "That's naughty" and she starts crying and says, "I'm sorry, Mammy, I won't do it again".'

Mothers continued to use similar methods of control over the years. Smacking seemed the obvious and right form of punishment to mothers of young children in both 1972 and 1981 studies when verbal warnings were ignored. Only two or three mothers in both studies insisted that they never smacked their children.

Fathers

There was still a tendency for mothers to consider their husbands were more lenient than they were themselves but more fathers were considered strict (see Table A11).

Table A11 *Approach to upbringing by fathers of the original sample and 1973–1975 cohort (% in brackets)*

	1964–1966 original sample in 1972[a]	1973–1975 Cohort in 1981[a]
Strict	5 (16)	9 (36)
Average	8 (26)	5 (20)
Lenient	18 (58)	11 (44)
Total	31 (100)	25 (100)

[a] Includes 1 stepfather.

Specific issues

On specific aspects of upbringing the trend was towards an upbringing more typical of the normal infant-school child. Differences between the older and younger cohorts, however, were not so marked as might have been expected.

Bedtime and sleeping arrangements

Down's syndrome children in the 1973–75 cohort were being put to bed rather earlier than those in the original sample had been, at a similar age. Differences, however, were not pronounced. The slight differences are, perhaps, accounted for by the presence of similar aged siblings rather than any changes in fashions (Table A12). There was, however, a distinct change in the sleeping arrangements made for the younger cohort: far fewer slept with parents (see Table A13).

Table A12 *Bedtime of the original sample and 1973–1975 cohort (% in brackets)*

	1964–1966 original sample in 1972	1973–1975 cohort in 1981
Before 7.00	9 (24)	9 (35)
7.00–7.59	16 (43)	10 (39)
8.00+	6 (16)	4 (15)
No specific time	6 (16)	3 (12)
Total	37 (99)	26 (101)

Going out alone

An important aspect of upbringing, because it has implications for the normality of a child's lifestyle, friendships and general development, is whether or not to allow the child out alone. It was an area that caused parents much anxiety and doubt in 1972. In

Table A13 *Sleeping arrangements made for the original sample and 1973–75 cohort (% in brackets)*

	1964–1966 original sample in 1972	1973–1975 cohort in 1981
Own room	10 (27)	17 (65)
With parents	16 (43)	5 (19)
With others	11 (30)	4 (15)
Total	37 (100)	26 (99)

'Own room' compared with the rest: $\chi^2 = 9.17$; df = 1; p < 0.01.

fact the proportion of children allowed out (beyond the curtilage) had scarcely altered (Table A14).

Table A14 *How far the original sample and 1973–1975 cohort were allowed out alone (% in brackets)*

	1964–1966 original sample in 1972	1973–1975 cohort in 1981
Allowed out alone	12 (32)	8 (31)
Not allowed out	25 (68)	18 (69)
Total	37 (100)	26 (100)

Of those who allowed their children out alone in 1981, the longest interval allowed to lapse before checking on the child was about 60 minutes, the shortest five minutes and the average 25 minutes. In fact others who could be left in the garden were only left on average seven minutes (excluding one who could be left a long time) and the longest period was 20 minutes.

Friendships

An area of considerable concern to parents, both when their children were young and when they were teenagers, was their offsprings' lack of friends. For the 1973–75 cohort the situation had improved (see Table A15) although two of the 'friendships' were of an extremely limited nature. As in 1972, friends of the Down's syndrome child tended to be older or younger than themselves and the extent of interaction, for a few, was confined to watching the play of others.

Table A15 *Friendships of original sample and 1973–75 cohort (% in brackets)*

Friends	1964–1966 original sample in 1972	1973–1975 cohort in 1981
No one	10 (27)	5 (19)
Siblings of similar age	14 (38)	7 (27)
Friends through siblings	8 (22)	4 (15)
Own friends	5 (14)	10 (39)
Total	37 (101)	26 (100)

Those with 'own friends' compared with the rest: $\chi^2 = 3.95$; df = 1; p < 0.05.

Friendships at school did not compensate for lack of friends at home. Even though the variety of schools the younger cohort attended was much greater than had been the case for the older cohort, most still travelled out of the local area to school. There was certainly more coming and going in 1981 than there had been in 1972, but only one child saw school friends regularly at home and only seven had any out-of-school contact at all. For three of these it was a single visit only.

Use of babysitters

A further example of the more 'normal' upbringing of the younger children was that parents were more prepared to use babysitters. In 1972 it had been younger mothers who used babysitters more frequently and so the trend in 1981 is not surprising. It is of interest that similar proportions used 'outsiders' to babysit in both years and the mothers of the younger cohort used relations more than anyone else (Table A16). Two mothers of the younger children had been offered County Sitters and one used the service.

Table A16 *Use of babysitters for original sample and 1973–75 cohort (% in brackets)*

	1964–1966 original sample in 1972	1973–1975 cohort in 1981
None	11 (30)	1 (4)
Relatives only	11 (30)	14 (54)
Others	15 (41)	11 (42)
Total	37 (101)	26 (100)

'None' compared with the rest: $\chi^2 = 6.7$; df = 1; p < 0.01.

4. CHANGES IN SERVICES

It is possible to say that services had improved dramatically for families with Down's syndrome children, as the following account shows. Standard practices, which affect all parents and children (e.g. early advice) had improved and those services that were used selectively (e.g. type of schooling) were more likely to be administered according to the needs of the child rather than on what was available, or on the application of a narrow stereotype of what a Down's syndrome child was considered to need.

Changes in how parents were told of their children's handicap

One of the most dramatic areas of service change between the two populations was when, how and what parents were told about the condition of their babies. At a time when health services are under some pressure it is gratifying to be able to report substantial improvements in some areas of practice. By the early 1970s it had clearly become standard practice to tell parents about the condition of their Down's syndrome babies within one or two days of the birth (see Table A17).

Table A17 *Changes in when parents were told their children had Down's syndrome (% in brackets)*

	Births	
	1964–66[a]	1973–75
Under 10 days	17 (32)	23 (89)
11 days to 3 months	18 (34)	3 (12)
3–12 months	13 (25)	—
Over 12 months	5 (9)	—
Total	53 (100)	26 (101)

'Under 10 days' compared with the rest:
$\chi^2 = 16.28$; df = 1; p < 0.001.
[a]Information not available for three parents.

It also follows from this earlier communication with parents that the venue for telling parents was, in the 1970s, firmly with the maternity hospital and their staff. Seventy-three per cent of parents in the 1970s were told by staff in the maternity hospital or by their own GP compared with only 32% of those who had their babies in the 1960s. This difference is significant.

In addition to these improvements more parents were told kindly and accurately about the condition. The importance of home background for determining the abilities of the child was also often stressed to parents. The situation was not yet perfect, however. One father was told, 'He's a mongol and he'll be a cabbage for the rest of his life and he'll be no use.' Another, 'He'll be virtually a cabbage, if he talks you'll be lucky. When he's 10 he'll be like 2, and he'll never work.' The comment that the doctor 'was very nice in his way' that followed this mother's account must be taken as an example of the extreme tolerance of parents. Again, however, parents who were given this sort of inaccurate and unhelpful advice in the 1970s were far more likely to have the benefit of more accurate information from other professionals, albeit at a later date.

Genetic advice

Only 24% of mothers in the older cohort were given genetic tests and advice on their chances of having a second Down's syndrome child, but 16 (62%) mothers in the younger cohort received this service. All except one of the 13 mothers of the younger cohort who went on to have further pregnancies after the Down's child had advice and tests, compared with only 47% of mothers of the older cohort who had more children. All the younger cohort mothers were also given the amniocentesis test on subsequent pregnancies, although one woman, by her own account, had the test at too late a stage in the pregnancy, and two others had had to insist on amniocentesis. Two mothers were given tests, but no advice.

Seven mothers had no genetic counselling. They included all the three women in social classes IV and V. Five of the parents had either vasectomy or sterilisation operations. It is of interest that two of these seven families, who did not have the advantage of genetic counselling, had Down's syndrome children among their extended kin.

Vasectomy (9 fathers (35%)) and sterilisation (4 mothers (15%)), had become a popular form of birth control among the younger mothers. Three mothers were considering sterilisation. This compares with nine mothers (26%) and one father in the original sample in 1972 who had used these methods of birth control.

Several factors contributed to mothers of the younger cohort being less inclined than mothers in the original sample to limit their families after the Down's syndrome birth: mothers were younger, the child was more frequently the first-born child, and the amniocentesis test was known to be available. Twelve (46%) mothers in the younger cohort had had children after the birth of the Down's syndrome child by the time of the interviews compared with 30% of mothers of the older cohort. Six (23%) mothers of the younger cohort said they were discouraged from adding to their families because of the Down's child.

Later help

Short-term care

Although slightly more of the younger cohort had opportunities for short-term care than the original sample (54% compared with 43%), more mothers were inclined to refuse the offers. Sixty-five per cent had refused, or would refuse, offers compared with 49% of the original sample in 1972. In fact only four (15%) of the younger cohort had taken short-term care placements compared with 38% of the original sample

Table A18 *Changes in the use of short-term care facilities (% in brackets)*

	1964–1966 original sample in 1972	1973–1975 cohort in 1981
Accepted	14 (38)	4 (15)
Would accept	5 (14)	5 (19)
Refused	2 (5)	10 (39)
Would refuse	16 (43)	7 (27)
Total	37 (100)	26 (100)

(Table A18). There are two possible explanations for the trend. The move towards normalisation for younger children may mean that, because young children are not usually sent away without parents, younger Down's children were also kept at home. On the other hand, the explanation may be that the original sample was biased towards the less able children and it is the mothers of these children who most frequently take advantage of short-term care.

Facilities were not, however, meeting all needs and at least two families would have appreciated more help. One woman, with severe family problems, and who had a regular monthly placement, still sometimes needed flexible and emergency care, which could prove unavailable. Another mother would have welcomed a family fostering arrangement for occasional weekends.

Future care

Care in the future had been a major worry for parents of the older cohort. In contrast, parents of the younger cohort were more optimistic and had a wider variety of ideas about care available in the future – hostels, community homes, farm and village communities. In addition, care away from home (partly perhaps because of this variety) was no longer seen as a wholly negative prospect. Some parents viewed it as a normal and natural progression for adults that would take care of future social, as well as physical, needs. The fact that parents were younger meant that it was not an urgent consideration and they could see that at least ideas about services, were improving. Consequently, while the actual percentage of parents who would look for some form of professional rather than family care had increased only slightly (Table A19), the approach to the issue had changed markedly: it was no longer automatically viewed as a last resort.

Table A19 *Changes in preferences for future care (% in brackets)*

	1964–1966 original sample in 1972	1973–1975 cohort in 1981
Residential care	15 (41)	13 (50)
Siblings or family	13 (35)	5 (19)
Don't know	9 (24)	7 (27)
Parents themselves	—	1 (4)
Total	37 (100)	26 (100)

Other help

Parents of the younger cohort were far more in touch with professionals than the parents of the original sample had been in 1972. Over half the mothers had had contact with a social worker – usually from the community but sometimes hospital based – although very few felt the service was very useful. The one or two who did appreciate social workers calling were mothers who felt the need to unburden themselves to someone. Other help included information on allowances and arranging short-term care.

Health visitors were similarly received: one or two individuals were clearly outstanding on information, support and advice but the service was not universally found to be helpful. Where the children were ill, understandably, health visitors could be very useful. One offered to arrange a night sitter for a mother who was coping with family illnesses.

Twenty-one (81%) of the families had contact with a psychologist. Eleven of these were in touch with two psychologists who were initiating parents' groups and home teaching schemes. Generally the parents benefited from this particularly skilled help. This was often the first intensive help that parents had and they were given positive advice rather than – as one mother put it – 'just carrying on in spite of the birth'. All told this sort of help was the reverse of that experienced by parents in 1972 when few had contact with psychologists at all and, for those who did, it was often confined to a brief assessment terminating in a depressing placement in a special school. The approach in 1972 was often considered by parents as merely confirming prejudged decisions, rather than assessing needs and finding solutions.

Speech therapy, too, was more widespread. Only two, both outside the special school 'safety net', had no such help: one child had home tuition and the other attended a normal Welsh-speaking school. Parents were still dissatisfied however and one or two marked it out as 'the worst service'. Sessions were felt to be too infrequent and the progress made was sometimes felt to be negligible.

The professionals who were particularly helpful to parents tended to be those who had skills directly relevant to the mentally handicapped population. Specialist, rather than generic workers were easily the most useful. One visitor attached to the local ESN(S) school was constantly referred to as the source of information and advice about allowances and services. Similarly the psychologists possessed very detailed knowledge of the needs of the children and how best to encourage their development. An example of the variety of help one worker could give is as follows. A mother had the advantage of visits from a community nurse who was attached to the mental handicap hospital. His practical and all round skills were immensely useful to the mother and he gave useful advice on stimulation, upbringing, future care and general services available. He attempted also to smooth parental relationships by discussions with the father on the causation of Down's syndrome and the services a Down's child needs. As well as this, he ensured that the child joined swimming classes and went on outings. The mother, too, by his efforts was involved in coffee mornings at the hospital. It must be said that a single professional involvement of this depth is of more value than three or four less intensive encounters.

Continuing problems with services

While services had improved greatly, there were still problems. A few parents still felt that they had to find out about things themselves and that it was up to them to mobilise services. A few commented that, although there was a rush of help straight after the birth (and it should be pointed out no parents of the older cohort had had this initial intensive help), this help then subsided leaving the mother isolated. As one said, 'In the end you realise you can only help yourself.' Even in the 1970s, parents could be ignorant of services or even be told (wrongly) that they would not qualify. Gaps in parents' knowledge included information on the attendance allowance, Family Fund, how to get pushchairs and incontinence services.

An important area of difficulty for mothers whose babies were ill was that, at that time, there was no help with transport to hospital or, if treatment was at a distance, hotel bills. Normally there is accommodation for mothers at hospitals and one can only wonder why this was not made available. One mother found she was entitled to help after her daughter was 2 years old but, by this time, the major problems had passed.

A predictable difficulty with services was lack of flexibility. Services need to be able to provide standard and constant care, but they also need to be able to respond to crises. Preventative intervention would have been a welcome development. The lack of flexibility found with services for Down's teenagers was also found with the younger cohort and non-standard problems were particularly likely to lack any formal or immediate solution. One example will illustrate this. A father was deserted by his wife and left to care for his Down's syndrome child and two other children. He also wished to continue to work. All the solutions he found to 'cover' for the time he was absent from home were organised through his own efforts and it was solely because of his own resourcefulness and personal contacts that any solutions were found at all. Even so, the arrangements were not ideal and worked only so long as the child remained fit and well. Over and above this, however, and strikingly important from the point of view of service provision, all the arrangements that were made (using professional services) were not official, and depended solely on the good nature of the professionals involved and so could, presumably, have been stopped at any time. In other words there was no official and formal solution to this, not uncommon, problem of the single parent.

A more optimistic note on the provision of services was that professionals seemed far more ready to give advice to parents in areas where, in the 1960s, professionals would have been unwilling to intervene. For instance, more authoritative and confident advice was given on discipline and workers tried to change parental attitudes that could be interpreted as over-protective. In general, professionals seemed more confident about the quality of their advice on upbringing and so were willing to be more directive to parents.

5. FINANCIAL BENEFITS

The attendance allowance

The attendance allowance was introduced in 1971 and, in 1972, the early allocation of the allowance to the original sample had been very unfair. This was not the case for the younger cohort in 1981 and all families received the allowance. Twelve (46%) received the lower rate and 14 (54%) the higher rate. Six of those who had the higher rate, however, did so only after they had appealed against being allocated the lower rate so that only 31% received the higher rate without argument. The younger cohort were also more fortunate than the older cohort in the age at which they received their allowance. Twenty-one (81%) received it at 2 years old – the earliest possible age – and all were in receipt of it by 5 years old.

The Family Fund

The Family Fund was not in existence when the original sample was interviewed in 1972. It had been established by the time the second group was interviewed. Fourteen (54%) of the younger cohort had applied to The Family Fund for help and all, eventually, received help. Three of them had initial refusals although these children did not seem substantially different from those who were helped immediately. Indeed their average Gunzburg score was slightly lower (35.3 compared with 38.2 for those helped immediately) and one of the most disabled children in the sample was initially refused help.

Three mothers did not know of the Fund or realise it could apply to them – all had children who scored above average on the Gunzburg PAC (an average of 74.7 compared with 44.1 for the cohort). Nine others did not feel they should apply: some felt they coped well enough, others that they would only apply for something substantial and one had been discouraged by a professional. Again, not all parents realised the money was not from a charity and some were certainly discouraged from applying because of this misapprehension. Those who had not applied were not substantially better on the Gunzburg PAC than those who had applied successfully (an average of 37.6 for those who applied compared with 44.1 for those who did not apply) and two had severe health problems.

Mobility allowance

The mobility allowance was not in existence when the original sample was interviewed in 1972. It had been established by the time the second cohort was interviewed.

Although there were only seven (27%) children with no mobility problems at all in the 1970s cohort only two children qualified for the mobility allowance. It should be said that one of these two had no more problems than others who were unsuccessful and the successful child could, for example, go on buses. Five others had applied but been refused. One of these, at least, had severe problems. She had very poor health, had a home teacher and went everywhere by taxi in order to avoid infections.

The simple measuring of the ability to walk along a corridor was felt by mothers to be a totally inappropriate measure of mobility in the real world that included steps and other hazards. All the other problems that made real barriers to mobility for mothers were ignored – e.g. heart, feet and bowel problems were unrecognised and, above all, decisions did not take into account behaviour and refusal to walk. Allocation was based on a very strict interpretation of the ability to walk rather than on how far the child did or would walk.

6. CHANGES IN EDUCATION

Home teaching schemes

A completely new development in South Wales for the under-fives, and one which would have been very welcome earlier, was the introduction of home teaching schemes. Sometimes these were combined with support groups for parents. Altogether 19 (73%) of the children had some contact of this sort, although six of these children had either a very short or very irregular programme of teaching. The availability of a scheme was obviously related to area. Often, too, the early schemes were arranged so that parents visited a central point, rather than being visited themselves at home. This could be a disadvantage for those mothers without transport or with less mobile children.

The schemes were almost universally popular with only one or two mothers who found the teaching inappropriate, or difficult because of needing to maintain the child's interest, or worrying for themselves in that lack of progress undermined their own confidence.

The schools

Not unexpectedly one of the major improvements following the 1970 Education Act was that school places became available both for all the children and at the same age that normal children were offered school places. All but one of the younger cohort attended a nursery or playgroup before they went to school and all were in school by 5 years old, most starting at three or four years. In 1972 only 34% of the 1960s cohort had begun school early and 30% started school when they were over $5\frac{1}{2}$ years old.

Children also attended a greater variety of schools (see Table A20). Whereas 71% of the 1964–66 cohort were in an ESN(S) school by 1972 only 31% of the younger cohort were in such schools by the same stage, although two had places arranged there for the following year. Overall services for parents with young Down's children had greatly improved. However, services as yet were not reaching them all, and part of the so called improvement was a function of the complete dearth of services which existed for parents in the 1960s.

Table A20 *Changes in school placements (% in brackets)*

	Births	
School	1964–66	1973–75
ESN (S)	40 (71)	8 (31)
ESN (M)	—	7 (27)
Special observation class in primary school or assessment unit	11 (20)	9 (35)
Ordinary	3 (5)	2 (8)
None	2 (4)	—
Total	56 (100)	26 (101)

'ESN (S)' compared with the rest: $\chi^2 = 12.2$; df $= 1$; p < 0.01.

In particular, services which would lead to integration of the children into normal patterns of life were not common. Most importantly, from this point of view, less than half the children were being educated within ordinary schools, and fewer still in their local schools. In addition to this, some special classes or units within regular school settings were, in practical terms, still very isolated from the main schools.

References

Aumonier, M. and Cunningham, C. C. (1984) Health and medical problems in infants with Down's Syndrome. *Health Visitor* **57** (May), 137–140.

Ayer, S. and Alaszewski, A. (1984) *Community Care and the Mentally Handicapped*. London: Croom Helm.

Barrera, M. E., Watson, L. J., and Adelstein, A. (1987) Development of Down's syndrome infants with and without heart defects in their caretaking environment. *Child: Care, Health and Development* **13**, 87–100.

Baumeister, A. A. (1968) Paired associates learning by institutionalised and non-institutionalised retardates and normal children. *Am. J. Ment. Defic.* **73**, 102.

Bayley, M. (1973) *Mental Handicap and Community Care*. London: Routledge & Kegan Paul.

Bayley, N. (1954) Normal growth and development. In Hoch, P. H. and Zubin, J., *Psychopathology of Childhood*. New York: Grune and Stratton (1959).

Bendix, S. (1975) Administrative and social management of the family with a new born spina bifida infant, within the Cardiff area. In Spain, B. and Wigley, G. (eds), *Right from the Start*. London: National Society for Mentally Handicapped Children.

Bernstein, B. (1971) *Class, Codes and Controls*. London: Routledge & Kegan Paul.

Bicknell, J. (1983) Mentally handicapped people: their rights and responsibilities. *Journal of Occupational Therapy* **46** (6), 157–160.

Boles, B. (1959) Personality factors in mothers of cerebral palsied children. *Genet, Psychol. Monogr.* **59**, 159–218.

Booth, T (1985) Labels and their consequences. In Lane, D. and Stratford, B. (eds), *Current Approaches to Down's Syndrome*. London: Holt, Rinehart & Winston.

Bradshaw, J. (1980) *The Family Fund*. London: Routledge & Kegan Paul.

Brinkworth, R. (1983) *Sexual Development and the Problems of the Down's Syndrome Child*. London: Down's Children's Association.

Buckle, J. (1984) *What of the Future?* London: D. I. G. Charitable Trust. Summer, no.6, 17–19.

Buckley, S. (1985) Attaining basic educational skills: reading, writing and number. In Lane, D. and Stratford, B. (eds), *Current Approaches to Down's Syndrome*. London: Holt, Rinehart & Winston.

Buckley, S. (1987) In Fawley, G. and Lane, D. (eds), *A Normal Life for Down's Adults. Alternatives to Current Practice*. Report of a conference, Down's Children's Association, November 1985.

Bytheway, W. R. (1975) The statistical association between social class and self-reported delinquency. *Inter. J. Criminol. Penol.* **3**, 243–251.

Byrne, E. A. and Cunningham, C. C. (1985) The effects of mentally handicapped children on families – a conceptional review. *J. Child Psychol. Psychiat.* **26** (6), 847–864.

Carr, J. (1970) Mongolism – telling the parents. *Devel. Med. Child. Neurol.* **12**, 213–221.

Carr, J. (1975) *Young Children with Down's Syndrome*. London: Butterworths.

Carter, C. O. (1958) A life-table for mongols with causes of death. *J. Ment. Defic. Res.* **2**, 64–67.

Centerwall, S. A. and Centerwall, W. R. (1960) A study of children with mongolism reared in the home compared with those reared away from the home. *Paediatrics* **25**, 678–685.

Central Statistical Office (1983) *Social Trends 13*. London: HMSO.

Central Statistical Office (1985) *Social Trends 15*. London: HMSO.

Cheseldine, S. E. and Jeffree, D. M. (1981) Mentally handicapped adolescents: their use of leisure. *J. Ment. Defic. Res.* **25**, 29–49.

Chumlea, W. R. and Cronk, C. E. (1981) Overweight among children with Trisomy 21. *J. Ment. Defic. Res.* **25**, 275–280.

Cleary, J. and Shepperdson, B. (1980) The Ffynone fathers. *Motherhood in Swansea*, Supplementary Paper No. 2. Medical Sociology Research Centre, University College of Swansea.

Cohen, P. (1962) The impact of the handicapped child on the family. *Social Casework* **43** (3), 137–142.

Corad Report (1982) Report by the Committee on Restrictions against People. London: HMSO.
Court Report (1976) *Fit for the Future*. Report of the Committee on Child Health Services. Cmdn. 6684. London: HMSO.
Coxon, A. P. M. (1985) The 'gay' lifestyle and the impact of AIDS. In *AIDS: The Latest Moral Panic*. BSA S.W. and Wales Medical Sociology Group Meeting, September 1985, University College, Swansea.
Craft, M. (1979) Chromosomal anomalies. In Craft, M. (ed.) *Tredgold's Mental Retardation*. London: Ballière and Tindall.
Crine, A. (1982) People said it would not work. *Community Care*. 9 December, pp.14–16.
Cunningham, C. C. (1982) *Down's Syndrome: An Introduction for Parents*. Human Horizons Series. London: Souvenir Press.
Cunningham, C. C. (1985a) Training and education approaches for children with special needs. *Brit. J. Med. Psychol.* **58**, 285–305.
Cunningham, C. C. (1985b) Early intervention for the child. In Craft, M., Bicknell, J. and Hollins, S. (eds), *Mental Handicap: A Multi-disciplinary Approach*. London: Ballière and Tindall.
Cunningham, C. C., Aumonier, M. E. and Sloper, P. (1982) Health visitor support for families with Down's syndrome infants. *Child: Care, Health and Development* **8**, 1–19.
Cunningham, C. C., Glenn, S. M., Wilkinson, P. and Sloper, P. (1985) Mental ability, symbolic play and receptive and expressive language of young children with Down's syndrome. *J. Child Psychol. Psychiat.* **26**, 255–265.
Cunningham, C. C. and McArthur, K. (1981) Hearing loss and treatment in young Down's syndrome children. *Child: Care, Health and Development* **7**, 357–374.
Cunningham, C. C. and Mittler, P. J. (1981) Maturation, development and mental handicap. In Connolly, K. and Prechtl, H. R. (eds), *Maturation and Development: Biological and Psychological Perspective*. London: Spastics International Medical Publications and William Heinemann Medical Books.
Cunningham, C. C., Morgan, P. A. and McGucken, R. B. (1984) Down's syndrome: is dissatisfaction with disclosure inevitable? *Develop. Med. Child Neurol.* **26**, 33–39.
Disability Alliance (1981) *Disability Rights Handbook 1981*. London: Disability Alliance.
Domino, G., Goldschmid, M. and Kaplan, M. (1965) Personality traits of institutionalised mongoloid girls. *Am. J. Ment. Defic.* **68**, 498.
Donnison, D. (1982) *The Politics of Poverty*. Oxford: Martin Robertson.
Douglas, J. W. B. (1964) *The Home and the School*. London: MacGibbon and Kee.
Dunnell, K. (1979) *Family Formation in 1976*. London: OPCS.
Eastwood, B. (1983) Care in the Community. *Nursing Mirror*, 12 January, 46.
Evans, D. (1973) Some language abilities and mentally handicapped persons, with special reference to Down's syndrome. Unpublished PhD Thesis. University of Exeter.
Farber, B (1968) *Mental Retardation: Its Social Content and Social Consequences*. Boston: Houghton Mifflin Company.
Farber, B., Jenné, W. C. and Toigo, (1960) *Family Crisis and the Decision to Institutionalise the Retarded Child*. Council for Exceptional Children. NEA Research Monogram Series, No. A-1.
Feinmann, A. J. (1983) Freed from hospital – why these children present no practical problems. *Medical News* **15** (5), 24–26.
Francis, S. H. (1971) The effects of home and institutional rearing on the behavioural development of normal and mongoloid children. *J. Child Psychol. Psychiat.* **12**, 173.
Fraser, F. C. and Sadovnick, A. D. (1976) Correlation of IQ subjects with Down's syndrome and their parents and siblings. *J. Ment. Defic. Res.* **20** (3), 179–182.
Gath, A. (1972) The effects of mental subnormality in the family. *Brit. J. Hosp. Med.* **8** (2), 147.
Gath, A. (1973) *Should retarded children be kept at home? Family considerations*. Paper given to Association for Child Psychology and Psychiatry, October 1973.
Gath, A. (1978) *Down's Syndrome and the Family: The Early Years*. London: Academic Press.
Gath, A. (1987) Implications of mental handicap for the family. Paper given to conference on 'Current topics – mental handicap'. Cardiff, June 1987.
Gibbs, M. V. and Thorpe, J. G. (1983) Personality stereotype of non-institutionalised Down's syndrome children. *Am. J. Ment. Defic.* **87** (6), 601–605.
Gibson, D. (1979) *Down's Syndrome: Psychology of Mongolism*. Cambridge: Cambridge University Press.
Goffman, E. (1963) *Stigma: Notes on the Management of Spoiled Identity*. Harmondsworth: Penguin.
Goldberg, P. and Huxley, P. (1980) *Mental Illness in the Community*. London: Tavistock.
Goldfarb, W. (1954) Emotional and intellectual consequences of psychologic deprivation in infancy: a re-evaluation. In Hoch, P. H. and Zubin, J. (eds), *Psychopathology of Childhood*. New York: Grune and Stratton (1959).
Goodman, L. A. and Kruskal, W. H. (1954) Measures of association for class classifications. *J. Am. Stat. Assoc.* **49**, 732–764.
Grant, G., Black, J., Wenger, C. and Humphreys, S. (1984) Care networks project: progress summary. Department of Social Theory and Institutions, University College of North Wales, Bangor.
Gregory, S. (1976) *The Deaf Child and His Family*. London: Allen & Unwin.

Gunzburg, H. C. (1963) *Progress Assessment Charts*. London: National Association for Mental Handicap.
Hall, V. and Russell, O. (1985) Community mental handicap nursing – the birth, growth and development of the idea. In Sines, D. and Bicknell, J. (eds), *Caring for Mentally Handicapped People in the Community*. London: Harper & Row.
Hannam, G. (1973) *Parents and Mentally Handicapped Children*. Harmondsworth: Penguin.
Hegarty, S. and Pocklington, K. (1981) *Educating Pupils with Special Needs in the Ordinary School*. Windsor: NFER-Nelson.
Heginbotham, C. and Day, K. (1983) Helping mentally handicapped people with psychiatric problems. In *Care in the Community: Keeping It Local*. (Report of MIND'S 1983 Annual Conference).
Hewett, S. (1970) *The Handicapped Child and His Family*. London: Allen & Unwin.
Hewett, S. (1975) Telling the family. A review of some of the relevant research and opinion. In Spain, B. and Wigley, G. (eds), *Right from the Start*. NCMHC.
Hill, P. (1981) Are there crises in adolescence? *Update* 2, 143–150.
Holt, K. (1957) The impact of mentally retarded children on their families. Unpublished MD Thesis. University of Sheffield.
Hughes, D. and May, D. (1981) Reconciling preferences and prospects: problems of management and carer awareness for the mildly mentally handicapped. Paper presented to BSA Medical Sociology Group Conference, University of York, 23–26 September, 1981.
Hughes, D. and May, D. (1983) Growing up in ward twenty: the everyday life of teenagers in a mental deficiency hospital. Unpublished draft paper. Department of Psychiatry, University of Dundee.
Hunt, N. (1967) *The World of Nigel Hunt*. London: Darwen Finlayson.
Hunt, S. (1980) Stereotyping children with Down's syndrome. *J. Mat. Child Health* 5, 328–332.
Hunton, M. (1979) *Medical Help for Children with Down's Syndrome*. Stourbridge: Mark & Moody.
Jackson, B. and Marsden, D. (1962) *Education and the Working Class*. London: Routledge & Kegan Paul.
Jaehnig, W. B. (1975) The handicapped child in the family. *Handicapped Person in the Community*. Milton Keynes: Open University Press.
Jeffree, D. M. (1968) *Masked deprivation in the nurture of severely subnormal children*. Unpublished MEd Thesis. Manchester University.
Jeffree, D. and Cheseldine, S. (1983) Working with parents of adolescents: the work of the Path project. In Mittler, P. and McConachie, H. (eds), *Parents and Professionals and Mentally Handicapped People*. London: Croom Helm.
Jenkins, E. (1954) *The Tortoise and the Hare*. London: Victor Gollanz.
Jervis, G. A. (1948) Early senile dementia in mongoloid idiocy. *Am. J. Psychiat.* 105 (2), 100–106.
Johnson, R. C. and Abelson, E. B. 1969. The behavioural competence of mongoloid and non-mongoloid retardates. *Am. J. Ment. Defic.* 73, 856–857.
Jolly, H. (1981) Continuing care for the children in hospital. Association for the Welfare of Children in Hospital Conference, Swansea, May 1981.
Jones, H. (1981) Do mentally handicapped people require specialist community nursing care? *Apex. J. Brit. Instit. Ment. Hand.* 8 (4), 122–123.
Jones, K. (1960) *Mental Health and Social Policy 1845–1959*. London: Routledge & Kegan Paul.
Kennedy, J. F. (1970) Maternal reactions to the birth of a defective baby. *Social Casework* 51 (7), 410–416.
Kew, S. (1975) *Handicap and Family Crisis*. London: Pitman.
King, R. D., Raynes, N. V. and Tizard, J. (1971) *Patterns of Residential Care*. (Sociological studies in institutes for handicapped children). London: Routledge & Kegan Paul.
Leeming, K., Swann, W., Coupe, J. and Mittler, P. (1979) *Teaching Language and Communication to the Mentally Handicapped*. London: Evans/Methuen Educational.
Lejeune, J. (1983) *Recent advances into research into Down's syndrome*. Lecture to the Down's Children's Association, London, 10 September, 1983.
Lemperle, G. and Radu, D. (1980) Facial plastic surgery in children with Down's syndrome. *Plastic and Reconstructive Surgery* 66, 337–343.
Leonard, C. O., Chase, G. A. and Childs, B. (1972) Genetic counselling: a consumer's view. *Genetic Counselling* 287 (9), 433–439.
Loxley, F. D. (1976) The child sterilisation case: some background issues. Occasional paper of the Division of Educational and Child Psychology of the British Psychological Society No. 9, Winter 1975/6.
Lyle, J. (1959) The effects of institutional environment on the verbal development of imbecile children. I. Verbal intelligence. *J. Ment. Defic. Res.* 3, 122–128.
Lyle, J. (1960a) II. Speech and language. *J. Ment. Defic. Res.* 4, 1–13.
Lyle, J. (1960b) III. The Brooklands residential family unit. *J. Ment. Defic. Res.* 4, 14–22.
May, D. and Hughes, D. (1986) An uncertain future: the adolescent mentally handicapped and the transition from school to adulthood. Report to Scottish Home and Health Department, Department of Psychiatry, University of Dundee.
MacAllister, R. J., Butler, E. W. and Lei, T.-J. (1973) Patterns of social interaction among families of behaviourally retarded children. *J. Marriage and Family* 35 (1), 93–100.

McConkey, R. and Jeffree, D. M. (1975) Partnership with parents. *Special Education: Forward Trends* 2 (3), 13–15.

MacKeith, R. (1973) The feelings and behaviour of parents of handicapped children. *Child. Develop. Med. Neurol.* 15 (5), 24–27.

Michaels, J. and Schucman, H. (1962) Observations on the psychodynamics of parents of retarded children. *Am. J. Ment. Defic.* 66, 568–573.

Miller, E. J. and Gwynne, G. V. (1972) *A Life Apart*. London: Tavistock.

Mitchell, D. (1976) Parent–child interaction in the mentally handicapped. In *Language and Communication in the Mentally Handicapped*. London: Edward Arnold.

Mittler, P., Cheseldine, S. and McConachie, H. (1981) *The Education of the Handicapped Adolescent. Roles and Needs of Parents of Handicapped Adolescents*. Paris: Centre for Economic Cooperation and Development.

Mittler, P. and McConachie, H. (1983) *Parents, Professionals and Mentally Handicapped People*. London: Croom Helm.

Moncreiff, J. (1966) *Subnormality in London*. London: PEP.

Moore, B. C., Thuline, H.C. and Capes, L. (1968) Mongoloid and non-mongoloid retardates: a behavioural comparison. *Am. J. Ment. Defic.* 73, 433.

Murdoch, J.C. (1984) The family care of the Down's syndrome child. *Maternal and Child Health* 9 (2), 69–72.

Newson, E. (1976) Parents as a resource in diagnosis and assessment. In Oppé, T. E. and Woodward, F. P. (eds), *Early Management of Handicapped Disorders*. Amsterdam: Associated Scientific Publishers.

Newson, J. and Newson, E. (1963) *Infant Care in an Urban Community*. London: Allen & Unwin.

Nisbet, J. (1963) Family environment – a direct effect on family size on intelligence. *Occasional Papers in Eugenics*, no. 8. London: Eugenics Council.

Oakley, A. (1974) *The Sociology of Housework*. Oxford: Martin Robertson.

Office of Population Censuses and Surveys (OPCS) (1977) *Classification of Occupations 1970*. London: HMSO.

Olshansky, S. (1962) Chronic sorrow: a response to having a mentally deficient child. *Social Casework* 43, 90–193.

Open University (1982) *Family Circles*. Unit 1. Handicapped person in the community. Milton Keynes: Open University Press.

Oswin, M. (1971) *The Empty Hours*. Harmondsworth: Allen Lane. Penguin Press.

Pahl, J. and Quine, L. (1985) *Families with Mentally Handicapped Children: A Study of Stress and Service Response*. Health Services Research Unit, University of Kent.

Pinker, R. (1971) *Social Theory and Social Policy*. London: Heinemann.

Pringle, M. L. K. and Fiddes, D. O. (1970) *The Challenge of Thalidomide*. London: Longman.

Quine, L. and Pahl, J. (1986) First diagnosis of severe mental handicap: characteristics of unsatisfactory encounters between doctors and patients. *Soc. Sci. Med.* 22, 53–62.

Record, R. G. and Smith, A. (1955) Incidence, mortality and sex distribution of mongoloid defectives. *Brit. J. Prev. Soc. Med.* 9, 10.

Roche, A. F. (1965) The stature of mongols. *J. Ment. Defic. Res.* 9 (2), 131–145.

Roith, A. R. (1963) The myth of parental attitudes. *J. Ment. Subnorm.* 9, 51.

Rosen, L. (1954) Selected aspects in the development of the mother's understanding of her mentally retarded child. *Am. J. Ment. Defic.* 59, 522.

Rutter, M., Graham, P. and Yule, W. (1970) *A Neuropsychiatric Study in Childhood*. London: Heinemann.

Ryan, J. (1973) Scientific research and individual variation. In Clarke, A. D. B. and Clarke, A. M. *Mental Retardation and Behavioural Research*. Study Group 4, Institute for Research into Mental Retardation. Edinburgh: Churchill Livingstone.

Ryan, J. M. (1978) *The Organisation of Soviet Medical Care*. Oxford: Basil Blackwell and Martin Robertson.

Savage, M. (1979) In Craft, M. (ed.) *Tredgold's Mental Retardation*. London: Ballière and Tindall.

Schaffer, H. R. (1964) The too cohesive family – a form of group pathology. *International J. Soc. Psychol.* 10 (4), 266–275.

Schonell, N. and Watts, B. H. (1956) A first survey of the effects of a subnormal child on the family unit. *Am. J. Ment. Defic.* 61, 210–219.

Shepherd, M., Cooper, B., Brown, A. C. and Kalton, G. (1966) *Psychiatric Illness in General Practice*. Oxford: Oxford University Press.

Shepperdson, B. (1973) Attending to need. *New Society* 24, 754.

Shepperdson, B. (1983a) Home or hospital birth. *Health Visitor* 56, 405–406.

Shepperdson, B. (1983b) Abortion and euthanasia of Down's syndrome children: the parents' view. *J. Med. Ethics* 9, 152–157.

Shepperdson, B. (1985a) Changes in the characteristics of families with Down's syndrome children. *J. Epid. Commun. Health* 39 (4), 320–324.

Shepperdson, B. (1985b) Parents' perceptions of their Down's syndrome children. Unpublished paper. Institute of Health Care Studies, University College of Swansea.

Sheridan, M. (1965) *The Handicapped Child and His Home*. London: National Children's Home.

Shotwell, A. M. and Shipe, D. (1964) Effect of out of home care on the intellectual and social development of mongoloid children. *Am. J. Ment. Defic* 65, 693.

Silverstein, A. B. (1964) An empirical test of mongoloid stereotype. *Am. J. Ment. Defic.* 68, 493.

Sines, D. (1985) Setting the scene. In Sines, D. and Bicknell, J. (eds), *Caring for Mentally Handicapped People in the Community*. London: Harper & Row.

Sinsen, J. and Wetherick, N. E. (1981) The behaviour of children with Down's syndrome in normal playgroups. *J. Ment. Defic. Res.* 25, 113–120.

Smith, W. R. and Berg, J. M. (1976) *Down's Anomaly*. Edinburgh: Churchill Livingstone.

Spitz, R. A. and Wolf, K. M. (1946) Anaclitic depression: an enquiry into the genesis of psychiatric conditions in early childhood. *Psychoanal. Study Child* 2, 313.

Spradlin, J. E. and Rosenberg, S. (1964) Complexity of adult verbal behaviour in a dyadic situation with retarded children. *J. Abnorm. Soc. Psychol.* 68, 694.

Stedman, D. J., Eichorn, D. H., Griffin, J. and Gooch, B. (1962) A comparative study of growth and development trends of institutionalised and non-institutionalised retarded children. Paper given to American Association of Mental Deficiency, May.

Thase, M. E. (1982) Reversible dementia in Down's syndrome. *J. Ment. Defic. Res.* 26, 111–113.

Thompson, W. A. R. (1971) *Black's Medical Dictionary*, 29th Edition. Book Club Associates.

Tizard, J. (1964) *Community Services for the Mentally Handicapped*. London: Oxford University Press.

Tizard, J. and Grad, J. (1961) *The Mentally Handicapped and Their Families*. Maudsley Monographs. London: Oxford University Press.

Tyne, A. (1982) Community care and mentally handicapped people. In Walker, A. (ed), *Community Care*. Oxford: Basil Blackwell and Martin Robertson.

Veall, R. M. (1974) The prevalence of epilepsy among mongols related to age. *J. Ment. Defic. Res.* 18 (2), 99–106.

Warnock, H. M. (1978) *Special Educational Needs*. Report of the committee of enquiry into the education of handicapped children and young people. Cmnd. 1712. London: HMSO.

Welsh Office (1978) *Digest of Welsh Statistics*. Cardiff: Welsh Office.

Welsh Office (1983) *All Wales Strategy for the Development of Services for Mentally Handicapped People*. Cardiff: Welsh Office.

Wertheimer, A. (1982) No places for children. *Community Care* 25 November, 18–19.

Wertheimer, A. (1986) Mental handicap: where do they go from here? *S. S. Insight* 12–19 April, 6–7.

Wilkin, D. (1979) *Caring for the Mentally Handicapped Child*. London: Croom Helm.

Wilkinson, G. (1985) Community care: planning and mental health services. *Brit. Med. J.* 290, 1371–1373.

Wing, J. K. (1979) Trends in the care of the chronically mentally disabled. In Wing, J. K. and Olsen, R. (eds), *Community Care for the Mentally Disabled*. Oxford: Oxford University Press.

Wolfensberger, W. (1980) Overview of normalisation. In Flynn, R. J. and Nitsch, K. (eds), *Normalisation, Social Integration and Community Services*. Baltimore: University Park Press.

Wolfensberger, W., Mein, R. and O'Connor, N. (1963) A study of the oral vocabularies of SSN patients. III. *J. Ment. Defic. Res.* 7, 38–45.

Wolfensberger, W. and Thomas, S. (1981) The principle of normalisation in human services: a brief overview. In *Research Highlights, No. 2. Normalisation*. Department of Social Work, University of Aberdeen.

Wunsch, W. L. (1957) Some characteristics of mongoloids evaluated at a clinic for children with retarded mental development. *Am. J. Ment. Defic.* 62, 122–130.

Younghusband, E., Birchall, D., Davie, R. and Kellmer-Pringle, M. L. (1970) *Living with Handicap*. London: National Bureau for Co-operation in Child Care.

Name Index

Subject Index

In the following index, 'children' refers to Down's syndrome children and 'teenagers' to Down's syndrome teenagers. 'Down's syndrome' is abbreviated to 'DS'.

213